What If We've Been Wrong?

Keeping my promise to America's "Abortion King"

TERRY

D1166855

What If We've Been Wrong?

Keeping my promise to America's "Abortion King"

by Terry Beatley

Printed in the United States of America.

ISBN 978-0-9841334-8-2

To order books, go to **AbortionKing.com**

Guiding Light Books, LLC

Printed with ecclesiastical permission
Arlington, Virginia
June 29, 2018
Nihil Obstat: Rev. Paul F. deLadurantaye, S.T.D.
          Censor Liborum

Cover Design

Terry asked me,
"How did you come up with this design for the cover art?"

I woke up in the middle
of the night with this completed
image in my mind.
Got up, sketched it out, and the next
morning created the art.

This is a "God design."

Mark Almas
kmDaniels, Creative Thinking

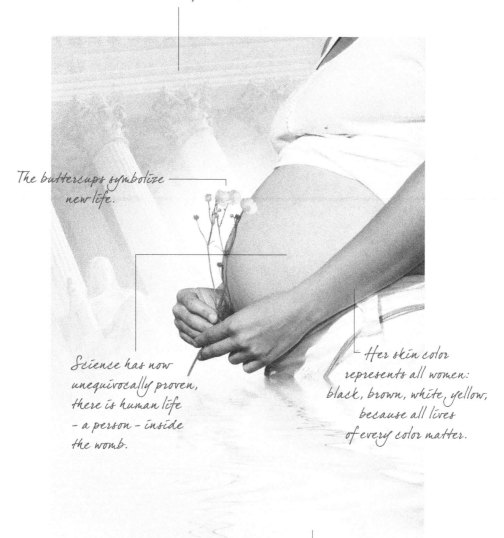

The Supreme Court: a brilliant, but secular body, capable of erring by diverging from our founding principles in the Declaration of Independence.

The buttercups symbolize new life.

Science has now unequivocally proven, there is human life – a person – inside the womb.

Her skin color represents all women: black, brown, white, yellow, because all lives of every color matter.

The waist high water represents the decades of tears, anguish and regrets since the 1973 Roe v. Wade decision.

The water reflection calls to mind the millions of babies lost.

Endorsements

"As a born again Christ follower, I am deeply moved by Terry Beatley's passionate pro-life response to America's most deadly battlefield since 1973: the womb of the American mother."

Ron Brown
*Former longtime Assistant Football Coach at University of Nebraska
Current Associate Head Coach at Liberty University*

"This book is a must-read! Dr. Bernard Nathanson's remarkable story of redemption and hope — and the alarm he sounded for our wayward culture — is far too important to be forgotten with his passing. Terry Beatley is faithfully, tenaciously keeping the cofounder of NARAL's message alive."

Marjorie Dannenfelser
President, Susan B. Anthony List

"Terry Beatley's work shines a bright light on the destructive seeds that have caused the coarsening of culture by devaluing life. Read it and be more equipped to lead the restoration of America."

Thomas P. McDevitt
Chairman, Washington Times

"The courageous message of Terry Beatley is critical to exposing the lies on which the abortion industry and the constitutional right to abortion rests. Truth, not ideology, should guide our judges and lawmakers. Terry's story of Dr. Nathanson, an abortion apostle, exposes the lies that masquerade as a women's health issue resulting in death, pain and suffering. Go tell it everywhere."

Mary Ellen Bork
Wife of the late Judge Robert H. Bork

"... What was the strategy of the abortion industry early on? How can knowing that strategy provide the key to changing abortion law and abortion culture? Terry Beatley has written a powerful book which answers those questions. Get What If We've Been Wrong?, *read it, and tell others about it."*

Dr. Jerry Johnson, Ph.D.
President and CEO, National Religious Broadcasters

"Dr. Bernard Nathanson left behind a very important mission for Terry Beatley. I enthusiastically support Terry's efforts to fulfill that mission by restoring a life-affirming culture through teaching America the truth of what 'The Abortion King' did to our country and what we can do to reverse it. If our country responds in conviction and repentance to Terry's efforts to bring Dr. Nathanson's message to our people, there is still a chance to return our great nation to the faith of our fathers where they truly believed, 'All men are created equal' and are 'endowed by their Creator ... with life, liberty, and the pursuit of happiness.'"

Dr. Richard Land
President, Southern Evangelical Seminary, Matthews, North Carolina
President Emeritus, Ethics & Religious Liberty Commission of the Southern Baptist Convention

"Terry Beatley's single minded determination to get the truth out is a timely and relevant gift to this country — and politically, a potential game changer."

Nancy Schulze
Founder, Congressional Wives Speakers
Cofounder of The American Prayer Initiative
Wife of 9-term Congressman Dick Schulze, Ret.

"I had the wonderful privilege of calling Dr. Bernard Nathanson friend. Terry Beatley has captured his parting and compelling message, a message the world desperately needs to hear during this National discussion of the Born Alive Abortion Survivor's Protection Act."

Congressman Trent Franks (Arizona)

"Terry was tasked by the cofounder of NARAL — Dr. Bernard Nathanson — to teach the truth of how he used propaganda to deceive Supreme Court justices, legislators, and the American public. He equipped Terry with the truth. Now it's our turn to listen, learn and respond to the truth."

Reverend Paul Scalia
Episcopal Vicar for Clergy, Diocese of Arlington

"Everyone – especially Catholics – should read this book! It is a tool to help all become well-informed and to respond to the promise that Terry Beatley made to the doctor who deceived America with the lie that abortion is health care."

Archbishop Joseph Naumann
Diocese of Kansas City, KS
Chairman, USCCB Pro-Life Activities Committee (as of 11/2018)

"This book has the most concise, clear description of the conversion of a heart that starts first with science. Nathanson's was a conversion of the mind first and then the heart … It's the clearest document I've ever read on the topic."

Congressman Kevin Cramer (North Dakota)

"I enthusiastically recommend this book! Terry Beatley keeps Dr. Bernard 'Bernie' Nathanson's extraordinary story alive with tenderness, honesty, and humility. All three flow through her writing and her own life example. Humility was the lifeblood of Bernie Nathanson — and I know that this book and film will ensure that his witness to truth continues to be heard until we all live in the culture of life and civilization of love that he so passionately desired. Bernie was a treasured friend, prophetic voice and powerful Christian witness to an age which has lost its soul. What If We've Been Wrong? will re-sensitize Americans' hearts and minds — if they are willing to be liberated with the truth."

Deacon Keith Fournier
Editor in Chief, Catholic Online
Catholic Deacon, Author, Constitutional Lawyer
Founder, The Common Good Foundation

"America, please read this book and take action now! Kenya does not need Planned Parenthood. Our girls need EDUCATION — not abortion."

Sister Rose Wangui, VHM
Founder, Mother of Mercy Girls' Secondary School in Kenya, Africa

"This beautifully written book shows the power of truth. Journey with Terry as she fulfills her promise while proving that pro-life politics is a ministry to unborn children."

Karen Cross
Political Director, National Right to Life

"The story of Dr. Bernard Nathanson is one that is as inspiring as it is heartbreaking. The power of a merciful God is shown in this fantastic book by Terry Beatley. Not only did she fulfill the task given to her by Dr. Nathanson, but she did it in a way that provides hope for all of us. Everyone needs to read this book."

James W. Sedlak
Executive Director, American Life League

"I knew Dr. Bernard Nathanson quite well as one of America's most amazing individuals. This riveting account of Terry's promise to him should be read by all in the pro-life community and shared widely with people on the other side of the issue. It is a well told, easy read that stirs your heart and makes you think about what if we've been wrong?"

Chris Slattery
Founder and Director, Expectant Mother Care-EMC Frontline Pregnancy Centers, New York City, New York

"With this book Terry not only completes a commitment she made to Dr. Bernard Nathanson, but has done her own not insignificant part to enliven the conscience of our nation."

H. W. Crocker III
Author, Triumph: The Power and the Glory of the Catholic Church

"With a powerful inside look at a sinister industry, What If We've Been Wrong? is a must-read that the millennial generation should not miss!"

Helena Ramirez
Recognized as 2015 Forbes 30 Under 30 in Law and Policy & 2015 Washington, D.C. "Leaders of the Future" by Latino Leaders Magazine

*In gratitude to many people
who helped make this story possible.
Many hands make light work.
(Appendix A)*

---

*This book is dedicated to
Mary, the Mother of the Savior of the world.
May this book exalt her 'feminine genius'
and help restore respect for the dignity
of unborn children in America.*

---

*In memory of the teenage girls who lost
their innocence, and then their lives.
(Appendix B)*

"I, too, would like to be a pencil
in God's hand."

Terry Beatley

Table of Contents

Foreword

By Fr. C. John McCloskey III

What If We've Been Wrong? promises what J.R.R. Tolkien once coined as a "eucatastrophe" — two Greek words that when combined mean "good destruction." Empower yourself and others with this easy-reading account as Terry deconstructs how Americans got duped by a worldview *incompatible* with liberty and justice for all. Discover the benefits of being liberated with the Truth as you experience a glimpse of Divine Mercy while this story unfolds with surprises. Like Tolkien said, it "pierces you with a joy that brings tears" and great hope for America, which has currently lost her moorings, her soul, and her conscience.

This should be read by every American, because we have *all* been affected by the exploitation of women and the heinous crime of abortion. By exposing the "Catholic Strategy," the loss of parental rights, the warping of "women's healthcare" and a stealthy racist population-control plan, Terry Beatley's pursuit to fulfill a promise that she made to the cofounder of NARAL is a game changer. She uses the commitment of a promise, her courageous spirit and the power of loving people with truth to change hearts and minds to defend the unborn and their mothers ... all the way to the voting booth.

Dr. Bernard Nathanson was no stranger to me. For many years I was his spiritual advisor and brought him into the Catholic Church in 1996, in part so that he might be saved, forgiven by the Lord, and so that he might make restitution for serious sins — most particularly the abortions that he performed. His testimony and parting message can unlock the stronghold that the abortion industry has on American politicians, media, healthcare, pro-choice feminists and the pulpit.

This true story about Love and Divine Mercy could very well heal the racial and political divide in our country and tip future elections in favor of candidates who are willing to be true voices for the most vulnerable — *women and children.* Terry proves that to make our country great again, it begins by admitting our errors and elevating the dignity of all lives — *not just some chosen by the few.* Without question, Dr. Nathanson's saga and message can help re-sensitize the heart of America.

You will be inspired by Terry's passion for justice and righteousness as her activism unfolds in a real-life drama. From meeting ex-offenders to exploited women to power-hungry politicians, her drive to fulfill the promise she made to "The Keeper of the Abortion Industry Keys" will motivate voters and awaken slumbering Christians. I agree with Terry that if Americans, particularly Catholics, Protestants, Evangelicals and people without any faith at all, would *learn* of Dr. Nathanson's strategy of deception and then *respond* to his parting message, the future of America will be much brighter.

Fr. C. John McCloskey is a priest of Opus Dei who writes for The Catholic Thing *and serves as a non-resident Fellow with the* Faith and Reason Institute *in Washington, D.C.*

CHAPTER ONE
The Medical Moral Thug

"Teach the strategy of how I deceived America ..."

Bernard N. Nathanson, M.D., *cofounder of NARAL*

What If We've Been Wrong?

"I don't think we've done enough to educate the American public what's really at stake in this debate over choice . . ."

Senator Hillary Clinton to Senator Rick Santorum on the U.S. Senate floor
as she defended partial birth abortion

What would you do if you made an audacious, but sincere, promise to
a dying doctor who admitted to being a former mass murderer? What if
you promised him that you would deliver his personal parting message
to America and reveal his national strategy of deception until they
became common knowledge? What if exposing his deception and making
his parting message widely known could help stop the exploitation of
American young women?

I made such a promise to the preeminent physician who admitted to
being America's medical moral thug — a man who ushered in the
Barbaric Age. He ". . . foisted an evil of incalculable dimensions"[1] upon
this country by intentionally hoodwinking the public and manipulating
the opinion of United States Supreme Court justices. His name was
Bernard N. Nathanson, M.D., a New York obstetrician-gynecologist,
and he deeply regretted his role in deceiving America with a stealthy
propaganda campaign that quite literally affects everyone.

What If We've Been Wrong? is based on the true story of my seven-year
odyssey into the warped world of "women's healthcare and reproductive
freedom," a racist population-control plan, the "Catholic Strategy,"

political-judicial fiat, and the assault on parental rights and motherhood. This story is a testimony to how the Lord uses "average Joe" kind of people and sometimes the worst of circumstances to advance His kingdom of love and life. Just as importantly, it is a journey into the power of prayer that is allowing me, with the help of many others, to deliver on my promise to reveal the extremely perilous course our country has taken. Lastly, *What If We've Been Wrong?* is a true love story that I hope can be a catalyst for healing the racial and political divide at a time when we all need the gift of mercy.

There's a segment of the culture, though, that doesn't want this story told because it thrives on deception, death and individual destruction. And its lifeblood — the exploitation of young women and their children — is found in the realm of electoral politics.

Dr. Nathanson died on February 21, 2011, desperately wanting Americans to be liberated from his lies and to respond to his personal parting message. I invite you, your family and friends along on this journey and, perhaps together, we can elevate the dignity of all lives and restore a *civil* society in which we care for our neighbors once again.

What motivated me to want to fulfill this promise? In April 2009, seven months before meeting Dr. Nathanson, a friend referred me to Pastor John Bibbens, the senior pastor of a primarily black Christian congregation in rural Virginia. He didn't know me, but he agreed to my request for a three-hour appointment, giving us time to watch *Maafa21: Black Genocide in the 21st Century America,* a documentary about the genesis of Planned Parenthood and the secular humanist worldview of its founder, Margaret Sanger. I wanted him to view this movie because it explains Sanger's strategy for controlling births of those *she* deemed less desirable.

In 1939, her organization, the Birth Control Federation of America, which would later become Planned Parenthood, called the population control strategy the "Negro Project."[2] With eugenicists, atheists and extreme racists running the organization, they aggressively promoted sterilization and the use of contraception in minority communities to weed out those she considered "the unfit," — that is, the poor. "In bringing birth control to the then largely poor (i.e. unfit) population of the South, with a few influential black ministers promoting the project as the solution to poverty, Sanger hoped to significantly reduce the black population. Martin Luther King, Sr., as the eldest son of nine children born into poverty in a family of sharecroppers, would have made the perfect target for 'elimination.' But his birth had already taken place."[3] *Maafa21* documents in great detail Sanger's unashamed desire for the "elimination of 'human weeds,' for the 'cessation of charity,' for the segregation of 'morons, misfits, and the maladjusted' and for the sterilization of 'genetically inferior races.'"[4] This was the atheistic, Darwinist worldview of Margaret Sanger who marketed her worldview in the name of "women's healthcare."

When the documentary was over, I asked Pastor Bibbens what he thought. He pointed his finger and declared, "I'll tell you what I think. I will *never* vote for a pro-choice candidate ever again, for if I do, I'm voting to annihilate my own race, and furthermore, abortion is just plain wrong. I did not know the truth about Planned Parenthood and Sanger's 'Negro Project', but I am more convinced than ever that abortion is the ultimate injustice. Terry, *all* Americans need this information, not just black Americans." He thanked me for sharing it with him and strongly encouraged me to continue sharing it with others.

As if a curtain had been pulled back just far enough for me to view inside, it seemed as though the unalienable right to life could be a leading issue to unite our broken country which has lost her way in a sea of secularism and propaganda. I saw how America might possibly uphold the dignity of human life again, so I told Pastor Bibbens that I would continue. What I didn't realize as I met with him was that in seven months I would be in New York City interviewing Bernard N. Nathanson, M.D. — the cofounder of NARAL who had, in 1970, implored Planned Parenthood to enter the industry of abortion and later trained its doctors how to kill. He was the physician who fast-tracked Margaret Sanger's racist population control plan featured in *Maafa21* turning it into something far more sinister, effective and deadly. Dr. Nathanson was once known as America's "Abortion King."

I invite you along on this journey as the veil of deception is lifted so we can restore a *civil* society that chooses love over violence once again.

"My name is Norma McCorvey and I reside in Dallas, Texas . . . Thirty-three years ago, I came before the United States District Court Northern District of Texas Dallas Division as the Plaintiff "Jane Roe," the young woman whose case legalized abortion in the United States, Roe v. Wade . . . Those judges who made the earlier decisions never had the advantage of the real facts to base their decision because the entire basis for Roe v. Wade was built upon false assumptions . . ."

From Norma McCorvey, formerly known as Jane Roe of the 1973 *Roe v. Wade* case, in her 2003 affidavit (Section 1 and 2) to the Supreme Court of the United States requesting a hearing to reverse the *Roe v. Wade* decision. SCOTUS refused to hear her case. (Appendix E)

What If We've Been Wrong?

CHAPTER TWO
The Thirteen Ounce Miracle and Assignment

"The abuse of the fiduciary relationship and the internal censorship of news hostile to editorial policy is especially dangerous when practiced by the mega-press ..."

Bernard N. Nathanson, *The Abortion Papers*

What If We've Been Wrong?

The Assignment

Not too long after this pivotal meeting with Pastor Bibbens, I learned that a *Rediscovering God in America* event was coming to the Virginia Beach area in June 2009, and I decided to attend. The day was filled with nationally known speakers who presented the providential history of America, attesting that God — not government — is the source of our rights. When the event adjourned something peculiar happened. A lady ran up to me as I was exiting the sanctuary and said she needed to tell me something. Feeling perplexed, I stepped aside from the large crowd now leaving the church and listened to her story.

Her name was Dianne, and she proceeded to explain that in 1989 her daughter's birth was the youngest gestational birth recorded at that time in U.S. history. While on vacation in Hawaii, she went into premature labor at twenty-one weeks and three days. Although doctors tried to stop her labor, it soon became apparent that delivery was imminent. Three doctors, including the chief neonatologist, urged Dianne to abort her baby because, in their opinion, "it" could not survive the birth process. She refused to take the life of her child and reminded each doctor of his Hippocratic Oath, which forbade him from doing harm. Dianne promised that any action or non-action on their part that would take the life of her child would be highly contested. Her baby girl, Chory, survived delivery and weighed in at the neonatal intensive care unit at *thirteen ounces.* She was so small that she could fit in the palm of a hand. With underdeveloped lungs, eyes still fused shut, and a host of medical issues, the odds of survival were deemed zero.

Dianne said her daughter was now a healthy twenty-year-old. I responded that her story was amazing, but I didn't understand why she was telling me. She explained that when her daughter was living in the NICU in an open bed warmer for twelve months in Hawaii, her grandfather would call her each day from Florida and Dianne would hold the phone up to her baby's ear as he prayed that the doctors and nurses would do their best to keep his granddaughter alive. Repeatedly, Dianne witnessed the baby noticeably respond to his voice, moving and wiggling more when the phone was brought near her baby's ear.

Dianne related that her father had died six months earlier and that he had always been a strong believer in the power of prayer. Before his passing, he told Dianne about a vision he had had twenty years ago, while his granddaughter was fighting for survival in the Hawaii hospital. In the vision, his granddaughter was standing beside a woman at the top of white steps of what looked like a federal building he had seen in Washington, D.C. In front of them and to the side stood pastors, and on the other side stood politicians and lawyers. In the middle, all the way down the steps, were thousands of people cheering and crying. The woman and her daughter stood with hands held high, as if celebrating some kind of a pro-life victory. And then Dianne said, "That woman, I believe, is you."

I felt astonished. This woman, a complete stranger, had no idea of my pro-life activity and the encouragement Pastor Bibbens had recently given me. She knew nothing of my church affiliation or even if I attended one, or my political persuasion. Exchanging phone numbers and a hug, we parted and I recall walking out of the building asking God what had just happened. It felt surreal, and I didn't know what to make of it.

For the next five months I frequently prayed, asking God for direction regarding what I was supposed to do with my research and findings about Planned Parenthood, black genocide, and how the abortion lobby had undermined parental rights and was endangering girls through legislation. One evening at a twenty-four-hour prayer vigil at my church, I sat alone in a candle-lit room and asked again. Then His answer came — a consistent and repetitive thought: *"Go and interview Dr. Bernard Nathanson, the doctor who had demanded that Planned Parenthood get into the abortion trade. Go and interview him."*

I was surprised and troubled by this idea. I knew the doctor's history as the cofounder of pro-choice politics, but I couldn't imagine why God would direct me to interview him. I argued that He had the wrong person for the job. It seemed unlikely that a stay-at-home mom from Virginia would even be granted an interview. But I had learned one lesson throughout my life — you don't say no to God.

"At that time, I was an uninformed young woman."

From Norma McCorvey, formerly known as Jane Roe of the 1973 *Roe v. Wade* case, in her 2003 affidavit (Section 2) to the Supreme Court of the United States requesting a hearing to <u>reverse</u> the *Roe v. Wade* decision which stripped unborn babies of all rights and protections. SCOTUS <u>refused</u> to hear her case. (Appendix E)

"Happy is he who not only knows the causes of things but who has not lost touch with their beginnings."

G.K. Chesterton
Illustrated London News, September 26, 1908

"I prefer to be true to myself, even at the hazard of incurring the ridicule of others, rather than to be false, and incur my own abhorrence."

Frederick Douglass, Father of American Civil Rights, former slave, abolitionist, minister, entrepreneur, advisor to five Republican presidents

CHAPTER THREE

The Ask, The Interview and My Promise

"Where are the churches?"

Bernard N. Nathanson, M.D., to Terry Beatley

What If We've Been Wrong?

The Ask

Dr. Bernard Nathanson was no ordinary doctor. Once known as the "Abortion King," he was the cofounder of the National Association for the Repeal of Abortion Laws, known today as NARAL Pro-Choice America, the first and most powerful pro-abortion political action organization in the United States. His public relations strategy was used to persuade voters to support (or at least not hinder) the cause of decriminalizing abortion and led to polarizing Americans over the issue for the past five decades.

Dr. Nathanson personally implored Planned Parenthood to enter the abortion industry and trained its personnel for two years in the early seventies in baby-killing techniques. He watched the birth control giant expand into a worldwide abortion organization that would eventually be caught on undercover video discussing how to "[alter] abortion methods in order to procure more salable parts …"[5] and streamline this revenue-generating aspect of their abortion business[6] — a clandestine industry he predicted long ago. Dr. Nathanson's deception was instrumental in paving the way for the *Roe v. Wade* Supreme Court decision, which decriminalized killing babies in the womb throughout *all* nine months of pregnancy.

God's instructing me to interview this daunting figure regarding the most central moral challenge to our culture was quite intimidating. As I contemplated what I would ask him, I could not help thinking of the people he had used, hurt or killed. I sympathized with the millions of mothers who thought they had no other choice but to choose violence. I especially felt compassion toward black Americans because, through my research, I was aware of the staggering statistical results and how the deception has affected the black population. In addition, I felt frustrated, yet sympathetic, toward Catholics and Protestants because so many of them had been hoodwinked by NARAL's "Catholic Strategy," a political tactic designed by Dr. Nathanson.

But something more stirred inside me. When I was a young woman, I had believed what the feminist movement had marketed — to strive in a male-dominated career, break the "glass ceiling" and postpone motherhood. I had done so in the investment brokerage business as the only woman in a newly hired group of thirty employees. The business treated me kindly as a woman, and then, as a young mother in my mid-thirties. But now, as a stay-at-home mother in my forties, I had made the discovery that feminists representing the abortion industry were legislatively stealing my parental rights to protect, guide and nurture my own children. It was a paradox to me: how had the women's movement, which clearly had helped me enter the male-dominated financial world, changed into something that now threatened my parental rights and advocated abortion?

It also concerned me that wealthy Americans who donate millions of dollars to the abortion population-control lobby were indirectly aiding in the legislative destruction of parental rights. I wondered if they knew that many teenagers had already died at the hands of abortionists — a little-known fact that the media suppresses. (See Appendix B: The Teenage Victims)

I felt guilty that I had given so little thought to this contentious issue, despite the fact that I believed, as a Christian, that all life is sacred. For most of my adult life I had given more consideration to buying a new car or deciding what to make for dinner than to protecting the sanctity of human life. I had also believed the propaganda that abortion was a personal decision that had nothing to do with me. I discovered I was wrong; it had everything to do with me.

Dr. Nathanson eventually discovered how wrong he had been as well. In fact, he issued a bold statement to America in 1983:

> *I believe the abortion ethic is fatally and forever flawed by the immorality of the means of its victory. A political victory achieved by an unscrupulous and unprincipled minority … I believe that an America which permits a junta of moral thugs to foist an evil of incalculable dimensions upon it, and continues to permit that evil to flower, creates for itself a deadly legacy: a millennium of shame.[7]*

So who was this minority? What were the means of its victory? Why was it allowed to grow? What are the consequences of a "millennium of shame" and what should we do now?

I nervously stepped out in faith and dialed the doctor's Manhattan, New York telephone number provided by a pro-life activist lawyer and friend. It seemed so odd that I was about to ask for an interview with Dr. Nathanson, who admitted to partnering with another "moral thug," Lawrence Lader. Together, they had changed the entire trajectory of "women's healthcare" for the next half-century, mutating it into something to which even original feminists were radically opposed. Both men were atheists, members of the cultural elite, and in 1967, they bonded over the issue of abortion. According to Dr. Nathanson, Lader despised the Catholic Church — and Christians in general — and both men believed there was no force more powerful than intellectuals and their ideas.

The soft voice of Mrs. Christine Nathanson answered my call. She informed me that her husband was very ill and frail, but recommended I fax a letter of request. Promising to present it to him, she said that it was highly unlikely he would grant an interview. So I sent the following letter, and I never expected to hear back from her again.

November 9, 2009

Dear Dr. Nathanson,

I am requesting an interview. To be able to say that I have met with you, listened to your first-hand experience, and caught your vision for a pro-life America can only positively impact my presentations.

I strongly believe that if Christians would do their part, the gates protecting this pagan practice will fall. I am meeting pastors who strongly support my endeavor and others who are timid but taking a chance. They are catching the vision of an America embracing life and opposed to abortion, the court reversing its Roe v. Wade decision and Personhood Amendments passed in all fifty states.

They are observing their congregations getting enthused and motivated to overcome this evil. Pastors, who have perceived abortion as a political issue and have shied away from it, are awakening from a deceptive slumber and complicit complacency.

Thank you for considering a visit with me and I surely hope to meet you soon.

In Christ,

Terry Beatley

Just a few days later, though, Christine Nathanson called and expressed her surprise that Dr. Nathanson had agreed to my visit on December 1, 2009. I would soon meet the doctor who changed the world in such an irrevocable way, and I felt scared, yet excited, at the same time.

The Interview: New York City

I arrived at the appointed time. Mrs. Nathanson greeted me and cautioned that she didn't know how long he could endure an interview because he seemed more stressed than usual. She made it clear that she would keep his best interests in mind and check on him throughout my visit. As she led me through the small kitchen to their living room, my curiosity increased with every step. My stomach felt jittery and the experience seemed surreal as I entered the dimly lit, 1970s-style living room.

"Your guest is here," she said. Dr. Nathanson was sitting on a long sofa that seemed to swallow his small frame, and he motioned for me to enter. His Chihuahua, Hillie, stood guard on his lap pillow and growled as I greeted him. He settled her down with a whisper and a few loving pats on the head.

Large glasses framed the 83-year-old doctor's face, and his eyes reflected a caring nature. With a slight smile, he stated that he rarely gave interviews anymore. I asked him why he had agreed to mine. Dr. Nathanson replied, "Your letter seemed so passionate that I was compelled to say 'yes.'" This made me feel a little more at ease.

As he reached for his glass of water with trembling hands, he told me that he suffered from anxiety. It took considerable effort for the doctor to hold his glass, so I awkwardly talked whenever he sipped. What I found so striking was that his mind was sharp and clear despite his considerable physical challenges. He pointed to the television where a popular 4 p.m. FOX News personality was talking about threats to America's sovereignty. Dr. Nathanson remarked, "He's a little too dramatic for me, but what comes out of his mouth is like liquid gold." With that comment he had revealed his quick wit, and I instantly liked him.

He then shifted to the interview and asked, "What would you like to know, Terry? I will answer anything you ask me. I have nothing to hide anymore."

His question caught me by surprise and all of my organized thoughts were scattered. Sensing my nervousness, he told me not to be afraid, and with that little bit of encouragement my questions flowed. He told me the saga of his miserable childhood, failed relationships, and details of NARAL's national plan of deception to manipulate the gullible public and decriminalize abortion. Dr. Nathanson also told me of his unexpected rethinking of abortion and his disavowal of the practice. Despite his change of heart, the evil he helped unleash continued to burden him greatly.

My Promise

When Dr. Nathanson admitted he had intentionally stripped the unborn child of all rights and protections, his voice was faint and raspy. I looked at his downcast eyes and felt a tremendous amount of sympathy for him. He had cancer, and it was clear that he did not have much time left. Facing his own mortality, he was anxious that so much needed to be done to slow down, if not completely eradicate, the abortion industry — an industry *he* created. He desperately wanted people to know *how* and *why* he had deceived America on this issue of abortion.

I felt sad that this would probably be the only time I would ever meet with Dr. Nathanson. He was genuine and open — a man of courage and extreme humility. There was an internal strength about him that I found compelling. I was so moved by him that I had to hold back tears, but I continued with one last question — this one was totally unplanned — and I had no idea how he would answer it.

"Dr. Nathanson, I know you are too sick to travel getting your message out. *If* you have something to tell America, I promise I will carry it across our nation for you."

Pausing to contemplate, he turned and looked at me. Slowly and carefully he responded, *"Yes. Yes, I do. Continue teaching the strategy of how I deceived America, but also deliver this special message. Tell America that the cofounder of NARAL says to ..."*

Dr. Nathanson's parting message was simple, yet powerful, and it could change the world for good. His tender eyes looked up at mine as we shook hands. I accepted his pro-life mantle and committed myself to this endeavor. There was no hesitation on my part, and I immediately believed God would make a way to reach the heart of America through the former "Abortion King's" final message. Victory in restoring respect for the dignity of human life throughout the United States suddenly seemed possible because his message cut to the heart of the matter.

He looked slightly more at ease and gave me a faint smile. I thought of the suffering Dr. Nathanson had endured as he watched the value of human life erode into the marketing of aborted baby organs. He accepted responsibility for his role in making this possible, but I was so thankful to see hope in his eyes; hope for a restored and united nation under God, which would one day return to reason and end the violence against humanity.

I had no way to gauge how his message would be received. Would millennials, who had grown up in a post *Roe v. Wade* culture, even care about his message? Would feminists be fired up when they learned that they had been lied to and used? Could the political stronghold that ensnares "men without chests" in Washington, D.C. be severed? Would the Church teach boldly so that alerted Christians would elect righteous leaders who, in turn, would appoint righteous judges?

Would future presidents of the United States courageously embrace Dr. Nathanson's parting message and defend the dignity of human life?

Eight months after our meeting, I moved to the Civil War town of Fredericksburg, Virginia, the district of State Senator Edd Houck. He chaired the Virginia State Senate Education and Health Committee, which Planned Parenthood called their "saving grace in the Virginia Senate." I knew it as the "Kill Committee" where almost every piece of pro-life, pro-family, pro-parental rights legislation died a quick death. His voting record suggested two things to me. First, he had surrendered the safety of Virginia's girls and women to the legislative agenda of NARAL and Planned Parenthood lobbyists; second, his voting record reflected the consequences of Dr. Nathanson's legacy. I had a strong sense that I was supposed to help remove this senator from office as the first step in fulfilling my promise.

A couple of years later, I realized that my pursuit to help defeat this state senator provided the ideal framework for a true story in which to tell about my promise to America's "Abortion King."

"In 1970, I told this court in the form of an affidavit that I desired to obtain an abortion never really understanding the ramifications . . . It is my participation in this case that began the tragedy, and it is with great hope that I now seek to end the tragedy I began."

From Norma McCorvey, formerly known as Jane Roe of the 1973 *Roe v. Wade* case, in her 2003 affidavit (Section 3) to the Supreme Court of the United States requesting a hearing to reverse the *Roe v. Wade* decision which stripped unborn babies of all rights and protections. SCOTUS refused to hear her case. (Appendix E)

"Civilization is only one of the things that men choose to have. Convince them of its uselessness and they would fling away civilization as they fling away a cigar."

G.K. Chesterton
Illustrated London News, October 21, 1905

For further study and resources:

Killer Angel
A short biography of Planned Parenthood's founder, Margaret Sanger
by George Grant
Highland Books, 2001

Life, Education and Resource Network (LEARN)
www.blackgenocide.org

Margaret Sanger's Eugenic Legacy
by Angela Franks
McFarland & Company, Inc., 1971

CHAPTER FOUR
The Survivor

*"We will be forced to buy and import unimaginable quantities
of human fetal tissue from the third world."*

Bernard N. Nathanson, M.D., *The Hand of God*

What If We've Been Wrong?

Fulfilling My Promise

After moving to Fredericksburg I arranged to watch *Maafa21* with another pastor, Rev. Hashmel Turner, to whom I had been referred. Before meeting him, I was unaware of his battle for religious liberty in a case, *Turner v. City Council of Fredericksburg, Virginia,* that would eventually be considered at the U.S. Supreme Court or that he had been featured in an extensive profile by *The Washington Post* called "The Trials and Tribulations of Hashmel Turner." He had been a Fredericksburg City Councilman and had an upstanding reputation in his community. Something truly remarkable happened that afternoon as we watched *Maafa21.* It began with the tears that dripped down his brown face.

"I'm sorry, Rev. Turner. We can stop the movie if it's making you so sad," I offered.

"No, Terry, these are tears of joy, not sadness. I'm crying because I thought my work for the Lord was mostly done after defending the name of Jesus Christ in the court system, but I see that it is not. Tell me, why are you passionate about this issue?"

I told him about my promise to Dr. Nathanson and how I intended to reveal his strategy of deception and deliver his parting message to Americans. Rev. Turner wiped away his tears and shared, "I'm going to tell you something I just recently learned from my godmother. She told me that sixty-three years ago, a couple of elder family members took my fourteen-year-old mother into Washington, D.C. for an illegal abortion." He smiled and explained in his smooth, baritone voice, "The abortionist searched for me with his tools, but he couldn't find me. The Lord had me buried too deeply in my mother's womb and my life was spared." As the slow realization of what he just told me settled in, I felt shocked. To think that he had survived an abortion was just astounding.

Rev. Turner continued, "My godmother told me the Lord anointed me in my mother's womb to do great things for Him. I guess she was right. Who would have thought that someone born into extreme poverty, fatherless, nearly aborted, and almost thrown away like trash in our nation's capital could have defended religious liberty and carried the name of Jesus Christ all the way to the United States Supreme Court?"

As I listened, I felt certain that the hand of God had arranged our meeting. A Fredericksburg friend had referred me to Rev. Turner, thinking he would be interested in watching the documentary and learning how their mutual senator had supported the legislative agenda of abortion for over a quarter of a century. My friend was right. Rev. Turner was very disturbed by Senator Houck's voting record. I explained to the pastor that the vast majority of Americans have no idea of the worldview underlying the work of Planned Parenthood, as well as the ways in which the organization imposes its philosophy through legislation, sex education, and indoctrination that undermine the value system set forth in the Declaration of Independence.

Following the movie, Rev. Turner said that he was willing to protect life over party politics. Once again, I experienced how the "life" issue transcends race and can unite disparate people around common beliefs. Rev. Turner agreed to help defend life in the womb and spread the truth, regardless of the potential backlash.

I was elated that God had arranged the meeting with an abortion survivor, who also became a staunch defender of religious liberty. But I needed to make sure that I was working in cooperation with God's plan. After leaving Rev. Turner, I drove through town and I began to pray. I asked the Lord to make it clear if I was supposed to help defeat Senator Houck as a step in fulfilling the promise to Dr. Nathanson. I got my answer at a red light.

The license plate in front of me was an abbreviation of Isaiah 30:21. I picked up my Bible from the passenger seat and read, *"Whether you turn to the right or to the left, your ears will hear a voice behind you, saying, 'This is the way; walk in it.'"* And the next verse said: *"Then you will desecrate your idols overlaid with silver and your images covered with gold; you will throw them away like a menstrual cloth and say to them, 'Away with you!'"* (NIV) It seemed like more than a coincidence that that particular verse appeared at that moment, so I decided to stay on course.

To me, the golden images were NARAL and Planned Parenthood, which were supported by millions of dollars, including *tax revenue.* The silver idols were the power-hungry elected officials who would rather hide behind the plastic slogans of "Choice, Women's Healthcare and Reproductive Rights" propaganda that Dr. Nathanson had helped create than stand firm to defend the defenseless. Perhaps it was a woman's instinct — the mother in me — but I intuitively knew that in order to desecrate the idols, this senator had to be defeated with a campaign strategy much broader than a focus on jobs and the economy. It would be necessary to appeal to the voters' hearts with the power of love, not just concern for their wallets.

A year and a half earlier God had shown me through Pastor Bibbens' response to *Maafa21* what the fruit of elevating the dignity of all lives would be: by loving people through showing them the hard, ugly truth of Planned Parenthood, many Christians would let go of political party labeling and vote for candidates who would protect the sanctity of all human life and help end violence against the human family. Now God had blessed me with the friendship of Rev. Hashmel Turner, who was willing to stand up for the gift of life in the political realm as well.

Although I felt small and ill-equipped, I was encouraged that God was making a way for voters to clearly respond to Dr. Nathanson's message by what would happen in the 2011 Virginia Senate election. It was a year away, but I felt confident voters could be made aware of the doctor's legacy and how the two candidates were polar opposites — the incumbent, whose voting record, in my opinion, seriously jeopardized the safety of minor children by voting to obliterate parental rights and inadvertently advance Sanger's "Negro Project," and the other candidate, a man who had promised to protect the gift of life, as well as the safety of children by preserving parental rights.

From the Civil War town of Fredericksburg, Virginia, Dr. Nathanson's message started to take hold and the voters began to set the stage for what could happen all across America.

"Previously, the courts, without looking into my true circumstances or taking the time to decide the real impact abortion would have upon women, used me, my life, and my circumstances to justify abortion . . . Because the courts allowed my case to proceed without my testimony, without ever explaining to me the reality of abortion, without being cross-examined on my erroneous perception of abortion, a tragic mistake was made – a mistake that this Court has the opportunity to remedy."

From Norma McCorvey, formerly known as Jane Roe of the 1973 *Roe v. Wade* case, in her 2003 affidavit (Section 4) to the Supreme Court of the United States requesting a hearing to reverse the *Roe v. Wade* decision which stripped unborn babies of all rights and protections. SCOTUS refused to hear her case. (Appendix E)

"I have one great political idea . . . It is in substance, 'Righteousness exalteth a nation; sin is a reproach to any people.' [Proverbs 14:34] . . . [T]his constitutes my politics - the negative and positive of my politics, and the whole of my politics."

Frederick Douglass
An Address Delivered in Ithaca, New York, October 14, 1852

Recommended viewing:

Maafa21

Black Genocide in the 21st Century America DVD or on YouTube
by Life Dynamics
www.lifedynamics.com

Blood Money

The Business of Abortion DVD
Narrated by Dr. Alveda King
www.ewtnreligiouscatalogue.com

CHAPTER FIVE

The Missing Love

"… a monster was germinating within me. The monster recognized nothing but utility, respected nothing but strength of purpose, craved love—and then perverted it."

Bernard N. Nathanson, M.D., *The Hand of God*

What If We've Been Wrong?

Dr. Nathanson's Upbringing

To appreciate the significance of Dr. Nathanson's parting message requires a basic understanding of his childhood and his domineering father. Bernard was born in New York in 1926 into a loveless home in which disdain toward his mother replaced oxygen in the household. His mother was constantly and unfairly berated and belittled by her husband. Consequently, young Bernard and his sister, Marion, under the tutelage of their controlling father who abhorred his wife, learned to do the same. Bernard's father was a Jewish atheist and a highly respected obstetrician-gynecologist. Although the father was difficult and demanding, young Nathanson and his sister worshipped him. It is fair to say the children spent their childhood thirsting for true, unconditional, authentic love from their father. They never received it.

Another element made their home life challenging. Although Nathanson's father was proud of his orthodox Jewish heritage, he spoke against the faith and criticized it whenever possible. To add to the confusion, his father enrolled his son in the best New York Jewish schools and mandated that he learn the Torah. Young Nathanson would then be subjected to his father's quizzing, judgment and condemnation of Judaism. Learning rigid laws was valued; learning values was not.

As Bernard grew older, he became aware of his father's extramarital affairs. This made Bernard's relationships with women difficult and strained. Eventually, he became driven to prove that he was no longer his father's puppet. Bernard wanted to leave his own mark on the world and make his father proud of him. His sister Marion, however, was not as strong. She had been manipulated by her father for too long. At the age of forty-seven, she committed suicide.

Through first-hand experience, Bernard knew loveless relationships and how the value of human life is constantly evaluated by the measures of the material world — a world that judges by apparent convenience or inconvenience, usefulness or uselessness, and value or disposability — thus rendering the gift of life and the dignity of the human person worthless — the root of secular humanism.

In this worldview, people seem *disposable*.

"In fact, I did not know what the term 'abortion' really meant."

From Norma McCorvey, formerly known as Jane Roe of the 1973 *Roe v. Wade* case, in her 2003 affidavit (Section 9) to the Supreme Court of the United States requesting a hearing to reverse the *Roe v. Wade* decision which stripped unborn babies of all rights and protections. SCOTUS refused to hear her case. (Appendix E)

"Train up a child in the way he should go, and when he is old he will not depart from it."

Proverbs 22:6 (KJV)

"Once thoroughly broken down, who is he that can repair the damage?"

Frederick Douglass
My Bondage and My Freedom

For a complete resource guide on life issues:

The Facts of Life

DVD 2016 Edition
Human Life International
www.hli.org

What If We've Been Wrong?

CHAPTER SIX
The Slow Sharp Chisel

"I had not a seedling of faith to nourish me."

Bernard N. Nathanson, M.D., *The Hand of God*

What If We've Been Wrong?

I explained to Rev. Turner how the abortion industry lobbyists hide behind complicit politicians who wreak havoc on parental rights and the authority of the family. Sometimes their legislative agendas are aggressive and other times they are like a slow, sharp chisel, systematically carving away the fundamental right of parents to direct the upbringing of their children. I was advocating that politicians, such as Senator Houck, needed to be held accountable by their constituencies. In an effort to depict the real and present danger, I shared my experience about what happened when I took my daughter to a pediatrician for a sports physical.

At one point the pediatrician turned to my daughter and asked, "May your mom stay in the room with us?" The doctor informed me that she was required to ask this of any child fourteen or older before providing medical services. I was at a loss for words, but replied, "You have to be kidding," even though it was clear she was serious. The physician explained that the law had been changed so that when a child turns fourteen years old in Virginia, she is deemed an adult for the purpose of consent to "certain healthcare." What kind of healthcare? The law provides complete confidentiality for nearly anything having to do with sex, pregnancy testing, sexually transmitted diseases, contraception, or drug testing and treatment.

The pediatrician described the extreme consequences of this law by saying a minor could have syphilis, be dying with gonorrhea, or pregnant, and the doctor could no longer legally inform parents *unless the fourteen-year-old would give permission*. After years of NARAL and Planned Parenthood's insistent lobbying to provide access to confidential sexual healthcare services for minors, at least thirty-eight states offer minors "judicial bypasses," a policy that allows judges to circumvent parental consent or knowledge in states where it is *mandatory*, and grant permission for minor girls to obtain abortion surgeries. (See Appendix B: The Teenage Victims) In fact, NARAL Pro-Choice Virginia promotes judicial bypasses on its website: "Teens in Virginia who can't get consent from their parents are supposed to be able to request approval from a judge instead, in a process known as a 'judicial bypass.'"[8] The policy endangers girls by removing the care and protection of parents, and it encourages them to act covertly by hiding important health information from their parents.

The pastor made the connection between the loss of parental rights and politics, knowing that voters are apt to remain loyal to political parties, particularly when *unaware* of the issues, proposed bills, incumbents' voting records and the consequences thereof.

The abortion industry had grown into something that wasn't satisfied with taking the lives of babies in the womb. It wanted more. It wanted control over minors as well and the surest way to secure that control was legislatively. Dr. Nathanson told me that he "never meant for it to go this far." Through politics and policy, the abortion industry seeks its victory bringing a whole new dimension to what Rev. Turner knew quite well: *"My people are destroyed for lack of knowledge."* Hosea 4:6 (KJV)

"I was very naïve. For their part, the lawyers lied to me about the nature of abortion."

From Norma McCorvey, formerly known as Jane Roe of the 1973 *Roe v. Wade* case, in her 2003 affidavit (Section 9) to the Supreme Court of the United States requesting a hearing to reverse the *Roe v. Wade* decision which stripped unborn babies of all rights and protections. SCOTUS refused to hear her case. (Appendix E)

"The fear of the Lord is the beginning of knowledge, fools despise wisdom and instruction."

Proverbs 1:7 (KJV)

For further study:

Learn how the abortion industry lobbyists have undermined parental rights in your state by searching on the internet
"NARAL judicial bypass and [your state]" *and*
"Planned Parenthood and parental consent and notification laws and judicial bypass."

What If We've Been Wrong?

CHAPTER SEVEN
The First

"The population of the nation won't grow if it's left up to you."

Bernard N. Nathanson, M.D., *Aborting America*

What If We've Been Wrong?

Dr. Nathanson's father had his sights set on two medical schools for his son — Harvard or McGill University. As an alumnus of McGill, Nathanson's father befriended an unsuspecting F. Cyril James, McGill's president. When President James visited New York City from Montreal, Nathanson, Sr., would invite the president out for a night of drinks and dinner, working hard to develop a close friendship. A problem with this plan was that the doctor rarely drank, but Mr. James was a daily drinker. In order to keep up, Nathanson's father would become violently sick, usually before returning home.

Months after applying to Harvard and McGill, Bernard received two rejection letters. His father was furious and he called Mr. James at just the right time — happy hour. Within twenty-four hours, Nathanson was notified that the school had reversed its decision; he was accepted. Thus, he learned the benefits of manipulation and the effectiveness of deceit from his father who taught him that the end justifies the means to achieve success — a twisted way of thinking. It did not matter how he won, as long as he won. Virtue was not a factor.

In 1945, during his second year at medical school, young Nathanson met Ruth. He was drawn to her innocence, intellect and radiance. They began dating and even spoke of getting married after medical school. After years of exposure to his parents' miserable relationship, the idea of being happily married to Ruth was appealing. However, their wedding never took place. Ruth became pregnant and young Nathanson was afraid of not being able to finish medical school. Ruth put his education first and went alone to an abortionist that Bernard had located in Montreal. When Ruth returned by taxi in a puddle of blood, he helped her out of the car and tipped the driver.

After the abortion, an emptiness grew between them, and within a month or two, they drifted apart. As I listened to him describe the experience, it was clear that Dr. Nathanson had deeply cared for Ruth.

It may have been his first experience of real love. Sadly, that love was lost and the relationship became disposable. Life moved on though, or so he thought. A full awareness of what he had thrown away would not surface until decades later.

During his first year of residency at a Chicago hospital in the 1950s, Nathanson bonded with other exhausted gynecology residents over cheap beer at a local pub where they would sing a jingle about the gold mine in performing illegal abortions. It was a crude and morally repugnant ditty, and he sang it:

> *There's a fortune in abortion*
> *Just a twist of the wrist and you're through.*
> *The population of the nation*
> *Won't grow if it's left up to you.*
> *In the daytime in the nighttime*
> *There is always some work to undo.*
> *Oh, there's a fortune in abortion*
> *But you'll wind up in the pen before you're through.*

> *Now there a gold mine in the sex line*
> *And it's so easy to do.*
> *Not only rabbits have those habits*
> *So why worry 'bout typhoid and flu?*
> *You never bother the future father*
> *And there are so many of them, too.*
> *Oh, there's a fortune in abortion*
> *But you'll wind up in the pen before you're through.*[9]

Bernard finished his year of training not knowing how this chorus foreshadowed his cold, hollow future — a future never spent behind bars, but one in which he would be held captive nevertheless.

He moved back to New York City to finish his training at the Women's Hospital in Harlem where his father still worked after twenty-five years. Dr. Nathanson made some disturbing discoveries while shadowing his father during surgery. With a patient lying on the operating table undergoing a complicated hysterectomy, his father would ask his son for guidance. Young Bernard realized that his father lacked sufficient surgical skills and confidence. His father realized that his son had discovered his professional insecurities, while the rest of the medical community in New York thought Dr. Nathanson, Sr., was an exceptional physician. This reality became a contentious issue between father and son; their lives seemed to be based on a big lie.

Dr. Nathanson was practically impoverished while employed by his father, who would later blackball his son's entrance into the prestigious New York Obstetrical Society. As his relationship with his father soured, he tried to rekindle his friendship with his mother. This further angered his father, making the son desperate to be free of him. The loveless relationship deteriorated further and nudged young Dr. Nathanson to move on with his life.

In the early days of his residency at Women's Hospital, he wondered why poor patients kept showing up in the emergency room suffering a disproportionate number of "spontaneous miscarriages." Compared to the lower rate among private well-to-do patients, who could afford to pay a doctor for services, the impoverished patients seemed so much more likely to "spontaneously miscarry." He assumed the disparity was attributed to poor nutrition and lack of prenatal care, and it truly bothered him that economics seemed to be causing unnecessary miscarriages.

A senior medical resident informed him of the *real* reason these women were coming into the emergency room. He taught Dr. Nathanson to look for the telltale signs of botched abortions by locating certain markings on the cervix. Sure enough, some patients were actually suffering the effects of criminal abortions induced by a derelict physician, nurse, midwife, or friend.

A typical night shift at the hospital would include a young woman, usually black or Puerto Rican, entering the emergency room with terrible cramps, bleeding (sometimes profusely), running a high fever, and perhaps experiencing septic shock. Raging temperatures and damaged body parts were treated with IV antibiotics, and most patients were prepped for a dilation and curettage surgery, better known as a D&C. The fortunate ones would be discharged in a day or two.

The unfortunate patients, those suffering from a punctured intestine or a perforated uterus, would need aggressive treatment. Sometimes this led to a hysterectomy that left them sterile. The only beneficiary for this emergency care was the resident on duty who needed, as part of his training, to get as many major operations under his belt as possible. The ward provided a rich environment to expand one's resume, and countless women were sterilized by surgery-happy residents.

On the other hand, Dr. Nathanson called private-patient medical care the *theatre of abortion.* Every day was a performance with staff physicians doing abortions for patients who could afford to pay for their planned "spontaneous miscarriages." The women would feign serious cramps having been instructed to appear as if they were in pain. Sometimes they were advised to bring a prop — such as a sanitary pad stained with cranberry juice. If the patients were good actresses, they would make it past the admitting nurse.

The entire drama required teamwork: persuasiveness on the part of the woman to convince her gynecologist to end the life of her child;

deception at the front desk to be admitted into the clinic; physicians willing to break the law; and young residents pressured into participating in the drama by turning a blind eye and doing what they were told to do for pre-op. The abortion would be recorded as a required D&C surgery because the patient was suffering a "spontaneous miscarriage."

Dr. Nathanson described his disdain toward what he perceived to be an injustice and inequality of services between poor and affluent patients. He felt contempt toward the doctors who participated in this charade. Early on, he vowed that once he graduated from residency, he would not take part in the theatre of abortion, at least not directly.

"[My attorney] convinced me, 'It's just a piece of tissue. You just missed your period.' I didn't know during the Roe v. Wade case that the life of a human being was terminated."

From Norma McCorvey, formerly known as Jane Roe of the 1973 *Roe v. Wade* case, in her 2003 affidavit (Section 9) to the Supreme Court of the United States requesting a hearing to reverse the *Roe v. Wade* decision which stripped unborn babies of all rights and protections. SCOTUS refused to hear her case. (Appendix E)

"Unless a man becomes the enemy of an evil, he will not even become its slave but rather its champion."

G.K. Chesterton
Illustrated London News, April 14, 1917

For further study and resources:

10 Abortion Myths

A talk by Dr. Brian Clowes on CD
Human Life International
www.hli.org

Charlotte Lozier Institute

www.lozierinstitute.org

CHAPTER EIGHT

The Political Overseer

"What we needed were a white establishment figure and also a black to counteract those who thought abortion was 'genocide' and also a female."

Bernard N. Nathanson, M.D., *Aborting America*

What If We've Been Wrong?

The door to the neighborhood community center swung open and in walked the former mayor of Fredericksburg. He had a scowl on his face and appeared to be agitated, but he didn't intimidate me. I fully intended on doing what I had set out to do. Having rented the community civic center in a minority neighborhood to show the film *Maafa21*, I thought at first he had come to watch the film. I soon realized he was there to canvass the room to see who from his neighborhood was stepping out of line to learn about the history of Sanger's "Negro Project" and of NARAL's propaganda campaign. Content that there were only a few people there, he abruptly left, muttering something to a clergyman on his way out.

Having received a written invitation, a small group of local residents came for the film presentation. I knew it was important to extend personal invitations, so that morning I had driven through the residential neighborhood as a last attempt to invite anyone I could meet in person. The first people I saw were a black mother and grown daughter out walking. So I pulled over my car and introduced myself.

I explained that I had rented the center to show a film that documented the history of Planned Parenthood and Sanger's population-control plan that she and her colleagues referred to as the "Negro Project."[10] In addition, I asked them if they would like to learn how their senator was supported by Planned Parenthood in his current reelection bid.

To my surprise, the mother shared how she had had an abortion eighteen years ago. The nurse had told her that her fetus "was not a baby yet," so she went along with the abortion. "Are you saying my 'Choice' decision was part of something much bigger?" the mother asked.

I told her the movie documents in great detail how the abortion industry has affected black Americans. I also explained that abortion is now the leading cause of death in the black community — more deaths than all diseases, accidents and homicides combined — a sobering statistic.

I could see the surprise on both of their faces, particularly when I pointed out that this is *not* by accident. The mother and daughter both agreed to attend, but the daughter skeptically asked me why I was doing this. I told her about how I had promised the cofounder of NARAL that I would carry his parting message and expose his national strategy of deception.

I was so pleased because they both attended the film viewing. The mother had a visceral response when she learned that many politicians and leaders of the NAACP have known about Sanger's "Negro Project" and have done little or nothing to inform its members to help stop it. She abruptly stood up and slammed the metal chair in front of her and groaned, "No. No!" Her response was a testament to the accuracy of Proverbs 29:2: *"When the righteous thrive, the people rejoice; when the wicked rule, the people groan."* (NIV) This mother understood that many women have been deceived and she wanted to know what she could do to help fight back. She was on the verge of tears. I was too, but I knew that by loving people with the truth, good fruit would be produced.

I told the group that we needed to share the information with love because we should care more about people and values, as opposed to protecting political parties. I explained that we needed to throw our support behind candidates who would protect our unalienable right to life and not support candidates who bought the lies of Margaret Sanger and fell for Dr. Nathanson's propaganda.

They agreed to help and asked for fifteen copies of *Maafa21* and hundreds of copies of Senator Houck's voting record. The mother-daughter team distributed more than five hundred information packs and became quite proficient at explaining the anti-parental-rights voting record of their legislator. Together, united by the truth that life is a gift, we set out to prove that parents will vote to protect their parental rights and not give those rights away to elected officials and the aggressive abortion industry lobbyists. Despite what appeared to be a brazen intimidation tactic of the former city leader to monitor who became enlightened and informed, the shadows over Fredericksburg didn't seem as dark that day.

As the sun set, I returned to my temporary home on top of a former Civil War Confederate encampment ridge. I went straight to a horse-shoe-shaped garden I had nicknamed the William Wilberforce Garden, after the famous British man whose activism served as the catalyst to end slavery in England. The garden was encircled by boxwoods and cedar trees that provided a tranquil sanctuary where I frequently prayed. Surrounded by yellow buttercups that seemed to stare up at me, I knelt in the grass and thanked God for people who respond to the truth — people who will put party politics on the back burner and unite to defend the American family and the gift of life. Clearly, God was producing fruit from my promise by uniting races, using sincere people and the laws inscribed on their hearts — that a life is a life no matter what race, no matter the mother or father's economic bracket and no matter how small.

The fact remained: *all* lives matter!

"I was under the false impression that abortion somehow reversed the process and prevented the child from coming into existence."

From Norma McCorvey, formerly known as Jane Roe of the 1973 *Roe v. Wade* case, in her 2003 affidavit (Section 14) to the Supreme Court of the United States requesting a hearing to reverse the *Roe v. Wade* decision which stripped unborn babies of all rights and protections. SCOTUS refused to hear her case. (Appendix E)

"I should like to know if taking this old Declaration of Independence, which declares that all men are equal upon principle, and making exceptions to it, where it will stop. If one man says it does not mean a Negro why not another say it does not mean some other man?"

Abraham Lincoln
Speeches, Letters, and Papers: 1860-1864

"We are not so very far off from even the sacrifice of babies—if not to a crocodile, at least to a creed."

G. K. Chesterton
Illustrated London Times News, December 4, 1920

For further study about black genocide:

Abort73.com

Black Genocide.org
www.blackgenocide.org

Concerned Women of America
"The Negro Project: Margaret Sanger's Eugenic Plan for Black Americans"
www.concernedwomen.org

Life Dynamics
www.lifedynamics.com

For further study about Frederick Douglass:

Liberty Messenger USA
www.libertymessengerusa.org

What If We've Been Wrong?

CHAPTER NINE
The Beginning of NARAL

"The uterus had been perforated and a section of the lower small intestine had been lacerated in several places."

Bernard N. Nathanson, M.D., *Aborting America*

What If We've Been Wrong?

Early in his practice Dr. Nathanson found the criminal field of abortion to be unjust, and he had a sense of urgency to fix the inequality. In his estimation it was a crisis: the 1960s sexual revolution produced too many out-of-wedlock pregnancies. As American culture thumbed its nose at authority, responsibility and healthy sexual boundaries, Dr. Nathanson thought what needed to be changed were the laws prohibiting abortion — not people's behavior. With improvements in antibiotics and anesthesia, Dr. Nathanson considered decriminalizing abortion the best fix for the "social ill" of unplanned pregnancies.

At that time very little was known about the baby in the womb. What had previously been observed in the 1930s was "… the liberation of a human egg from the ovary. In 1944, through a microscope, was seen the union of the human sperm and ovum. In the 1950s, the events of the first six days of life were described, those critical first steps in a prodigious journey."[11] In fact, so little was known about the "fetus" — a Latin word meaning "baby" — that in *The Cumulative Index Medicus,* a medical journal "which lists every article published in every medical journal in the world … the 1969 edition … under the heading of 'fetus, physiology and anatomy of,' there were five articles in the world's literature."[12] Only five! When Dr. Nathanson began working toward a final solution for unplanned pregnancies, fetology — the study and science of the human unborn — was just beginning.

On June 2, 1967, he met the dynamic Lawrence Lader at a dinner party. Lader had been a close friend of Margaret Sanger, who had died eight months earlier. Sanger had had close connections with leading Nazis, such as Ernst Rudin, who wrote for her *Birth Control Review* pamphlet. Sanger wanted to control the population of those she deemed "dysgenic stock,"[13] which, in her opinion, included poor people, minorities, and a long list of others.

Lader held Sanger in high esteem, agreed with her philosophy of controlling births of "undesirables," and he was *openly* pro-abortion. In fact, he was such an abortion advocate that it was nearly the only

topic he wished to discuss that night over dinner. He impressed
Dr. Nathanson with his opinion that all anti-abortion laws should be
struck down in every state — a radical idea for its day. Lader was
ready to unite a fractured pro-abortion movement into a powerful
political organization, but he needed a medical professional to be the
front man — the face — of this radical idea. Who better than a
pro-abortion obstetrician-gynecologist who needed no persuading?

Dr. Nathanson had just enough defiance against the medical
establishment and their theatre of abortion. He longed to strike down
the existing anti-abortion regulations in New York State. The doctor also
quietly admired the sixties' youth movement that disdained authority
and boundaries. Knowing that the media would willingly embrace
a physician's "enlightened" ideas, Lader thought Dr. Nathanson the
ideal partner. According to Dr. Nathanson, he had a few other useful
credentials: he had learned well from his father the sinister skills of
deception, intimidation, and manipulation.

As Lader shared his enthusiasm for decriminalizing abortion, the seeds
of a vision were planted — a vision that would lead the two men
to organize the National Association for the Repeal of Abortion Laws
(NARAL). They were *not* interested in marketing new discoveries in
embryology and fetology. They had a different agenda — creating an
eight-point propaganda "pro-choice" campaign to persuasively promote
decriminalizing abortion. Soon thereafter, the standard of justice that
applies to all people everywhere would no longer apply to the unborn
child. Voiceless babies — and their mothers and fathers — would be
caught in the crossfire of the deadliest propaganda campaign in
human history, where America would embrace intrinsic evil contrary
to her founding principles.

"After three or four pitchers of beer, we started with the letter 'a' and eventually we reached 'r' and agreed on 'Roe.'"

From Norma McCorvey, formerly known as Jane Roe of the 1973 *Roe v. Wade* case, in her 2003 affidavit (Section 10) to the Supreme Court of the United States requesting a hearing to reverse the *Roe v. Wade* decision which stripped unborn babies of all rights and protections. SCOTUS refused to hear her case. (Appendix E)

"Even as I have seen, those who plow iniquity and sow trouble reap the same."

Job 4:8 (KJV)

"America is like a healthy body and its resistance is threefold: its patriotism, its morality and its spiritual life. If we can undermine these three areas, America will collapse from within."

Frequently attributed to Joseph Stalin, mass murderer,
Marxist Communist dictator of the Soviet Union (1929 - 1953)

For webinars and live presentations about Dr. Bernard Nathanson:

Hosea Initiative
Terry Beatley
www.hosea4you.org

What If We've Been Wrong? Study Course
Becoming a Witness for Life

CHAPTER TEN

The Shadows and United Nations' Treaties

"We've got to keep the women out in front. You know what I mean ... and some blacks. Black women especially. Why are they so damn slow to see the importance of this whole movement to themselves?"

Lawrence Lader to Dr. Bernard Nathanson, *Aborting America*

What If We've Been Wrong?

Sitting among the senator's staff at Senator Houck's town hall meeting was a young, attractive college student. She smiled as the senator complimented his team for keeping him organized and on task. Her inclusion on that team made me shudder, and I was aware that only a few people in attendance knew she had been a NARAL Pro-Choice America political intern, who also presided over a chapter of VOX: Voices for Planned Parenthood, a pro-choice college activist group notorious for encouraging promiscuity and advocating abortion rights.

My heart pounded as I walked up to the microphone for the public question period. I could see a couple of volunteers engaging in our first public skirmish with the senator as they distributed my flyer that contained his voting record *against* the family and *for* the abortion special interest group. Having documented his voting record summary and printed a couple hundred copies on bright orange paper, I felt confident that his days as a senator were numbered. I could hear his voting record being distributed to the crowd of a hundred or more local citizens as they passed the copies along.

Before I spoke at the podium, the senator, who stood about fifteen feet away, casually walked to the front row, took a copy and began to read it. It wasn't long before his face reddened and his forehead glistened with beads of sweat. Senator Houck's voting record against parents and the safety of girls was made clear with the General Assembly bill numbers and respective years in which he had voted:

- *Against* parents being notified of after-school medical treatment;
- *Against* making it a crime to coerce a girl or woman into having an abortion surgery;
- *Against* making ultrasound sonograms available to every woman considering an abortion;

- *Against* stricter health regulations, safety protocols, and inspections at abortion centers;

- *Against* parents being notified of their children's after-school activities;

- For *allowing* partial-birth abortion;

— the list went on and on.

I felt nervous, but I knew the questions needed to be asked to get his response on record, so I proceeded with a question similar to this: "Senator, for the benefit of your constituency, I'd like to review your voting record before asking my question. You have repeatedly voted to allow minor girls to have abortion surgeries and take dangerous abortifacient chemicals without parental consent or knowledge. These surgeries and drugs have major health risks, including infection, perforated uteruses, hemorrhaging, blood clots, stroke and death. Children can't even take a Tylenol pill at school without parental permission, so I simply want to know *why* are you voting to undermine and usurp our parental rights to guide and counsel our own children, and *when* are you going to stop?"

The senator stood speechless. He took cover behind his timekeeper who fussed at me for taking too long with my question. I turned and walked toward my seat expecting to hear his answer, or at least, his feeble excuse. To my surprise, he ignored my questions and invited the next person up to the microphone. About one hour later, and I assume after he was informed that he had been videotaped disregarding my inquiry, he returned to my question and provided his self-righteous answer. He said something akin to this bold statement:

"Now, concerning the question about young women obtaining abortions, I believe minors can make those decisions for themselves."

Excellent! I now had him on record sanctioning the divestment of parents from their responsibilities to raise and form their children into adulthood. I wanted to stand up and ask him, "If that minor child is running a high fever the following morning, how is a mother to know it is because her daughter has a perforated uterus due to a secret abortion? How is a parent to know that the depression her daughter suffers a month, a year, or decade later is because of this surgery unknown to the parent?" This is what Dr. Nathanson had warned me about! The industry will do whatever is necessary to obtain abortion revenue and advance the notion of controlling the population with the most altruistic reasons using politicians who acquiesce to the demands of an unscrupulous industry.

Evidently, Senator Houck was confident that he had enough loyal constituents attending his town hall meeting and that there would be no pushback to his audacious answer. He was right. Citizens in attendance sat like zombies as if they did not even hear his answer or comprehend the far-reaching, trickle-down consequences of what it means for our children to be treated like wards of the state. Not one father or mother stood up and questioned the senator's usurpation of their rights in making surgical and pharmacological decisions for their young daughters. I found their apathy more shocking than his answer, and my desire for his defeat intensified. Right then I resolved to use every tool at my disposal to live up to the promise I had made to Dr. Nathanson. I was determined that these issues would become the catalyst to retire the well-financed Chairman of the Senate Education and Health Committee. The questions remained: Would voters care? Could they be moved to defend the family and the dignity of human life if they were to learn how aggressive the abortion industry really is?

I looked at the young woman on his team. She smiled at the powerful senator again, and I assumed she admired how he had stood his ground. This college student probably thought she was advocating

enlightenment when, in reality, she was participating in darkness.
I felt sure she had no idea who Dr. Nathanson was and how her political activity was wreaking havoc on women, men and their children. She probably had no idea either how her activity, combined with the activity of lawmakers who truly believe that the government should have ultimate authority over children, could lead as far as permanently losing American sovereignty.

This is how it could happen: Under Article VI of the U.S. Constitution, international treaties become *supreme law* in America when ratified by two-thirds of the U.S. Senate and the President of the United States. (The House of Representatives does not vote on international treaties.) There is a United Nations' treaty called the *Convention on the Rights of the Child* (UNCRC), which, if ratified, transfers authority to an international tribunal to decide what is in the "best interests of the child."[14] It removes parents as the ultimate authority over their children and grants unlimited authority to the the United Nations Committee on the Rights of the Child, consisting of eighteen members from countries around the world who will monitor compliance. *"Article IV — Implementation of Rights — places the primary responsibility of ensuring the child's right to life, health, and security on the government, not the parents. Article V — Parental Guidance — [ensures] that the government will define the role that the parent should be playing and enforce that role to its standards. Article XVI — Right to Privacy — states that children have the right to privacy [and that] governments should enact and implement laws that protect children from attacks on their privacy, reputation, family, home, and way of life."*[15] It sounds altruistic, but the concern, though, is due to its ambiguous wording leaving open the possibility of enforcing this right of privacy even against concerned parents. It's already happening in state law; the UNCRC Treaty would enshrine the threat under international law.

What does this have to do with the abortion industry and Dr. Nathanson? Many abortion lobbyists, pro-choice feminists and activists want this treaty ratified because it will, in effect, secure the right for minors to receive confidential abortion and sexual healthcare services under international law *without parental consent or notification.* In addition, it would be a boon to Planned Parenthood's abortion business and would help spread Sanger's population-control ideology.

Here's the risk: When this treaty comes up for a vote, *all pro-choice U.S. Senators* will be pressured to support ratifying the UNCRC Treaty, or other treaties like it. If the senators don't support it, they will very likely be reminded by NARAL, Planned Parenthood, and other pro-abortion lobbying groups and activists that they will lose campaign support — financial donations as well as boots on the ground — and they will be warned of reelection defeat with a primary candidate. This stiff-backed reminder by the abortion lobbyists takes about one minute behind closed doors. This is the way abortion politics works — acquiesce or else.

Sadly, uninformed American voters, many of whom are loving, caring parents, will have sacrificed their parental rights — and their little girls and boys — on the demonic altar of "reproductive freedom" without any recourse because of treaty status under the U.S. Constitution. It is a serious threat marketed under the umbrella of altruism and one that former President Bill Clinton and Hillary Clinton fully supported, though, during Bill Clinton's presidency, the UNCRC Treaty lacked enough U.S. Senate support to pass. Should this treaty or a similar one (there are many threatening treaties) surface again under leadership that believes it takes a village and the United Nations to properly raise a child, as opposed to parents and policies which promote marriage and strong families, Dr. Nathanson's campaign of lies will have toppled American sovereignty and the family unit.

I had learned about the world of politics — where shadows live, deception thrives, darkness reigns and the drive for power consumes people. Unless politicians are grounded in virtue and morality, the shadows can overcome even those who start out with the best intentions. As the NARAL intern continued to smile at Senator Houck, who unashamedly supported stripping *my* right to protect *my* children, I wondered if there were any more Rev. Turners ready to stand up for family values and for the gift of life in this voting district.

I would spend the next few months finding out. I was in for a big surprise.

"*At no time did they tell me that I had to read [the affidavit in the Roe v. Wade case] before they accepted my signature. I told them I trusted them.*"

From Norma McCorvey, formerly known as Jane Roe of the 1973 *Roe v. Wade* case, in her 2003 affidavit (Section 13) to the Supreme Court of the United States requesting a hearing to <u>reverse</u> the *Roe v. Wade* decision which stripped unborn babies of all rights and protections. SCOTUS <u>refused</u> to hear her case. (Appendix E)

"To comprehend the history of thing is to unlock the mysteries of its present, and more, to disclose the profundities of its future."

Hilaire Belloc
Notes of a Curmudgeon, Albright's Ltd., 1956

For further study and action:

American Life League *"Hooking Kids on Sex"* video; www.all.org

Americans United for Life www.aul.org

C-Fam www.c-fam.org

Clare Booth Luce Policy Institute www.cblpi.org

Eagle Forum www.eagleforum.org

Family Research Council www.frc.org

Heritage Foundation www.heritage.org

Human Life Action www.humanlifeactioncenter.org

What If We've Been Wrong?

CHAPTER ELEVEN

The Evil Deeds of Darkness

"We put a spin on the information."

Bernard N. Nathanson, M.D., *to Terry Beatley*

What If We've Been Wrong?

Prior to meeting Dr. Nathanson, Lader had befriended the rising star of feminism, Betty Friedan. She had been "a political activist and professional propagandist for the Communist left for a quarter of a century before the publication of *The Feminist Mystique* ..."[16] Her book was published in 1963 — the year I was born — and is credited with starting the second wave of feminism. Before the wave turned into a tsunami, the vast majority of feminists seeking equal pay for equal work and increasing job prospects were *not* in favor of decriminalizing abortion. Friedan worked hard marketing discontent, though, persuading American suburban housewives and mothers that their lot in life was "a comfortable concentration camp" unless they break free of it in the form of working outside the home. In 1966, Friedan organized the National Organization for Women. (NOW) At that time Friedan had been opposed to abortion, but within a year of Lader's crafty persuasion, Friedan pivoted on the abortion issue and embraced the slogan Lader was peddling: "No woman can call herself free who does not own and control her own body."[17]

By the second annual NOW Convention held on November 18, 1967, and in a Lader-sort-of-way, Friedan railroaded the pro-abortion, pro-contraception plank into NOW's platform. This is well documented in the book *Subverted.* "... NOW simultaneously became both the national organization for women and the national organization against motherhood, a living contradiction."[18] Many of its leaders and members were furious, and some even quit; but from that day forward the "sexual revolution had hijacked the feminist movement,"[19] and NARAL's cofounder, Lawrence Lader, and his Communist-friendly cohort, Betty Friedan, had won.

Early in his career Lawrence Lader "... had worked for Vito Marcantonio, the only card-carrying Communist [up to that time] ever to be elected to the U.S. House of Representatives."[20] Therefore, embracing a radical agenda to fundamentally transform American society was nothing new for him. According to Dr. Nathanson, Lader adhered to revolutionary politics in which virtue, boundaries and honesty were *not* prerequisites.

Lader was knowledgeable, clever, and scrupulously precise. Dr. Nathanson said that his partner may have engrossed himself in this battle to decriminalize abortion as much for the benefit of promiscuous *men* as for the women he portrayed himself as interested in helping. Sex without consequences or responsibilities seemed to be Lader's ultimate motivation. It seemed as though Lader thought pregnancy was a curse and the closest thing to a dreaded disease. When I spoke with Dr. Nathanson, he had nothing favorable to say about his former partner.

The two men set out to organize the National Association for the Repeal of Abortion Laws (NARAL) over the next fifteen months, and they recruited Friedan. NARAL was the first political organization dedicated to pooling financial resources, equipping professionals with strategies to push toward decriminalizing abortion, marshaling activists, and synchronizing efforts in multiple states in which decriminalizing abortion was politically possible. The Lader-Nathanson-Friedan trio formed a dominant voice in the marketplace targeting women, legislatures, the Catholic Church, Protestants and the court of public opinion.

Even though NARAL's goal of stripping all rights and protections from the unborn was predetermined, perception in the media meant everything. They agreed that in order to advance the cause, it needed to *appear* that women were in control. "The first thing we did when I was involved with the founding of NARAL ... We allocated the majority of our budget in 1969 to a [female] public relations person" and they maximized Friedan's notoriety on NARAL's board of directors.

NARAL's first public comment organizational meeting was on February 14, 1969, and it plummeted in pandemonium. Screaming militant feminists shouted profanities and spewed anger at any *pro-abortion* speaker who expressed thoughts of a more restricted or slower path toward abortion decriminalization. They were crude, agitated and unruly. Dr. Nathanson did not like the dogmatism of the violent supporters and detested the militant feminists, but he and Lader *needed* them to

advance the cause, always keeping the activist women out in front.
By providing a public forum for these women, the feminists felt
empowered, but the forum was merely a smokescreen. Answers to all
of the important issues were predetermined. More importantly, by using
the women, NARAL's leaders were provided a greater opportunity for
media exposure, which is a requirement for political success. Although
their debut was not front page, it earned them a respectable amount of
coverage for NARAL's conception.

For the remainder of 1969, NARAL began executing an eight-point
strategic propaganda campaign. It targeted the state of New York
with the goal of overturning its anti-abortion law. The leaders would
then take their strategy national. NARAL's goal was "Total Repeal.
No more laws regulating abortion."[21] Trained in target messaging by
a public relations firm, the NARAL executives knew how to appeal to
Americans' emotions and to the coddled and defiant sixties generation.
Dr. Nathanson entered the public arena with the argument of "Choice,"
intentionally shifting attention from the reality of what that choice *does
to a baby* to focus solely on what they touted as "women's healthcare."

The team also used catchy phrases such as "Women Demand Equality"
and "Children by Choice" to tap into Americans' sense of justice and
fairness. Crafting emotional slogans, they intentionally masked the
extremism of removing all rights and protections for the preborn child.
NARAL needed additional media coverage to advance its misinformation
campaign, so they established citizen action committees, earned
endorsements from prestigious people in business and healthcare,
and created surveys and position statements, which were frequently
"dripped" to the press as they rolled out, according to Dr. Nathanson —
a well-orchestrated battery of lies. He explained how NARAL's public
relations representative would "... in turn court the media. It was
made up of young radicalized college graduates involved in *opposing*
the Vietnam War. Abortion was a cause they could *support*."
(Emphasis added)

Eager for ready-made stories, particularly those about women's rights, reporters accepted Dr. Nathanson's expert opinion and his data as facts. They rarely second-guessed him or NARAL's public relations representative. Capitalizing on the reporters' antagonistic feelings toward authority, tradition, faith, and boundaries, he guided the movement to the place where NARAL needed to go. Dr. Nathanson used these young, inexperienced and politically less-informed journalists as pawns in the mounting war. They made it so easy for him.

NARAL worked overtime at "spinning the information" to increase support for abortion-on-demand. By claiming that *one million* women annually were risking their lives by having back-alley abortions and that *five to ten thousand* American women a year were dying because of it, Dr. Nathanson ginned up sympathy for the cause of abortion law repeal. In addition, knowing every political strategy needs an alarming statistic, he told the media that *sixty* percent of Americans wanted abortion-on-demand legalized. It sounded like an unstoppable majority and that women's healthcare was in a major crisis. Throughout the misinformation campaign, facts, reliable statistics and logic were mere casualties.

In his book *The Abortion Papers,* Dr. Nathanson admits that many of the NARAL board meeting minutes included "nonsensical medical and scientific claims."[22] He purposely, frequently and boldly distorted the facts and figures to sway public opinion. He acknowledged that the more accurate numbers were approximately a hundred thousand criminal abortions annually — not one million — and closer to two hundred and fifty women died each year — not five to ten thousand! Prior to the campaign, only one half of one percent of the United States electorate was in favor of unrestricted abortion — not the reported sixty percent.[23]
Dr. Nathanson acknowledged that the bigger the lies, the more likely Americans would believe them. He also knew that false statistics needed to be greater than fifty percent in order to create the impression of a majority. Intentionally, he pulled America's compassionate heartstrings while coat hangers became synonymous with botched

abortions. By simply repeating the slogans and false data, the media created its own narrative and the doctor's lies became the marketed "truth." Criminal abortion seemed to be at epidemic levels with dead women down every city alley. It was propaganda, and it worked.

Supported by a multi-million-dollar budget, Lader and Nathanson worked with other organizations and began targeting politicians and candidates who could be pressured to support decriminalizing abortion. If the candidate or politician resisted, his political career or aspirations were subject to the full wrath of NARAL's negative campaigning. Dr. Nathanson often thought Lader's tactics were too extreme, but Lader lived for the extreme. NARAL was about to launch its most aggressive political maneuver yet — against the Catholic Church.

Both Lader and Nathanson viewed Catholic pro-life doctrine as a major impediment to decriminalizing abortion. They knew the Catholic Church was the most authoritative voice in protecting innocent life, so they set out to paint Catholic leadership in the worst possible light. When reflecting on NARAL's plan to fool enough Catholics for political victory, Dr. Nathanson wrote, "Many [Catholics] ended up in [NARAL's] camp, and [NARAL] used them with great effect ..."[24]

NARAL called their four-prong Catholic manipulation plan the Dr. Nathanson "Catholic Strategy." It was covert, politically effective, destructive to the parent-child relationship, and it perfectly advanced Sanger's "Negro Project."

The human toll would be *catastrophic.*

"My lawyers never discussed what an abortion is, other than to make the misrepresentation that it's only tissue.'"

From Norma McCorvey, formerly known as Jane Roe of the 1973 *Roe v. Wade* case, in her 2003 affidavit (Section 14) to the Supreme Court of the United States requesting a hearing to <u>reverse</u> the *Roe v. Wade* decision which stripped unborn babies of all rights and protections. SCOTUS <u>refused</u> to hear her case. (Appendix E)

" [Myths] are lies, carefully designed to reinforce a particular philosophy or morality within a culture. They are instruments of manipulation and control."

George Grant
Grand Illusions, Highland Books, 3rd Edition, 1998

For further study:

The Marketing of Evil
How Radicals, Elitists, and Pseudo-Experts Sell
Us Corruption Disguised as Freedom
by David Kupelian
WND Books, 2005

For regular updates on the battle for life:

Life Site News
www.lifesitenews.com

The Stream
www.stream.org

For pro-life action in your local area:

Pro-life Action League
www.prolifeaction.org

What If We've Been Wrong?

CHAPTER TWELVE

The People Who Make the Laws Rule the Culture

*"NARAL opposed on principle the involvement
of religious groups in politics, conveniently ignoring the
leadership role clerics had played in that other pivotal
revolutionary movement of the 1960s – the civil rights action."*

Bernard N. Nathanson, M.D., *The Abortion Papers*

What If We've Been Wrong?

"Oh, my God, I had no idea!"

This was one of many responses that I heard among the gasps of the 275 ethnically-diverse pastors and community leaders attending a breakfast gathering in Fredericksburg that I organized with the Virginia Christian Alliance and a group of volunteers. Breakfast sponsors included Regent University, Liberty University School of Law, The Heritage Foundation, the Center for Security Policy and ParentalRights.org. Exhibit sponsors included Concerned Women of America, The Frederick Douglass Foundation, Urban League, Reagan Institute, Virginia Coalition for Life, Virginians for School Choice, Bethany Christian Services and the Religious Freedom Coalition.

The pastors were responding to the data I presented showing the evidence of uninformed voters. I recited some of Senator Houck's most egregious votes over the past twenty-eight years and contrasted his record with the records of senators in nearby jurisdictions. Clearly, Houck strongly favored NARAL's abortion lobbyists over the wishes of his constituency. The looks of dismay on the pastors' faces as I peeled away Houck's family-friendly rhetoric spoke volumes as I demonstrated a political reality — *the people who make the laws rule the culture.*

"Now, pastors, do you see who gets hurt when you remain silent in your pulpits about defending the right to life in the political realm? Women and children become the immediate victims. The founder of NARAL told me so and explained how they used Christians' political ignorance, apathy and silence to advance the culture of death in America."

The room was dead silent, and I reminded them, "Jesus said, 'You will know them by their fruit ...' The fruit for an incumbent is how he votes on bills, *not* what he says to get reelected. Congregations need to be taught because that is part of loving God with all of our hearts, souls and minds. These are *moral* issues — not political — and we should have the most persuasive voice because America is founded on the Judeo-Christian value system. Protecting political party brands is not important. Protecting human life is non-negotiable."

Two guests of honor spoke before me. Virginia Attorney General Ken Cuccinelli presented the enormous legal latitude pastors actually have in the pulpit, in lieu of remaining silent about moral issues. He said:

> I would encourage those of you who are pastoring in black churches to look at the history of that [abortion] movement. Go read Margaret Sanger's letters about the Harlem Project and what she wanted to do. And I would also challenge you to pull out the map of Virginia and look at where the abortion clinics are. Go look at that. And if that doesn't make you mad, well then, you are a lot calmer person than I am. That makes me mad. Margaret Sanger is alive and well, or at least her legacy is.[25]

Attorney General Cuccinelli had exposed Sanger's racism in a factual way, and I could tell that the audience did not doubt him. He ended his speech by reminding the ministers that too many pastors stay away from politics thinking that it is scary, dirty or illegal. He added, "Well, guess what? You just left the field to the other side!" I sensed that his message resonated with the crowd.

Our second guest, Bishop Harry Jackson of the International Communion of Evangelical Churches, spoke of applying our Christian faith in the real world as citizens and impacting government. Both Jackson and Cuccinelli's presentations addressed the manner in which to apply eternal principles to protect our national creed as outlined in the Declaration of Independence: "We hold these truths to be self-evident, that all men are created equal, that they are endowed by their Creator with certain unalienable Rights, that among these are Life ..."

Prior to wrapping up my talk, I explained that Dr. Nathanson had said his strategy of deception worked only because the clergy was not united, nor determined, to combat this evil. So, in an effort to show how we must unite on a fundamental principle of American liberty and stop divisions based on race, I invited the crowd to stand and greet someone from a different race. The room filled with laughter, hugs and hand-shaking as leaders made friendly overtures to one another. From the podium I witnessed a restored and united America in which people can shift the pendulum away from division, lies and tyranny by first honoring the unalienable right to life in the voting booth.

As I scanned the crowd, I saw the smiling face of Rev. Turner. I asked the attendees to turn their attention to him, and I shared his story of surviving abortion. "Pastors and leaders, Rev. Turner could not have entered the battle to uphold the name of Jesus Christ in the Fredericksburg City Council meeting if the abortionist had had his way sixty-three years earlier! This is another reason why protecting the gift of life is so important. How many witnesses for Christ have been destroyed?" The room burst into loud applause for this humble man of God. I quietly thanked the Lord for this well-deserved recognition of Rev. Turner. His godmother was right. He *had* been anointed in his mother's womb to do great works for the Lord. We smiled at each other and I appreciated his reassuring nod. The truth was finally being told, and the political civil war on motherhood, fatherhood, and love suffered a major defeat that morning.

When the breakfast adjourned another minister, who was sitting with Bishop Jackson, walked over to me and clasped my shoulders. He introduced himself and said, "I want to encourage you to fulfill your promise to Dr. Nathanson, and if you can figure out a way to help the disenfranchised ex-offender in the process, you will have a way to reach broadly into the black community with your message because the criminal justice system has affected fifty percent of all households ...

even more than abortion at thirty-six percent." I sensed his sincerity, but I didn't know any ex-offenders at the time, and I definitely didn't understand how to connect the two issues. God did. He had another small miracle in store for me with an ex-offender I would soon meet.

I had hoped that the event would get at least a little bit of coverage in the local paper. It got more than that. The pastor breakfast appeared above the fold on the front page of *The Free Lance Star* with a full-color photo of Attorney General Cuccinelli, and the online articles went viral with tens of thousands of views. This became another answer to my prayers — media coverage.

It was a fabulous lesson for me that "God had my back," and I needed to leave the victory to Him. My job was to trust Him and continue pressing forward to fulfill my promise to Dr. Nathanson.

"The courts did not ask whether I knew what I was asking for."

From Norma McCorvey, formerly known as Jane Roe of the 1973
Roe v. Wade case, in her 2003 affidavit (Section 15) to the Supreme Court
of the United States requesting a hearing to reverse the *Roe v. Wade*
decision which stripped unborn babies of all rights and protections.
SCOTUS refused to hear her case. (Appendix E)

"The modern world is full of the old Christian virtues gone mad. The virtues have gone mad because they have been isolated from each other and are wandering alone. Thus some scientists care for truth, but their truth is pitiless. And thus, some humanitarians only care for pity, but their pity – I am sorry to say – is often untruthful."

G.K. Chesterton
Orthodoxy, Dodd, Mead, and Company, 1908

For further study:

Setting the Record Straight: American History in Black and White
Book or DVD
David Barton
Wallbuilders, Inc., 2010

Center for Bio-Ethical Reform
www.abortionno.org

CHAPTER THIRTEEN
The God of Second Chances

*"… when faced with complex public questions in a free
and democratic society an educated electorate will always
make the morally correct decision."*

Bernard N. Nathanson, M.D., *The Abortion Papers*

What If We've Been Wrong?

Less than a month later, my friend Angela and I were distributing the senator's voting record in a minority neighborhood. We arrived at the first house where three men were sitting on the front porch. Angela engaged them in conversation about the importance of family and how thirty-six percent of all abortions are of black babies, yet childbearing-age black women are *only* three to four percent of the population. Shaking their heads in dismay, all the men said they did not agree with killing babies. What surprised me is that they all wanted what we were carrying in a basket — a little card which explained fetal development at the various weeks of gestation and ten-week gestational baby models that fit in the palm of a hand. One man sent his young daughter down the steps to retrieve a card and model for each of them.

While holding the models in their hands, the men listened intently as Angela told them about the senator's voting record against life and how he supports the agenda of the abortion industry. They wanted to know how we knew this information. I told them it could be found on a legislative report card, and I asked if I could show them one, so they invited me up onto the porch.

What happened next was amazing.

As they carefully studied the record, they started pointing at different names of senators and delegates whom they knew and expressed their disgust at discovering these elected officials voted *for* the abortion industry and voted *against* family values, *against* parental rights, *against* school choice and *against* religious liberty.

Then I made my discovery. They were all disenfranchised.

The men told me that they were ex-offenders and they had never had their voting rights restored. All three of them, though, said that if they could vote, they would gladly vote *against* Senator Houck and vote *for* the pro-life, pro-family candidate. We didn't talk about political parties;

we talked about what unites us as a people. The difference in our skin color didn't matter either; instead, we saw what we had in common as part of God's family — our faith, a desire to want the best for our families, and a respect for the dignity of *all* life. Thanking Angela and me for sharing this information, they encouraged us to continue into their community telling others. I was overjoyed by their response and how eager they were to learn. It was at this moment I thought how much I'd like to start a school for ex-offenders and teach civic and U.S. Constitution courses and help these men become informed citizens. We had more doors to knock on, so we said our good-byes and walked to the next house.

This is when we met a man named Wilson.* He was a street-savvy guy who bore the scars of a hard life. Although he was in good humor, Wilson was guarded with us and impressed me as someone with whom I would always want to be on good terms. Wilson seemed to be friendly but more concerned with political party labels, and he avoided the issues we were trying to address. "Are you a Democrat or a Republican?" I responded that first and most importantly I was a "Christocrat" bringing truth because votes had been taken advantage of for twenty-eight years. Secondly, I was a *Frederick Douglass Republican* — not just a Republican. We parted on good terms, but unlike the response from the first three men, neither Angela nor I felt like he responded to the information. What I didn't know was that I would see Wilson on my return trip into his community in just a couple of weeks.

I prayed and asked God to send me people who would help knock on doors in this community. I didn't know where to find them. Two days later I received a phone call from a man at an organization. He wanted to know how they could be of help. I responded, "People who will pound

(*Name is changed.)

the pavement. Please send me as many people as you can on Saturday." Amazingly, about twenty millennials arrived and we went back into Wilson's neighborhood. This trip would bear even more fruit.

When I passed Wilson's house, I did not plan to bother him again, but he surprised me by turning off his lawnmower. He shouted, "Welcome back to my neighborhood! What information do you have for me today, Terry?" He remembered my name. I thought that might be a sign of something positive. I handed him a bright orange flyer that three black ministers had approved for distribution. It read, *"Do You Support Killing African American Babies?"* He read through the seven bulleted facts that explained how Sanger's organization started the "Negro Project," how she boasted of speaking to the Ku Klux Klan, and how Planned Parenthood was a major supporter for Senator Houck. It detailed Houck's voting record and provided evidence that he did the bidding of the abortion industry's chief lobbyists — NARAL and Planned Parenthood. The flyer also referenced the *Maafa21* film and how to access it online. It ended with a simple request to vote *against* the long-term politician. None of my materials mentioned the other candidate's name or political party. I just wanted the senator's voting record exposed, believing that if enough people had the knowledge, they would vote *against* him.

"Wilson, should American laws support what God says or what man wants?" I asked.

"Of course, what God says," he answered.

"Well, that's exactly what Frederick Douglass, one of the fathers of civil rights in America, believed. He wanted government to leave the black man alone so that he could thrive in liberty, provide for his family and be industrious. Douglass believed in limited government and personal responsibility, and he respected the Constitution and the sanctity of *all* human life, including life in the womb.[26] He never would have supported Sanger's "Negro Project" if it had existed in his day or the feminist pro-abortion agenda which emasculates fathers. Well, I'm exposing this tragedy and I do it because the Word says to expose evil and love my neighbor. You, Wilson, are my neighbor."

He stared at me and I could tell something had changed.

"Tell me about that doctor again," he said.

"I made a promise to Dr. Bernard Nathanson, who admits to fast-tracking this evil, and I'm tired of politicians hiding in the shadows taking cover under the slogan 'Choice,' while families are being destroyed, parental rights are undermined, women are hurt and millions of babies lose their lives. Abortion is now the number one killer of black Americans. Think about it. Abortion kills more black Americans than all illnesses, accidents and homicides combined in the black community. The numbers are staggering and it is not an accident. Planned Parenthood is controlling populations through abortion and proliferation of contraception."

Wilson recapped what we discussed and I confirmed his assessment. Then he made a profound declaration, "Well, I'll tell you what; I'll join your team. No one ever brings us this kind of truth, and families are falling apart here. We need representation that will strengthen families, not break us apart. Thank you for coming into my neighborhood."

I had never been so happy to high-five and hug a stranger. Wilson and I had connected on a most basic human level by recognizing that the worth of a person does not depend upon whether others think his or her life is significant. Wilson then asked more questions and shared with me what it was like to grow up in a community in which the family unit has nearly disintegrated. He wanted to learn more, and he asked me for books rather than DVDs. Again, I was just amazed at what was transpiring.

Loving others with bold truth and saving lives made for quick friendships, trust and the surest way to end racism. What I began to experience at this moment was what it would look like in a practical way when my promise to Dr. Nathanson is widely known and the truth of Planned Parenthood and Sanger's "Negro Project" is exposed on the national scale. Political strongholds and the destruction of the family unit would end as a renewed respect for the dignity of all human life would sweep America and unite this country that has lost its moorings. These were my thoughts as I stood looking up at Wilson, who was now my friend.

My surprises for the day were not over yet. A truck pulled up beside us. The driver was a distinguished professional whom Wilson knew. He explained to the driver what I was doing and gave him the paperwork. After glancing at the information, the driver declared it was about time someone came into this neighborhood with the truth and that it was exactly what was needed and long overdue. "This community and others like it all over America are desperate for this truth and no one ever reaches in and shares it with us." He encouraged me to keep going.

Wilson and I took the issue of race off the table; we both knew it was incongruous — in fact, impossible — to be a racist while actively pursuing saving the lives of children from another race. We united over the most basic principles of liberty — protecting the gift of life and the role of parents in the lives of their children. He joined my team and informed more than *three thousand five hundred voters* of the facts on the senator's voting record. Unbeknownst to me, he even entered the hospital with which the senator had been affiliated and distributed leaflets to the kitchen and janitorial staff until he got kicked off of the property! Many of them were Wilson's friends and cousins who appreciated receiving the senator's voting record. They were equally disappointed, and many vowed to vote for the pro-life, pro-family candidate.

Wilson informed me that he was disenfranchised too and that he had never given much thought to voting anyway, but now he would.
He understood that to vote was an opportunity to honor God and His gift of life. I valued his friendship and I thanked God for His purposeful plan for us — *the human race.*

He truly is the God of second chances.

"The courts never took any testimony about this [that abortion terminates the life of an actual human being], and I heard nothing which shed light on what abortion really was."

From Norma McCorvey, formerly known as Jane Roe of the 1973 *Roe v. Wade* case, in her 2003 affidavit (Section 14) to the Supreme Court of the United States requesting a hearing to reverse the *Roe v. Wade* decision which stripped unborn babies of all rights and protections. SCOTUS refused to hear her case. (Appendix E)

"Our nation cannot continue down the path of abortion, so radically at odds with our history, our heritage, and our concepts of justice. This sacred legacy, and the well-being and the future of our country, demand that protection of innocents must be guaranteed and that the personhood of the unborn be declared and defended throughout our land."

President Ronald Reagan
Personhood Proclamation, January 14, 1988

For leadership training:

CURE – Center for Urban Renewal and Education
www.urbancure.org

Frederick Douglass Leadership Institute
www.dlinstitute.org

Generation Joshua
www.generationjoshua.org

The Gloucester Institute
www.gloucesterinstitute.org

The Leadership Institute
www.leadershipinstitute.org

National Right to Life Academy
(A training course for pro-life college students)
www.nrlc.org/site/academy/

Patriot Academy
www.patriotacademy.com

CHAPTER FOURTEEN
The Few Perfidious Priests and The Catholic Strategy

*"… the church helped us in NARAL …
we used them with great effect."*

Bernard N. Nathanson, M.D., *The Abortion Papers*

Dr. Nathanson's second chance would come much later. It was now 1970 — the year that NARAL would crush a 141-year-old New York State law protecting children in the womb. Following that milestone, Dr. Nathanson would introduce to New Yorkers a new concept — ambulatory abortion services. Walk-in, walk-out same-day surgery. It would ultimately usher in the dawn of the mass, assembly-line slaughter of American babies. It was NARAL's cunning "Catholic Strategy," though, which would polarize politics, making a *long-term* abortion victory possible. In order to understand the magnitude of NARAL's success for swaying Catholics, one must first understand the timeline and historical religious context — particularly with what happened to the Kennedys.

> *There was an intentional, systematic, concerted effort on the part of a group of dissenting Catholic theologians (including Fr. Richard McCormick, Fr. Charles Curran, Fr. Joseph Fuchs, Fr. Robert Drinan, and Fr. John Courtney Murray), who spent a good deal of time with the Kennedys in the mid 1960s employing bogus moral theology arguments to convince them they could 'accept and promote abortion with a clear conscience' ... Once this was accomplished, these same Judas priests undertook to literally coach the Kennedys on what to say and how to vote in favor of abortion in their public lives. Given the Kennedys' enormous influence over American politics, it was diabolically logical for those dissenting Catholic theologians to have targeted this renowned and respected Catholic family for 'conversion.'* [27]

In July 1968, though, two years before NARAL's first legislative victory and at the height of the sexual revolution, Pope Paul VI released an encyclical which exploded like an atomic bomb. Today, it could possibly be the *most* prophetic document written in the 20th century. Written for Catholics and "to all men [and women] of good will on the regulation of birth," he titled it *Humanae Vitae,* which in English means *"Of Human Life."* (See Appendix G: Excerpts from *Humanae Vitae)* He warned of four societal consequences if cultures became closed to the gift of life by their acceptance of widespread birth regulation. (1) Pope Paul VI cautioned that the use of contraceptives would place a "dangerous weapon ... in the hands of those public authorities who take no heed of moral exigencies." In other words, governments would get involved in healthcare — *population control in particular* — without any moral constraints. (2) He also cautioned that birth regulation would "lead to conjugal infidelity and the general lowering of morality." (3) He forewarned that "the man" would lose respect for "the woman" and "no longer [care] for her physical and psychological equilibrium" and would come to "the point of considering her as a mere instrument of selfish enjoyment and no longer as his respected and beloved companion." Pope Paul emphasized that the Church's historical teaching on contraception was designed to protect the good of conjugal love and protect against treating each other as objects of pleasure.[28] (4) His final warning was that contraception would lead man to think that he had unlimited dominion over his own body — in other words, the age of hedonism, impurity, euthanasia, mad science — where one's faith is criminalized and freedom of conscience is a crime.

"Though there was much support for the encyclical, no document ever met with as much dissent, led to a great extent by Fr. Charles Curran..."[29] — the same priest who had previously guided the Kennedys to politically support abortion. In addition, he is the same priest who was finally removed in 1986 from his professor position at Catholic University of America because of his opposition to the Church's moral teaching.

Unfortunately, most Catholics have never read *Humanae Vitae. But all of the pope's predictions have come true.* For example, in the realm of science, researchers are now mixing together the genes of animals and humans. On the healthcare front, big government tried to force Little Sisters of the Poor, an order of Catholic nuns, to provide birth control and abortifacient pharmaceuticals to its employees through its healthcare plan, though to do so violates the nuns' religious beliefs. In fact, the federal government tried strong-arming the nuns with a seventy million dollar fine. Additionally, we live in an age of skyrocketing divorce, rampant pornography, the hook-up culture, and an epidemic level of sexually transmitted diseases with over half of the twenty million new cases every year being young people between the ages of fifteen and twenty-four years old;[30] but this *is* the religious doctrine of Margaret Sanger and her contemporary, Dr. Alfred Kinsey.

The world began following *their* worldview and rejected the truth found in *Humanae Vitae*.

Kinsey was America's first "sexologist" who recorded sexual experimentation on children as young as five months old to support his theory that children are sexual from birth.[31] He supported Sanger's worldview of sexual hedonism, but openly broadened the scope to normalize abortion, pornography, masturbation, no fault divorce, and, of course, homosexuality.[32] So as the Sanger/Kinsey contagion spread from the sixties forward — and some priests and theologians, like Fr. Curran, embraced Kinsey's pseudo-science — much of the American Catholic leadership, whether intentionally or not, failed to *proactively* and *boldly* support the Catholic Church's teaching regarding contraception. Now the warnings look like a fulfilled prophecy. A large percentage of Catholics use contraception — married or unmarried — and Kinsey's ideas have warped the thinking of too many Catholic pastors, parents and politicians. In fact, this led to some Catholic theologians and eventually lay people "... dissenting not only about contraception but also about homosexuality, masturbation, adultery, divorce and many other issues."[33] The true teachings of the Church provide a strong foundation for the American family, but far too many Catholic leaders have been mum as the Sanger/Kinsey worldview — a contagion — devoured American culture. The weakest among us — women and children — were hurt and the world continues to disdain Pope Paul VI's wise counsel despite the overwhelming evidence of its *accuracy*. This was the historical setting in which NARAL was organized.

Within two years of *Humanae Vitae,* NARAL and other abortion advocates launched a "political blitzkrieg,"[34] stripping away all rights and protections for the unborn baby up through the twenty-fourth week of pregnancy in New York State. NARAL's founders had anticipated that a win would springboard their political action organization onto the national platform with Dr. Nathanson at the medical helm. They were correct.

Known as the 1970 Cook-Leichter bill, this legislation first succeeded in the New York Senate, passing with a 31 to 26 vote. In the New York Assembly's Codes Committee, two concessions were added: a 24-week limitation and a parental consent requirement. On the first of three rounds of voting in the Assembly, the bill was defeated and tabled. NARAL's blitzkrieg went into overdrive pressuring assemblymen to pass the bill by rallying support with enlisted activists. Some Protestant and a few rogue Catholic clergymen joined in the battle as well.

While Lawrence Lader pressured the politicians, Dr. Nathanson tried to enlist help from Planned Parenthood's New York chapter. He asked its board of directors for the opportunity to present his case. They invited Dr. Nathanson to a meeting at which he strongly encouraged them to align themselves with NARAL, join the effort to legalize abortion, prepare to offer abortion services, and channel dollars to NARAL for future political and legislative battles. Quite discouraged, he left the meeting with the impression they would *not* join in the fight. They didn't – at first.

Ten days after being tabled and undergoing a tie vote with the full barrage of NARAL's campaigning, the Cook-Leichter bill passed, and Lader's friend, Governor Nelson D. Rockefeller, signed it into law on April 11, 1970. The victory was huge. The impossible had just happened, and the NARAL team was euphoric! They, along with others, had created a political-cultural climate based on propaganda and savvy political pressure to overturn a law that they thought was outdated and unjust. Dr. Nathanson and Lader were interviewed on TV and radio and often appeared in press conferences, finding support at every turn. Though not the first state to legalize abortion, New York was the first to pass such a radically liberal bill.

The doctor was building his legacy when he received a request from Planned Parenthood of New York not too long after the law had changed. They asked if he would mentor their doctors as they expanded their services to include abortion. I can only surmise Planned Parenthood calculated the enormous revenue they were missing out on by not providing abortions. Why? Because just a few years before this request, Planned Parenthood's World Population leaflet circa 1965 warned women not to abort their children! *"An abortion kills the life of a baby after it has begun. It is dangerous to your life and health. It may make you sterile so that when you want a child you cannot have it."*[35] Regardless of Planned Parenthood's bold, factual warning, Dr. Nathanson taught its medical personnel for the next two years. He said they took copious notes as he taught them how to perform abortions and manage abortion facilities. He had no idea that the organization would one day far exceed all of his expectations in revenue growth and the human toll. Planned Parenthood was well on its way to slaughtering over three hundred thousand children per year, providing over a *third* of all abortions. NARAL's propaganda had won.

Many of NARAL's dirtiest tactics are documented in Dr. Nathanson's collection of thoughts and notes from high level NARAL meetings in his book *The Abortion Papers.* The most disturbing was the "Catholic Strategy." By manipulating Catholic candidates and incumbents and, ultimately, persuading enough Catholic voters to secure a pro-abortion majority in the legislature, NARAL was able to to pass, ratify and maintain the new law which stripped all rights and protections from unborn children. It worked perfectly in New York where so many Catholics resided. Nathanson and Lader quickly strategized ways to implement it in other states in which decriminalizing abortion seemed remotely possible.

I listened to his condensed version of the "Catholic Strategy" and how they took a page right out of Margaret Sanger's marketing manual on how she spread the cultural acceptance of contraception and eugenics on a national scale. Sanger had needed a villain to blame for holding back what appeared to be progressive "women's healthcare." She chose the Catholic Church, even though until the 1930 Anglican Lambeth Conference in England, Protestants were as much against artificial birth control as Catholics. Like Sanger, Lader also chose Catholic Church leadership as NARAL's villain. According to Dr. Nathanson, "... the anti-Catholic warp was a central strategy, a keystone of the abortion movement."[36]

This stratagem employed a brazen, multi-tiered approach to secure Catholic support for pro-abortion candidates, which was an issue the Catholic voter had *never* had to consider until 1970. If NARAL couldn't secure enough Catholic votes for "Candidates for Choice," the organization knew it risked serious long-term defeat with every election cycle. If the will of the New York voters was to return to protecting children in the womb and supporting adoption services, NARAL would ultimately lose its recent victory. Keep in mind, this was the era before the Supreme Court's judicial fiat — the 1973 *Roe v. Wade* decision — which effectively silenced the voice of the people by unconstitutionally legislating from the bench.

NARAL's "Catholic Strategy," which was eventually used nationwide, included, first, blaming the Catholic Church hierarchy every time a woman died from complications due to an illegal abortion. Second, they supported the few Catholic candidates who were open to abortion law repeal or modification. Third, NARAL emphasized in the media the pro-choice Catholic minority opinion, which made Catholic support appear vastly larger than it actually was. Lastly, and most importantly, they devised a tactic called the "Catholic Straddle" "to separate religious conviction from legislative judgment."[37] This four-part strategy, which I'll explain in greater detail, became NARAL's ultimate conquest and triumph over a significant portion of the Catholic vote to favor — without remorse, guilt or shame — pro-choice candidates. This is why Dr. Nathanson described to me that the "Catholic Strategy" has been "the most brilliant political strategy of all time." Rightly so. NARAL has never released the political stronghold it has held on many Catholic voters since the early 1970s — despite the death tally, loss of parental rights, black genocide, and a culture of increasing violence.

Dr. Nathanson would later write,

> *It was, in a sense, the self-fulfilling prophecy: knowing that the Catholic Church would vigorously oppose abortion, we laced the campaign with generous dollops of anti-Catholicism, and once the monster was lured out of the cave in response to the abortion challenge and the nakedly biased line, we could make the Catholic Church the point man of the opposition. The more vigorously the church opposed, the stronger the appeal of the anti-Catholic line became to the liberal media, to the northeastern political establishment, to the leftist elements of the Protestant Church, and to Catholic intellectuals themselves.[38]*

On a relentless, aggressive offensive, the cofounders took turns charging Church leadership with being insensitive, ignorant, archaic and unresponsive. It certainly was not the first time in nineteen hundred years the hierarchy had been called names, so the Church chose to ignore the anti-Catholic rhetoric. Interestingly, in Dr. Nathanson's opinion, this lack of response and passivity worked in NARAL's favor. "What continually surprised us in the planning sessions and strategy meetings … was not only the comparatively mild quality of organized Catholic opposition [to abortion], but also the virtual absence of response to what was blatantly an anti-Catholic campaign … the religious bias was unmistakable."[39] Had African Americans or Jews been the object of NARAL's wrath, the media would have blistered the political organization, but because the villain was the Catholic Church hierarchy, NARAL got an easy media pass.

The duo claimed the Catholic leaders were turning the issue into a "religious war," when in reality, the leadership was merely standing firm on the deposit of truth that all human life deserves dignity. The Church's position was not new, nor was it evolving. Catholic leadership was unapologetic, steady, and without fanfare in their defense of life, but NARAL aggressively leveraged the minority opinion of the few wayward Catholic leaders.

Among other charges, including challenging the Church's tax exemption status, NARAL claimed that the Church lacked humanitarian understanding — an odd claim that could not be substantiated considering more than nineteen hundred years of pro-life, pro-family doctrine, historical writing and activism. Somehow, Lader and Nathanson missed the history lesson that the early Christians civilized a brutal and barbaric world — one in which babies were burned alive when being sacrificed to pagan gods in blazing pyres and a culture in which fathers practiced infanticide by abandoning their unwanted newborns, *usually girls,* out in the elements to be eaten by wolves, baked to death in the sun, or picked up by another to be raised as slaves. It was a global culture in which life was treated as if it was disposable until the early Christian church changed the culture with their message that *all* human life is valuable — not just some lives chosen by the few.

Because of the effective overall strategy, NARAL succeeded in persuading the media to portray pro-life Catholics as just a "fanatical minority of one religious faith suddenly determined to impose its dogma on the majority."[40] Victory! The villain was being boxed in by the misinformation campaign and NARAL was enjoying more media support.

Lader considered Catholics to be in either one of two camps: one was second generation, blue-collar immigrants who closely obeyed Church doctrine and the other was the "educated, fashionable Kennedy-style 'cool' Catholics who lived unencumbered by the fetters of traditional Catholicism ..."[41] The latter had rejected Pope Paul VI's warnings in *Humanae Vitae* — or more likely never knew about them — siding instead with Sanger's contraception dogma. Dr. Nathanson wrote that "... it was not a long step for [cool Catholics] to [embrace] the public position of 'pro-choice.' To maintain their appearance as enlightened and progressive while still retaining their bona fides as Catholics, we provided them with the now classic straddle for Catholics in public positions [and for voters]: *Abortion is personally abhorrent, but everyone must be free to make their own choice. Now we were ready to use them to call over the more traditional, less trendy Catholics to our cause*"[42] (author italicized).

Relying on Betty Friedan's keen sense of estimating the degree to which men could be stripped of their role as protectors over their families, NARAL began using the slogan, "Abortion is a decision between a woman and her doctor."[43] It complemented the "Catholic Straddle" quite easily. NARAL believed Catholics would be much more willing to vote for a "pro-choice" candidate if Catholics thought abortion was a medical decision. Killing babies became sugarcoated under the description of "women's healthcare" — making it out to be a *medical* issue, not a *moral* one. The "Catholic Straddle" and its accompanying slogan were powerfully persuasive, as they still are today.

The voting booth, though, was the object of NARAL's control. If the Catholic voter felt guilty or shamed for considering support for a pro-choice candidate, this feeling could be white-washed with NARAL's frequently repeated "Catholic Straddle" slogan that "… abortion is personally abhorrent but everyone must be free to make their own choice."[44] According to Dr. Nathanson, unsuspecting Catholics fell perfectly into the NARAL trap by means of his stealthy and deceitful political tactics. "The anti-Catholic tactic was not only fruitful in rallying the most influential and the most articulate elements of American political life to our side in the late 1960s, it was also central to the maintenance of the unity with the High Command of the movement."[45] Catholic politicians — and their loyal Catholic voters — became powerful pawns in a well-orchestrated crusade to decriminalize killing unborn babies under the banner of "women's healthcare, reproductive rights and choice" propaganda. NARAL's "Catholic Strategy" with its "Straddle" component, has ensnared American politics and completely separated the Christ follower from legislative judgement.

Dr. Nathanson wrote of the Catholic Church,

> *Let it be said: The Church [inadvertently] helped us in*
> *NARAL. The Papal encyclical of 1968 denying both abortion*
> *and contraception to Catholics was a bonanza for us at*
> *NARAL at precisely the correct moment in history.*
> *By linking abortion and contraception in the encyclical,*
> *the Vatican made it impossible for those Catholics who*
> *were using birth control to split off the abortion issue,*
> *therefore leaving them to pick their own way through the*
> *confusing ethical and theological landscape.[46]*

To confuse matters even more, NARAL "... sweeten[ed] the appeal and support[ed] those wavering Catholics who wanted to look around and see others of their ilk joining us, [NARAL] supplied them with fictitious polls and surveys designed to make it appear as if American Catholics were deserting the teachings of the Church and the dictates of their consciences in droves."[47]

For one thousand nine hundred and seventy years, Catholics had supported a culture of life, until a few perfidious priests deceived the Kennedys and NARAL's political strategy drove a wedge between religious conviction and legislative judgment. According to Patrick Madrid, an American Catholic author, apologist and radio/television host, "... this strategy worked so well that, today, it is [nearly] impossible to find a Catholic politician holding national public office who is pro-life. Thanks to these dissenters and those Catholics they duped, 'Catholic' is synonymous with 'pro-abortion' in politics."[48] This is why Dr. Nathanson could write that "Many [Catholics] ended up in [NARAL's] camp, and [NARAL] used them with great effect ..."[49] He didn't have to write about Protestants. By the 1970s, many of the mainline Protestant denominations had already fallen to Sanger's controlling-birth creed and were eager for, if not already ardently demanding, the decriminalization of abortion. In addition, they could take great comfort knowing that the popular "Catholic" Kennedys were pro-choice too.

Whether they knew it or not, Christians were championing the hedonistic dogma of Margaret Sanger and Dr. Alfred Kinsey. Both were atheists who felt accountable to no higher power than themselves and who institutionalized their practice of promiscuity and sexual deviancy in America. Lawrence Lader and Dr. Nathanson simply capitalized on Christians' gullibility, and the most vulnerable people — preborn children and their mothers — would suffer the violent consequences of secular humanism. This worldview would soon inundate America, leaving millions of angry and wounded people and families in its path.

Their broken lives became the evidence that worldviews have real consequences.

Worldviews matter.

"The abortion decision that destroyed every state law protecting the rights of women and their unborn babies was based on a fundamental misrepresentation."

From Norma McCorvey, formerly known as Jane Roe of the 1973 *Roe v. Wade* case, in her 2003 affidavit (Section 15) to the Supreme Court of the United States requesting a hearing to <u>reverse</u> the *Roe v. Wade* decision which stripped unborn babies of all rights and protections. SCOTUS <u>refused</u> to hear her case. (Appendix E)

"The church must reassert its priestly and prophetic roles, guarding and guiding the land in the schools, in the media, in the local governments and courts."

George Grant
Grand Illusions, Highland Books, 1998

For further study:

The Abortion Papers
(Chapter 3 – Catholics)
By Bernard N. Nathanson, M.D.
Frederick Fell Publishers, 1983

Sexual Sabotage: How One Mad Scientist Unleashed a Plague of Corruption and Contagion on America
By Judith A. Reisman, PhD.
WND Books, 2010

For further study on worldview education:

Apologia – Worldview Course
www.apologia.com

Colson Fellows Program
www.colsonfellows.org

Faith and Reason Institute
www.frinstitute.org

St. Paul Center for Biblical Theology
www.stpaulcenter.com

Summit Ministries
www.summit.org

Theology of the Body Institute
www.tobinstitute.org

CHAPTER FIFTEEN

The Belly of the Beast

"... it was medical fact that something was in there, but also it was an article of faith, and at that time I rejected faith. We were doing abortions and we had to minimize the ethical and moral impact of what we were doing ..."

Bernard N. Nathanson, M.D., to Terry Beatley

What If We've Been Wrong?

Dr. Nathanson had accurately estimated that 250,000 abortions would take place in New York City in the first year, but he had little idea *where* these abortions would be performed. What he did not anticipate was the degree to which "medical rogues and ruffians"[50] would fill the void. This was not what he had in mind when NARAL fought so hard to have the anti-abortion laws struck down without any state regulations or oversight.

The New York State Medical Society, as well as the Association for the Study of Abortion, had tried to limit the procedure to hospital settings, but this was not how the law was written. The hospitals were rationing how many abortions they would perform per day, making it impossible to meet the demand. So Dr. Nathanson began advocating for outpatient, ambulatory abortion services to be offered at freestanding "clinics" and at doctors' offices — a daring idea for its time. He envisioned freestanding, professionally run "clinics," perhaps franchises. In his opinion this would be the missing link to assembly-line abortions that would liberate the hospital from the unending demand for post-abortion beds.

Another issue of concern was the inherent danger of rushing through an abortion. Most abortionists were still doing it the "old-fashioned way" with a razor-sharp curette blindly scraping the delicate walls of the uterus, risking laceration and puncturing the woman's intestines. Forceps would extract the baby's body parts, and each surgery took a minimum of a half hour, but usually much longer because the abortionist had to account for each arm, leg, abdomen and skull, as well as any other shredded body parts. About the same time that New York was changing the law, Dr. Nathanson was introduced to an abortion technology which had been improved upon in a country *not* known for its humanitarian concerns — Communist China. Doctors there had mastered the suction curettage — basically a vacuum — that made "cheap, mass-scale abortion possible."[51] Snuffing out the lives of preborn children was now possible in an outpatient, assembly line fashion. In an effort to increase the number and "quality" of doctors trained to perform abortions using the new apparatus, Dr. Nathanson organized the "First Symposium on Non-Hospital Abortion Procedure" for July 1, 1970. He invited every doctor in New York City, regardless of his field of medicine. Eighty doctors attended. NARAL was pleased considering how politically averse doctors were and how the procedure was *not* a generally accepted surgery in the medical field.

Dr. Nathanson did not hold back. He lectured on how to perform late-term saline abortions on babies sixteen weeks or older. In this procedure amniotic fluid is removed with a long needle stuck through the mother's abdomen. It is replaced with a salt solution. After the baby swallows the saline poison, the baby's lungs are burned and the outer layer of the baby's skin is stripped away. After the baby suffers a gruesome, painful death for about one hour, the baby's heart stops beating and the mother's labor soon begins. He taught that the abortion is a "medical success" if the child arrives dead. I do not know if he explained that the baby also arrives burned and shriveled up.

Another doctor, who had very limited experience using the Chinese suction method, taught doctors how to use this technology. Both he and Dr. Nathanson presented the two methods like pros. No one knew that the second presenter was a mere novice. Quietly, though, Dr. Nathanson was deeply concerned about the risks of surgeries being done in non-hospital settings, but there seemed to be no other choice.

Malpractice was NARAL's greatest "risk" associated with the recent legislative victory, and the organization's leaders were conscious of this imminent threat. If it became public knowledge that even a few women were maimed or died under legalized abortion in the Big Apple, it could result in an avalanche of bad press. There was also an additional threat. Consider the disturbing purpose of a NARAL executive committee meeting Lader called for January 9, 1971, just a mere eight months after New York decriminalized abortion. He was in a frenzy over the most embarrassing new reality, which was a "... serious threat to abortion advocacy: the increasing number of live-born infants emerging from second-trimester saline abortions. Lader saw these abortion survivors as an embarrassment to NARAL and was concerned that the press had made much of them and that the opposition elements were seizing upon them as a tactic in the abortion wars."[52] To think that any human being or an entire organization would consider a child struggling for his or her life as an *embarrassment* is almost unfathomable. In fact, it is inhumane.

But the NARAL leaders marched forward hoping to dodge these sorts of incidents so that the abortion industry would not be subjected to activists wanting to regulate it with standards of safety and care — the very thing NARAL lobbied *against* (and still does).

In an attempt to reduce the possibility of regulations, Dr. Nathanson, as the medical director for NARAL, sought to inspect independent abortion facilities. He would make suggestions regarding ways to decrease patients' injuries. However, he encountered an insurmountable problem: this cash-cow industry also attracted scavengers out for a quick buck, eager to prey on scared, vulnerable young women. This bothered him greatly for he had wanted to decriminalize abortion because he thought it would be good for women. He truly had *not* meant them harm.

Dr. Nathanson recalled the days of visiting abortion centers with hippies high on pot posing as medical personnel. This was quite in contrast to affluent women arranging for "spontaneous miscarriages" in a sterile hospital environment or in some reputable women's gynecology offices. These new freestanding "abortuaries" were inherently more risky and endangered even more women than before the law had changed. The Abortion King's idea of clean, outpatient, professionally managed women's health centers was a grand illusion, similar to the situation today in which *thousands of health violations* are cited in abortion facilities across America and countless more are likely being committed in states that do not even require inspections.

Regardless of the facility Dr. Nathanson inspected, contamination was common: from unsterilized equipment and blood-splattered walls and floors to a lack of procedures for "waste removal" and dozens of other risks. Even the most basic protocol was missing, such as changing bed linens in between patients and cleaning door handles. Dr. Nathanson was persistently distressed over the reality that without accountability and health department oversight, he had secured a far greater health risk for women.

While he was running his regular obstetrics-gynecology practice, delivering babies at a local hospital, and serving on NARAL's executive team, he also accepted the job as director of the Center for Reproductive and Sexual Health, better known as C.R.A.S.H. or Women's Services. The "services" were abortions — lots of them. It was here at C.R.A.S.H. that Dr. Nathanson presided over 110-120 abortions a day — an average of 800 per week. He had thirty-five doctors and eighty-five nurses reporting to him. With ten operating rooms and a facility open from 8 a.m. to midnight 364 days a year, millions of dollars were streaming into the "non-profit" practice.

In an effort to weed out the derelict physicians in C.R.A.S.H., he changed the pay structure to a flat hourly rate of $90 per hour, as opposed to a hefty per-abortion commission, which encouraged doctors to perform hasty surgeries. He hired a new group of professionals, but with a restricted income and eventual boredom from performing the same procedure thousands of times, many of these doctors eventually left to pursue the rapidly growing field of fetology — the exciting new area of science and healthcare. Dr. Nathanson knew the easy-to-enter abortion trade would forever draw sketchy doctors, as well as young, inexperienced ones eager to pay off college debt from the profits of instant clientele. Minimal effort was required to build this practice — just an advertisement and a persuasive receptionist, many of whom doubled as a "counselor" ensuring frightened women that abortion was the right choice. To his credit, he tried to clean up the C.R.A.S.H. abortion mill, which he did, but the practice of abortion remained a magnet for greedy practitioners without morals, as it still is today.

Near the end of 1972, Dr. Nathanson was exhausted from working excessive hours and from a never-ending list of demands. He was drained both physically and emotionally, and he resigned as medical director of C.R.A.S.H. Quitting was a fairly easy decision but not a small one. C.R.A.S.H. was probably the busiest abortion facility in the Western Hemisphere. In fact, it was busier than surgery units in New York's finest hospitals. On January 1, 1973, just a few weeks before the U.S. Supreme Court *Roe v. Wade* decision, he took a new job as chief of obstetrics at St. Luke's Hospital in New York City. Just a few weeks after stepping down from C.R.A.S.H., the Supreme Court handed down the *Roe v. Wade* and *Doe v. Bolton* decisions on January 22, 1973, which when read together decriminalized killing babies in the womb for *any* reason whatsoever during *all* nine months of pregnancy in all fifty states — two rulings that would more closely align America with other countries known for violating human rights — Communist North Korea and Communist China.

Mission accomplished! In the words of Dr. Nathanson, the Supreme Court justices and NARAL cofounders had succeeded in *"dismissing any rights or protection or anything to do with the fetus."*

Working as chief of obstetrics at the hospital, his pace was much slower than the prior five years as medical director of NARAL, medical director of C.R.A.S.H., inspector, lobbyist, abortionist, obstetrician and gynecologist. He had some time to be still, to contemplate, and to reflect on what he had accomplished for American women and admits to having been "... kept too busy to contemplate in any critical way the quintessential brutality of permissive abortion."[53]

Sitting with Dr. Nathanson, I began to feel limp. We were discussing the *human life toll,* and I knew I had to ask: how many babies did he abort? When he answered, we were no longer looking at each other's eyes. He stared straight ahead and said, "I am responsible for the death of seventy-five thousand children. Five thousand by my own hands. I taught doctors how to perform abortion surgery on another ten thousand babies and, on my watch, an additional sixty thousand children were killed by my team; that's seventy-five thousand human lives."

As I peered over at his distraught face, I knew he was fully aware that fifty million unborn children had lost their lives since 1973.

"My lawyers never discussed what an abortion is, other than to make the misrepresentation that 'it's only tissue.' I never understood that the child was already in existence. I never understood that the child was a complete separate human being. I was under the false impression that abortion somehow reversed the process and prevented the child from coming into existence."

From Norma McCorvey, formerly known as Jane Roe of the 1973 *Roe v. Wade* case, in her 2003 affidavit (Section 14) to the Supreme Court of the United States requesting a hearing to reverse the *Roe v. Wade* decision which stripped unborn babies of all rights and protections. SCOTUS refused to hear her case. (Appendix E)

For further study:

"NYC's tanning salons inspected more regularly than abortion clinics."
www.nypost.com/2014/04/07
New York Post, April 17, 2014

"A Haunting Look into Abortion Doctor Kermit Gosnell's 'House of Horrors'"
(Warning : very graphic)
The Blaze, April 15, 2013
www.theblaze.com/stories/2013/04

Abuse of Discretion: The Inside Story of Roe v. Wade
By Clarke D. Forsythe
Encounter Books, 2013

For policy and legislative action:

American's United for Life
www.aul.org

Heritage Foundation
www.heritage.org

Human Life Action
www.humanlifeactioncenter.org

National Right to Life Legislative Action Center
www.nrlc.org

Susan B. Anthony List
www.sba-list.org

CHAPTER SIXTEEN

The Cinder Blocks and Militant Feminism

"The 'modern' Kennedy Catholics needed little persuasion from us."

Bernard N. Nathanson, M.D., *The Abortion Papers*

What If We've Been Wrong?

One of the millions of American women Dr. Nathanson impacted is Leslie, the daughter of a former Washington Redskins football player. When I met her, Leslie had just recently shared a secret she had been carrying for thirty years. "Imagine carrying a cinder block or two every day of your life and everywhere you go. You have it with you on your wedding night. You carry it with you all day at your job and to nieces' and nephews' birthday parties. You even carry the blocks with you to the hospital during the birth of your children." I asked her if she would tell me more about her secret and ultimate triumph over personal destruction. As I listened, I knew her story resonated the pain of millions of other women in America. She kindled a deep empathy in me for women who have had abortions. She challenged me to understand the heaviness of the burden that had been sold as a solution to their problem.

Leslie had grown up in the Washington, D.C. suburbs, enjoying the privileges that came with her father's NFL football career. Her family was Catholic — the "cool Catholics" Dr. Nathanson had described. They attended Mass almost every Sunday and she was enrolled in Catholic schools from elementary grades through high school. Like so many women today, and despite her religious upbringing, she had believed the lies of the 1960s self-actualizing feminist movement. She participated fully in the sexual liberation revolution, drinking, drugging and sleeping around throughout college.

Before graduating in 1980, this gorgeous blond, blue-eyed communications major had just landed her dream job as a TV talk show host when she found out she was pregnant. Knowing her career would evaporate because she was an unwed pregnant woman, Leslie was panic-stricken and in crisis when she decided to abort what appeared to be a major inconvenience. She thought that with a few bong hits, sleep, time and her growing career, she could leave this chapter of life behind her.

Relishing her new celebrity status as a bubbly, twenty-two-year-old personality on morning television, Leslie partied non-stop on off-hours with drugs and guys. Within a year and a half, she found herself pregnant again, but this time the stakes were much higher as there was a bigger career hanging in the balance. A friend arranged for a second abortion. This young Catholic woman's secrets kept piling up in her heart.

Abandoning Catholic pro-life doctrine, Leslie left the Catholic faith. She found a church in a different denomination where she never heard a pro-life sermon preached, and she began her involvement in pro-choice politics. Validating her own two choices, she spent years fervently fighting to protect "women's reproductive rights" and became an outspoken advocate for pro-choice politics. At times she became militant with anyone who didn't agree with her opinion. The radical feminist inside of her angrily argued that the *only* issue was a woman's "right to choose." Working as a media advisor for a pro-choice candidate, Leslie lobbied lawmakers in the Virginia General Assembly and helped organize pro-choice events. Her activism was so valued by the Virginia League for Planned Parenthood that they invited her to serve on its board. She ultimately declined the invitation just a short time before a spiritual transformation of epic proportion would drive her to her knees. It would eventually and providentially link her life with my mission to fulfill my promise to Dr. Nathanson.

As I hung on every word of Leslie's story, I saw a nation of wounded women filling church pews and bar stools. They once thought a baby would be a heavy burden, but were now saddled with cinder blocks, courtesy of Dr. Nathanson, either directly or indirectly. He and his colleagues had had utopian intentions without *any* concept of what would happen to the hearts and minds of women and men — days, weeks, years and decades after having an abortion. The NARAL leaders never considered the long-term effect of marketing "disposable life."

I prayed that God would make a way for people to learn the rest of Dr. Nathanson's story.

"Weddington and the other supporters of abortion used me and my circumstance to urge the courts to legalize abortion without any meaningful trial which addressed the humanity of the baby, and what abortion would do to women."

From Norma McCorvey, formerly known as Jane Roe of the 1973 *Roe v. Wade* case, in her 2003 affidavit (Section 15) to the Supreme Court of the United States requesting a hearing to <u>reverse</u> the *Roe v. Wade* decision which stripped unborn babies of all rights and protections. SCOTUS <u>refused</u> to hear her case. (Appendix E)

"For you created my inmost being;
you knit me together in my mother's
womb. I praise you because
I am fearfully and wonderfully made;
your works are wonderful,
I know that full well. My frame
was not hidden from you when
I was made in the secret place,
when I was woven together in the
depths of the earth. Your eyes saw
my unformed body; all the days
ordained for me were written in your
book before one of them came to be."

Psalms 139:13-16 (NIV)

"Abortion kills twice. It kills the body of the baby and it kills the conscience of the mother. Abortion is profoundly anti-woman. Three quarters of its victims are women. Half of the babies and all of the mothers."

Saint Teresa of Calcutta

For a concise summary of the Roe v. Wade erroneous assumptions:

Roe v. Wade: An Exercise in "Assumicide"
Appendix C
By Samuel B. Casey, J.D. and Allan Parker, J.D.

What If We've Been Wrong?

CHAPTER SEVENTEEN
The Eucatastrophe and Suicide

*"The change in my thinking resulted almost entirely
because of science."*

Bernard N. Nathanson, M.D., to Terry Beatley

What If We've Been Wrong?

Dr. Nathanson looked up at me after repositioning Hillie on his lap pillow and said quite seriously, "You need to understand this . . ."

He was about to describe his eucatastrophe moment, a term that J.R.R. Tolkien coined to depict ". . . the sudden happy turn in a story which pierces you with a joy that brings tears . . . it produces its peculiar effect because it is a sudden glimpse of Truth . . ."[54]

It was 1973, just a few months after the *Roe* and *Doe* U.S. Supreme Court decisions. He was working as chief of obstetrics at St. Luke's Hospital when a new technology arrived. It was *not* an improved Communist Chinese abortion technology, but a radical and revolutionary Scottish invention.

"Terry, the bombshell was real-time ultrasound. It made everything come alive."

Dr. Nathanson disclosed that for the first time he and the mother could actually see the baby yawn and stretch in real-time motion. Moving images of his second patient sucking her thumb and wiggling her toes declared the humanity of the baby in the womb, and this awakened Dr. Nathanson's inner voice, a voice he had long forgotten or perhaps never known — the voice of conscience. The baby's pounding heart, once hidden and only heard, was now being *seen* beating on the monitor as early as five weeks when most pregnant women do not even know they are carrying a child yet. This new scientific breakthrough allowed him to *see* life and truly *bond* with it.

> *"As a result of all of this technology — looking at this baby, examining it, investigating it, watching its metabolic functions, watching it urinate, swallow, move and sleep, watching it dream, which you could see by its rapid eye movements via ultrasound, treating it, operating on it — I finally came to the conviction that this was my patient.*

This was a person! I was a physician, pledged to save my patients' lives, not to destroy them. So I changed my mind on the subject of abortion." [55]

It was scary as the memories slipped out of the shadows, including those of his college sweetheart, Ruth, and their unplanned baby. Had the baby been a girl or a boy?

The images also brought back his recollection of performing an abortion on another girlfriend after his relationship with Ruth. Yes, his hands had personally killed his own child and, when he had finished the procedure, he had felt only pride in his adept skill. Real-time ultrasound brought him face to face with the humanity of his own dead children and the fact that he was responsible for caring for his second patient, the baby. He didn't argue with what science had just proven. Dr. Nathanson responded to the science with a human response — recognizing there was another person's life to consider. He commented, *"Ultrasound opened a window into the womb."*

When I heard him describe this part of his journey, I couldn't even think of a question to ask. I just wondered while sitting next to him how it must feel to be eighty-three years old, knowing that at that moment, approximately fifty million American babies had been brutally killed by abortion since 1973; countless women had suffered emotionally and physically; and fathers had lost their right to protect their children. I felt great sympathy for this old man whose remorse was carved so deeply into his tired face. Sorrow filled the room.

I thought the interview might be over, but he turned to me and asked, "Did you know *The New England Journal of Medicine* published my article in 1974 titled *'Deeper into Abortion'*?" Explaining that he had wanted doctors to be aware of what real-time ultrasound had revealed, Dr. Nathanson had written what proved to be a hotly contested article.

His reflections on decriminalizing abortion included,

> *Life is an interdependent phenomenon for us all. It is a*
> *continuous spectrum which begins in utero and ends*
> *at death – the bands of the spectrum are designated by*
> *words such as fetus, infant, child, adolescent and adult.*
> *We must courageously face the fact – finally – that human*
> *life of a special order is being taken. And since the vast*
> *majority of pregnancies are carried successfully to term,*
> *abortion must be seen as the interruption of a process*
> *which would otherwise have produced a citizen of the*
> *world.* [56]

The article in *The New England Journal of Medicine* did not go over well. Bags of mail arrived, much of it hate mail from doctors full of contempt who were now profiting from the practice. They did not want the new scientific proof that "It's a baby and alive," nor the moral pressure to cease the practice. Dr. Nathanson also received hate mail from pro-life doctors who chastised and condemned him for unleashing the culture of death onto America and then changing his mind. Things got ugly.

As it was in his childhood, his life had returned to a tumultuous cyclone of emotions. Like Leslie and millions of other women and men, Dr. Nathanson carried the weight of cinder blocks. For the next seventeen years, a shadow would slowly pull him deeper into emotional darkness and down into the "valley of tears," suggesting that suicide would be the best way out of his new reality.

"As the class action plaintiff in the most controversial U.S. Supreme Court case of the twentieth century, I only met with the attorneys twice. Once over pizza and beer, when I was told that my baby was only 'tissue' and another time at Coffee's office to sign the affidavit. I had no other personal contacts."

From Norma McCorvey, formerly known as Jane Roe of the 1973 *Roe v. Wade* case, in her 2003 affidavit (Section 16) to the Supreme Court of the United States requesting a hearing to reverse the *Roe v. Wade* decision which stripped unborn babies of all rights and protections. SCOTUS refused to hear her case. (Appendix E)

"The wisdom of man alters with every age; his prudence has to fit perpetually shifting shapes of inconvenience or dilemma. But his folly is immortal: a fire stolen from heaven."

G.K. Chesterton
Illustrated London News, October 8, 1910

"It is a poverty to decide that a child must die so that you may live as you wish."

Saint Teresa of Calcutta

For further study and for resources:

Anglicans for Life
www.anglicansforlife.org

Priests for Life
www.priestsforlife.org

CHAPTER EIGHTEEN
The Acknowledgement

"I went through a transitional time ... when I felt the burden of sin growing heavier and more insistent. It was as if the contents of the baggage of my life were mysteriously absorbed in some metaphysical moisture, making them bulkier, heavier, more weighty, and more impossible to bear."

Bernard N. Nathanson, M.D., *The Hand of God*

What If We've Been Wrong?

Leslie, the television talk show host, carried her two cinder blocks for thirty years. While ignoring and denying what was eating her up inside, she battled depression, eating disorders, and substance abuse — textbook issues for post-abortive people who never connected the dots. One evening while walking under the weeping willow in her back yard, she unexpectedly heard what she calls the voice of God: *"I am the Creator of Life. I am the seed."* Instinctively, Leslie understood, and fell to her knees and wept. "I realized I had taken the lives of two of God's children through my abortions, and for the first time in three decades I acknowledged what I had done as a college student and as a career-driven television personality."

Leslie knew her "right" had no validity since her unborn children were human beings too. What the sexual revolution feminists — and the U.S. Supreme Court — had told her was her "right" was a destructive lie. "Abortion rights are not reproductive rights, but child-killing rights"[57] and the propaganda of NARAL, which had been propped up by the liberal media and Kennedy-style politicians, simply disintegrated. Like millions of American women who suffer the consequences of post-abortion trauma, Leslie now recognized that "whenever one group of human beings affirms its rights to determine the fate of other human beings, it is the beginning of oppression."[58] As Leslie processed this revelation, the long branches of the willow surrounded her like the arms of God as she asked for forgiveness and vowed that she would spend the rest of her life fighting for the unborn.

After enrolling in Rachel's Vineyard post-abortive healing retreat, which helped her work through her personal grief, Leslie agreed to serve as a Virginia coordinator for the Silent No More campaign. In this position she helps women and men break their silence and join others in speaking the truth about abortion's negative consequences and the hope found in healing.

It is interesting to note Leslie's prior perception that abortion would solve her "problems," yet in reality, abortion caused her so much grief, anger and self-loathing. Americans need to ask why no one at either abortion center bothered to tell Leslie before she made her decisions that ultrasound existed, or that the *The New England Journal of Medicine* had published Dr. Nathanson's article explaining that ultrasound opened a window into the womb and there was life inside.

"I was never invited into the court. I never testified. I was never present before any court on any level, and I was never at any hearing on my case. The entire case was an abstraction."

From Norma McCorvey, formerly known as Jane Roe of the 1973 *Roe v. Wade* case, in her 2003 affidavit (Section 16) to the Supreme Court of the United States requesting a hearing to reverse the *Roe v. Wade* decision which stripped unborn babies of all rights and protections. SCOTUS refused to hear her case. (Appendix E)

". . . and you will know the truth, and the truth will set you free."

John 8:32 (NCAB)

For post-abortion healing:

Rachel's Vineyard
www.rachelsvineyard.org

Redemptive Healing
www.redemptivehealing.net

Surrendering the Secret
www.surrenderingthesecret.com

For a story about the redemptive power of Christ:

Leslie Blackwell
www.leslieblackwell.com

For a video of Norma McCorvey telling her story of being exploited:

Reversing Roe

The Norma McCorvey Story video
www.vimeo.com/90179334
Dan Donehey

CHAPTER NINETEEN

The Resignation Letter and the Hubris of Certainty

*"What an incalculable injustice will have been perpetrated.
What an immeasurable irretrievable loss will have been suffered."*

Bernard N. Nathanson, M.D., *excerpts from his letter of resignation from NARAL*

What If We've Been Wrong?

NARAL's Board of Directors did not like Dr. Nathanson's article in *The New England Journal of Medicine.* The abortion leaders did not want to consider his pressing scientific questions and ethical concerns about the deliberate taking of life. In fact, Dr. Nathanson described NARAL's temperament for inquiry as "Communistic-Stalinist"[59] and morally evasive, but his questions and prodding were inescapable. According to Dr. Nathanson, NARAL made it very clear that his concerns over the ethics of human sacrifice were not welcome — at all.

What was also inescapable were his roots, which connected him to another time in history when people in power refused to recognize the humanity of Jews. His relatives, just thirty years earlier, had not *chosen* Hitler's Holocaust and the result was an unparalleled loss of human life. Dr. Nathanson acknowledged preborn babies were not *choosing* abortion — someone else was choosing it for them — and the result would also be cataclysmic. No longer able to ignore the prenatal phase of life or maintain the arrogance required to sustain an unwavering commitment to a pro-choice position, he decided to resign from NARAL.

Few people beyond the NARAL board of directors have ever read Dr. Nathanson's resignation letter. The following thought-provoking excerpts culminate with a question every American should answer:

January 22, 1975

Mr. Lawrence Lader
Chairman of the Board National Abortion Rights Action
League (NARAL)
250 West 57th Street
New York, N.Y. 10019

Dear Mr. Lader,

… The termination of human life – even human life
of a special order at any band in its spectrum — is a grave
and irrevocable act … My fears are more disturbing.
Our society has historically been organized around the family.
The integrity of the family as a unit has suffered a series of
hammer blows in the past two decades – abolition of laws
regulating contraception, the passing of the extended family,
the loosening of divorce laws; the permissive abortion
climate may conceivably be the coup de grace, the final insult.
Shall we watch passively, while imperceptibly but surely,
the fabric of our society continues to unravel?

… The 1954 decision of the Supreme Court desegregating
public education ushered in an era of social change
unparalleled in our time, and touched off shameful spasms
of civil disorder in our towns and cities … The decision
to strike down all laws regulating abortion in all the

states of this union is of the same order of magnitude of social change and in my opinion has within it the same seeds of chaos. We must brace ourselves to endure another generation of public turmoil and internal violence.

When the Supreme Court spoke on the abortion issue two years ago it struck down all abortion statues in this country. But the Courts spoke on the matter of race in 1892 affirming that segregation by race of train passengers was constitutional (and moral?). In 1954 it reversed itself in effect by striking down all laws respecting segregation in public education in the matter of Brown vs. Topeka School Board of Education. *The judgments of the Supreme Court were never meant to be infallible or eternal. And **what if we've been wrong** – if the Court should soon reverse itself on the abortion issue in the light of changing times and/or new scientific evidence? What an incalculable injustice will have been perpetrated. What an immeasurable irretrievable loss will have been suffered.*

The annual dues of NARAL are ten dollars and the hubris of certainty. Regretfully, I can no longer meet those dues.

Sincerely,
Bernard N. Nathanson, M.D.

(emphasis added)

No one has described the consequences of a society indifferent to abortion better than Mother Teresa in her keynote address to over three thousand five hundred attendees at the 1994 National Prayer Breakfast in Washington, D.C. At the head table sat President William (Bill) Clinton and First Lady Hillary Clinton as the little nun addressed the crowd with her famous speech called "WHATEVER YOU DID UNTO ONE OF THE LEAST, YOU DID UNTO ME." Here is an excerpt:

> But I feel that the greatest destroyer of peace today
> is abortion, because it is a war against the child, a direct
> killing of the innocent child, murder by the mother herself.
> And if we accept that a mother can kill even her own child,
> how can we tell other people not to kill one another?
> How do we persuade a woman not to have an abortion?
> As always, we must persuade her with love and we remind
> ourselves that love means to be willing to give until it hurts.
> Jesus gave even His life to love us. So, the mother who
> is thinking of abortion, should be helped to love, that is,
> to give until it hurts her plans, or her free time, to respect
> the life of her child. The father of that child, whoever he is,
> must also give until it hurts. By abortion, the mother does
> not learn to love, but kills even her own child to solve her
> problems. And, by abortion, that father is told that he does
> not have to take any responsibility at all for the child he
> has brought into the world. The father is likely to put other
> women into the same trouble. So abortion just leads to
> more abortion. Any country that accepts abortion is not
> teaching its people to love, but to use any violence to get
> what they want. This is why the greatest destroyer of love
> and peace is abortion.

When Mother Teresa was finished with her message of love — spoken nineteen years after Dr. Nathanson resigned from NARAL — the crowd erupted into a loud and long standing ovation. The Clintons, on the other hand, sat with their hands folded during the long, roaring applause. Mother Teresa's powerful message did not change their minds. The Clintons continued to support abortion "rights" — and, as of the publishing of this book, still do. Mrs. Clinton even zealously defends the right for women to "choose" the gruesome late-term, partial-birth abortion procedure up until just prior to the birth of the baby. This is when the baby girl or boy is intentionally delivered alive and feet first, but right before the head exits the mother's body, a pair of scissors stabs the back of the baby's neck and severs the brain from the spinal cord. Brains are suctioned out, head collapsed and the baby is *technically* born dead — no crime against humanity committed.

Twenty-two years after Mother Teresa's famous speech and forty-one years after Dr. Nathanson resigned from NARAL, Mrs. Clinton would run for President of the United States in 2016, strongly supporting the right for what is essentially child sacrifice to the "god of choice." It is legal homicide. Regardless of what science had proven or the benefits of building a culture of love that Mother Teresa so eloquently shared, Hillary Clinton, along with other misguided feminists, dug their heels in as one political party pretended to represent all women, *while over half a million female babies die each year in a very barbaric procedure.* Because baby girls don't vote and their cries are not heard, NARAL and Planned Parenthood advanced their agenda with the help of thousands of boots-on-the-ground — young women indoctrinated with feminist pro-choice political propaganda using the same lies that Dr. Nathanson had developed years earlier. In fact, Planned Parenthood would pay people $720 a week to promote presidential candidate Hillary Clinton in its drive to keep unfettered abortion legal.

Like the warnings from Pope Paul VI on what would happen to relationships between men and women in a world closed to the gift of life, Dr. Nathanson's warnings have all come to pass: (1) the continuing disintegration of family, (2) more public turmoil, and (3) internal violence.

"The facts about abortion were never heard. Totally excluded from every aspect and every issue of the case, I found out about the decision from the newspaper just like the rest of the country."

From Norma McCorvey, formerly known as Jane Roe of the 1973 *Roe v. Wade* case, in her 2003 affidavit (Section 16) to the Supreme Court of the United States requesting a hearing to reverse the *Roe v. Wade* decision which stripped unborn babies of all rights and protections. SCOTUS refused to hear her case. (Appendix E)

"Now, it shall come to pass, if you diligently obey the voice of the LORD your God, to observe carefully all His commandments which I command you today, that the LORD your God, will set you [a nation] high above all the nations of the earth."

Deuteronomy 28:1 (NKJV)

For further study:

Watch **Senator Rick Santorum rebut Senator Hillary Clinton's defense of partial-birth abortion** in a debate captured by C-SPAN on the U.S. Senate floor on March 12, 2003, C-SPAN.

https://www.youtube.com/watch?v=ItafBMuuy70 Minutes 5:23-5:27

https://lifedynamics.com/hillary-clinton-defended-partial-birth-abortion/

What If We've Been Wrong?

CHAPTER TWENTY

The Deceptive Snare of Disposabale Life

*"After my exposure to ultrasound, I began to rethink
the prenatal phase of life."*

Bernard N. Nathanson, M.D., *The Hand of God*

What If We've Been Wrong?

Paul Acors, *The Free Lance Star* opinion page editor, met me for coffee
at Hyperion, a local café. "So, Terry, what do you want from me?"
He tossed that question my way after listening to me explain how the
abortion lobbyists depend on compliant legislators.

Jokingly, I responded, "I thought you'd never ask! I'd like for you to
publish my guest editorial in which I'll explain the link between the
loss of parental rights, our senator's voting record and the legacy
of Dr. Nathanson."

"Sure, we can do that. Just don't go over eight hundred words.
I look forward to reading it."

I was surprised, but once again I recognized God in the driver's seat.
Everyone had told me I didn't stand a chance of getting an editorial
published, except for Gloria. She was the first friend I made in
Fredericksburg. Gloria is the nurse who performs real-time sonograms
and provides counseling at a local pregnancy center. Urging me to ask
Mr. Acors out for coffee, she reminded me, "Terry, you have nothing
to lose and much to gain. He can either say yes or no, but if he says yes,
you'll be able to reach thousands of voters with the truth."

Her passionate pro-life stance resonated from her daily pursuit of
providing positive alternatives to abortion. She was also motivated by
a personal family tragedy that had involved her daughter and services
rendered at a Planned Parenthood facility eight years earlier.

While enrolled as a college student, Gloria's twenty-one-year-old
daughter embraced what feminists and the sexual revolution had
promoted — "consequence-free promiscuity." Privately, the young
woman became concerned that she and her partner had contracted
HIV/AIDS, which in 1997 meant an early death, so she visited a
Planned Parenthood facility near her college for testing. The following day
her daughter phoned for the lab results, and the receptionist told

her that she would have to come *into* the office to get the results. Interpreting this to mean the results were positive, her daughter took her own life at gunpoint. As a painful conclusion to Gloria's catastrophe, Planned Parenthood eventually provided the lab results to her. All tests were *negative.*

Because of Gloria's personal and professional experience defending life in a culture of death, this mother's passion was the major catalyst for the newspaper's publishing a half-page, full-color editorial titled *"Houck's votes against family values."* Mr. Acors chose a silhouette picture of a dad, mom and small child walking hand in hand down a beach, which drew thousands of readers to the article. The picture perfectly depicted what Dr. Nathanson so deeply desired — the restoration of family and the building of a civilization of love.

In a twist of irony, Gloria has joyfully and enthusiastically helped save dozens of parents and their preborn babies from the deceptive snare of the disposable-life industry, which today's radical feminists so angrily defend. Not a day goes by that Gloria doesn't think about the full cost of sexual promiscuity and the deception of the abortion industry profiteering on the fear of young, American women.

"The view that is presented is the view of what the abortion industry thinks is good for women. The reality of women's experiences is never presented."

From Norma McCorvey, formerly known as Jane Roe of the 1973 *Roe v. Wade* case, in her 2003 affidavit (Section 17) to the Supreme Court of the United States requesting a hearing to reverse the *Roe v. Wade* decision which stripped unborn babies of all rights and protections. SCOTUS refused to hear her case. (Appendix E)

"Have nothing to do with the fruitless deeds of darkness; but rather expose them ..."

Ephesians 5:11 (NIV)

**Save children from abortion by supporting your local pregnancy
resource centers, like Fredericksburg Pregnancy Center**
www.fredericksburgchoices.com

To locate a pregnancy resource center in your state:
http://www.lifecall.org/cpc

For further study about Planned Parenthood:

American Life League
www.all.org

CHAPTER TWENTY-ONE
The Rare Cases

*"Perhaps the pregnancy may not be convenient, but I want
women to know that killing their children is not a
humane decision. Adoption is a far better choice for the mother,
father and all of humanity."*

Bernard N. Nathanson, M.D. to Terry Beatley

What If We've Been Wrong?

After Dr. Nathanson resigned from NARAL in 1975, he struggled
with such tough cases as rape. However, by the beginning of 1979,
logic and the advances in medicine moved him to a position where
he could not justify *any* reason why a woman should abort a child,
including one conceived in rape. He saw an inconsistency in logic
if he let live babies who were wanted but sanctioned death for babies
unwanted because of rape. He thought the rapist should receive all
of the punishment, not the child.

Recalling his emotional whipsaw days in the hospital setting,
Dr. Nathanson explained that he would strive to save the life of a
premature baby in the obstetrics unit and just minutes later abort a
baby of the same gestational age on a different floor in the hospital.
It was confusing — was he there to save or was he there to kill?
It no longer made any sense to him. *A life was a life no matter how
it came into existence.*

I think if he had met someone like Tricia, my new Puerto Rican friend
in Fredericksburg, he would have more quickly embraced life for children
conceived in rape, as well. Tricia was conceived when her fifteen-year-old
mother was statutorily raped by a forty-five-year-old man in 1968.

When I met Tricia through my parental rights activity, she was a happy
mother of two young daughters, totally devoted to her husband and family,
living a middle-class American life. Keenly aware that she had been
born a "statistic" that the Secular-Postmodern culture deems worthless,
Tricia shared her unique perspective on the gift of life and the lessons
she learned along the way. It is an amazing journey of being made whole
again in a secular world that demands her status as a disposable "choice."

When she was conceived, abortion was still illegal. Her mother and
grandparents, though, never considered seeking an illegal abortion
because they believed that her life had inherent worth. Furthermore,

abortion would not punish the father, so her grandparents and mother decided to provide a future for her through adoption. However, when Tricia entered the world, her mother had second thoughts and chose to keep her. Tricia became a blessing to her Puerto Rican family, and not an ounce of love was lost due to the circumstances surrounding her conception.

What was lost for Tricia, though, for a season of her life after moving to the states and away from her close-knit family, was the value of a pro-life perspective during *her* teenage years as the second wave of feminism indoctrinated her into a hedonistic "me first" lifestyle. From music and television to *Cosmopolitan* magazine articles, the messages promoted promiscuity and a self-centered mentality. It created a vicious cycle of exploitation, particularly to a young teenage girl living in a fatherless home with a mother working two to three jobs. It was the perfect storm for Tricia to believe what the media had told her: she controlled her body, and sex was merely recreational fun. When Tricia became pregnant at seventeen in 1986, abortion had become so normal that she made her choice as easily as breathing. It would be eighteen years before the memory of her choice would come back to haunt her while lying in a hospital bed.

At thirty-five and married, she had just lost her baby to an unexpected miscarriage. While the doctor was performing what he thought to be a post miscarriage ultrasound in preparation for a D&C, he suddenly paused over an image on the monitor and declared, "Wait! There's a baby here!" She had been carrying twins.

Tricia recalled looking at the sonogram images. "There in front of me was the most beautiful image of another baby dancing and wiggling as if to say, 'Here I am. I'm alive.' Her little arms and legs were in constant motion, and this was when I had my William Wilberforce moment. Like many Christian women sitting in the pews of denial, so was I. I knew that what I had done wasn't right, but I didn't realize just how wrong I had been. It was at this split second I recognized the humanity of my child and the tragic mistake I had made years ago when I had aborted a baby at the same age — twelve weeks old. I came face to face with the so-called 'blob of tissue' except this 'tissue' had arms, feet and 'danced.'" Tricia described the remarkable sight while a whirlwind of mixed emotions set in as she wept for taking the life of her child so many years ago.

Tears of joy, though, followed for the little girl growing inside her and gone were the delusions of "women's reproductive rights," so destructive to the family. Tricia has gone on to teach her children the value of chastity and the miracle of how women are uniquely gifted to bring forth life.

She also credits the Lord letting her and her children experience how — when she trusted Him — He did in fact make something beautiful out of ashes. For her family's reunion, Tricia's grandmother told her to invite her biological sister — the other daughter of the man who raped Tricia's mother. Though Tricia's grandparents had met her sister in 1988 and knew that Tricia visited her during her trips to the island, this was the first time that Tricia's grandmother personally extended the invitation to bring Tricia's sister into the family fold.

In a pro-abortion world that says Tricia should never have been born in the first place, her life is a testimony to the power of prayer and how God can make all things new. He redeemed her "unredeemable story" as only He could and blessed her with a sister who attends the family reunions. Tricia and her experiences illustrate the multi-generational blessings given to families who open their hearts to the gift of life.

In another twist of irony, the year Tricia was conceived — 1968 — Dr. Nathanson had been referring patients to Puerto Rico for late-term illegal abortions.

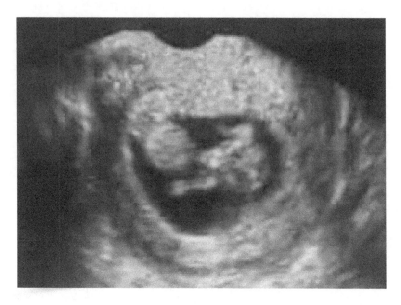

Tricia's daughter "dancing in her womb" at 11 weeks 0 days

Picture courtesy of Tricia Powell

"I never had an abortion and gave the baby up for adoption."

From Norma McCorvey, formerly known as Jane Roe of the 1973 *Roe v. Wade* case, in her 2003 affidavit (Section 18) to the Supreme Court of the United States requesting a hearing to <u>reverse</u> the *Roe v. Wade* decision which stripped unborn babies of all rights and protections. SCOTUS <u>refused</u> to hear her case. (Appendix E)

"The knot of Eve's disobedience was loosed by the obedience of Mary. The knot which the virgin Eve tied by her unbelief, the Virgin Mary opened by her belief."

St. Irenaeus
The Bible and the Virgin Mary: Journey Through Scriptures
St. Paul Center for Biblical Theology 2014

For a story about the redemptive power of Christ:

Tricia Powell
www.triciapowell.com

What If We've Been Wrong?

CHAPTER TWENTY-TWO
The Silent Screams, The President and The Baby Girls

"The baby draws back . . ."

Bernard N. Nathanson, M.D., *The Silent Scream film*

What If We've Been Wrong?

"Have you watched the two films I made?" Dr. Nathanson asked me. I told him I had seen one, but I was unaware of the second. "Make sure you do. Both of them sent gyrations through the pro-abortion side in the 1980s. Many minds were changed to protecting the unborn."

He was referring to *The Silent Scream* and *Eclipse of Reason*, films he narrated while studying what actually happens to the baby during the abortion procedure. In 1984, he asked Dr. Jay Kelinson, an abortionist in New Jersey, if he would record an ultrasound video of the baby during the extraction. What they discovered on the images was "shocking" and drastically and permanently changed their lives. Dr. Kelinson, as well as his nurse, who were performing about twenty abortions a day, immediately quit doing the procedures. As for Dr. Nathanson, he recognized that he now had hard scientific evidence that abortion supporters would never be able to honestly refute.

Beginning at minute 14:30, *The Silent Scream* video, which can still be seen on YouTube, reveals a child resting peacefully in her mother's womb as Dr. Nathanson narrates the step-by-step abortion. The child shifts around, and her thumb periodically moves to her mouth; however, the calmness shifts to agitated movements as the baby senses aggression. Her heartbeat increases significantly and her movements become rather violent as she tries to move away from the abortionist's suction tip, the lethal instrument, which had not even punctured the amniotic sac yet. The ultrasound captures the child opening her mouth in what Dr. Nathanson describes as the *"... silent scream of a child threatened imminently with extinction."* [60] After the sac is punctured, the viewer sees the body being tugged by the suction tool and then systematically dismembered from the baby's head as her life is savagely taken.

He explained that the baby sensed danger; she willed to live; and then ... love died.

To Bernard Nathanson with best wishes, Ronald Reagan

Dr. Nathanson meeting President Ronald Reagan at the White House

Courtesy of Christine Reisner-Nathanson

When Dr. Nathanson showed *The Silent Scream* to President Ronald Reagan at the White House, he was sincerely moved by the content. President Reagan said, "... if every member of Congress could see that film, they would move quickly to end the tragedy of abortion."[61] It catapulted the pro-abortion advocates into a defensive, marketing tizzy.

To Bernard Nathanson
With appreciation and best wishes, Ronald Reagan

Dr. Nathanson serving on a high level health committee with President Ronald Reagan, Surgeon General C. Everett Koop, M.D. and other leaders

Courtesy of Christine Reisner-Nathanson

Their argument that the fetus was only a mass of tissue was utterly defeated. "It" was a person. The President of the United States recognized that fact and befriended Dr. Nathanson to help promote a culture of life, love and civility — not violence.

The pro-choice lobby accused Dr. Nathanson of tampering with the film to make it appear that the child screams. To prove that he had not, he sent the original footage to the scientist in Scotland who invented the technology. The inventor's findings: the footage was original and it had never been tampered with. The inventor and Dr. Kelinson even signed affidavits stating that fact.

Dr. Nathanson explained that eighty-five to ninety percent of all women will choose life for their child if they can see the baby on a clear ultrasound image because they will bond with the child and recognize his or her humanity. It only takes about fifteen seconds to get a clear image. Dr. Nathanson elaborated, "This is why the abortion industry *vehemently opposes* mandatory laws requiring ultrasound imaging. It is an immediate catalyst for the loss of millions of dollars in revenue."

In 1987, he coproduced a second film that captures the inhumane practice of dismembering a five-month-old *viable* child. It was filmed using a fetascope placed inside the uterus. It is so graphic and grotesque that the content most assuredly provided the producers with an appropriate movie title: *Eclipse of Reason*. Dr. Nathanson entered this twenty-seven-minute film into five major film festivals. It became a finalist in the International Film and TV Festival of New York; and *Eclipse of Reason* was actually nominated for an Academy Award. Even *Newsweek* magazine wrote that it was "... disturbingly stark and may prove harder for critics to dismiss as misleading."[62]

This film, too, became the subject of debate. It included a lengthy introduction by actor Charlton Heston addressing the degradation of the twentieth century via the mass slaughter of babies through abortion.

On January 14, 1988, President Reagan issued his official *Personhood Proclamation*. I suspect that Dr. Nathanson may have helped write it. At the minimum, he probably reviewed it. Here is an excerpt from the Proclamation whose author clearly understood the Laws of Nature and Nature's God and how the Court's decision is at odds with science, history and justice:

> *That right to life belongs equally to babies in the womb,*
> *babies born handicapped, and the elderly or infirm.*
> *That we have killed the unborn for 15 years does not nullify*
> *this right, nor could any number of killings ever do so.*

*The unalienable right to life is found not only in the
Declaration of Independence but also in the Constitution
that every President is sworn to preserve, protect,
and defend. Both the Fifth and Fourteenth Amendments
guarantee that no person shall be deprived of life without
due process of law.*

*All medical and scientific evidence increasingly affirms
that children before birth share all the basic attributes
of human personality — that they in fact are persons.
Modern medicine treats unborn children as patients.
Yet, as the Supreme Court itself has noted, the decision
in* Roe v. Wade *rested upon an earlier state of medical
technology. The law of the land in 1988 should recognize
all of the medical evidence.*

*Our nation cannot continue down the path of abortion,
so radically at odds with our history, our heritage,
and our concepts of justice. This sacred legacy, and the
well-being and the future of our country, demand that
protection of the innocents must be guaranteed and that
the personhood of the unborn be declared and defended
throughout our land.*

But the silent screams continued. In fact, they multiplied while our
nation never paused to question how killing five hundred thousand baby
girls annually is considered "women's healthcare."

"Being unskilled and uneducated, with alcohol and drug problems, finding and holding a job was always a problem for me. But with my notoriety from Roe v. Wade, abortion facilities usually paying a dollar an hour more than minimum wage, were always willing to add 'Jane Roe' to their ranks."

From Norma McCorvey, formerly known as Jane Roe of the 1973 *Roe v. Wade* case, in her 2003 affidavit (Section 18) to the Supreme Court of the United States requesting a hearing to reverse the *Roe v. Wade* decision which stripped unborn babies of all rights and protections. SCOTUS refused to hear her case. (Appendix E)

"Law is a statement or a testimony of the health of a society. It is more than a restriction. If a society fails to protect the weakest members through law and charity of heart, it is a very sick society."

Dr. Bernard Nathanson to Terry Beatley

For further study:

ProLife Answers to ProChoice Arguments
By Randy Alcorn
Multnomah Publishers, 2000

Watch *Eclipse of Reason* video on YouTube:
https://www.youtube.com/watch?v=Q_qxveSahcw

Watch *The Silent Scream* video on YouTube:
https://www.youtube.com/watch?v=gON-8PP6zgQ

Watch *When They Say, You Say* (Episodes 1-5)
by Olivia Gans Turner
(Available on YouTube and from EWTN)

To help abortion center employees, including abortionists, leave the industry:

And Then There Were None
www.abortionworker.com

To read about a former Planned Parenthood manager who quit the industry:

unPlanned
by Abby Johnson
Tyndale Momentum, 2014

CHAPTER TWENTY-THREE

The Prayer Warriors and the Big Apple

*"Most disastrous, however, has been the legal
and extralegal campaign to shut down pro-life protests,
or even pro-life speech."*

Bernard N. Nathanson, M.D., *The Hand of God*

What If We've Been Wrong?

"The doctors at Planned Parenthood's Margaret Sanger Center in New York killed three of my babies," stated the young black woman.

She was one of about twenty women who participated in a monthly prayer gathering in Fredericksburg, asking the Lord to protect the unborn, help troubled children and restore broken families in America. The group's leader had heard me speak a few months earlier at the pastor breakfast meeting and had asked me to teach the prayer team about the abortion industry. She wanted her team of prayer warriors to lift up specific prayers, not generalities. Without hesitation I eagerly agreed to teach the legacy of Dr. Nathanson, the history of Sanger's "Negro Project" and her controlling-birth philosophy. God had a plan for this prayerful group of women.

After I presented the information and fielded questions, the women broke into four small groups to pray. This is when I discovered some of the prayer warriors were wounded. Soft crying resonated from one or two women in each group whose buried heartache from prior abortions began to surface. I kept my head bowed as quiet tears turned to loud wailing. The Old Testament Bible verse repeated over again in my mind, *"... if my people, who are called by My name, will humble themselves and pray and seek My face and turn from their wicked ways, then I will hear from heaven, and I will forgive their sin and will heal their land."* 2 Chronicles 7:14 (NKJV)

The young black woman mentioned above stopped crying and explained that she had recently been given a free airline ticket to visit her family in New York. She said she wanted to return to the Planned Parenthood facility in New York where she had lost her children to the lies that they were not babies yet — just "masses of tissue." She knew the workers *could* have told her that at nine weeks her babies already had little faces and fully-formed eyes, along with developing earlobes, fingers and toes. Regret ran deep, and she admitted that her children were victims of

Dr. Nathanson's "Choice" campaign and Sanger's "Negro Project." Carefully, I told her how important it is for women to heal from the psychological damage of abortion through experienced ministries like Rachel's Vineyard. She expressed interest in attending but vowed, nevertheless, to be on the sidewalk protesting while on vacation in the abortion capital.

A few weeks later I learned that she had indeed protested on the sidewalk in front of the large abortion mill and had encouraged pregnant women not to enter the facility, but to choose life and adoption instead. This woman was most likely ridiculed and cursed at by people passing by, but she saved the life of a baby and helped heal her own wounds.

When I received this good news, I paused to reflect on the message God had sent me after meeting Rev. Turner. *"Whether you turn to the right or to the left, your ears will hear a voice behind you, saying, 'This is the way; walk in it.'"* The next verse said: *"Then you will desecrate your idols overlaid with silver and your images covered with gold; you will throw them away like a menstrual cloth and say to them, 'Away with you!'"* Isaiah 30:21-22 (NIV) I felt so encouraged knowing that fulfilling my promise to Dr. Nathanson was bearing fruit — a life had been saved and women were being set free from the cinder blocks of shame — and they were silent no more.

The New York City Bureau of Vital Statistics published its data within the following year. Of course mainstream media and pro-choice politicians ignored the shocking figures: In 2012, 24,758 black babies were born alive in NYC and 31,328 were killed by abortion. Gross revenue for killing these little babies was approximately $14,700,000. It's big business for the silver-plated idols —the pro-choice politicians— and the gold-plated molten images — NARAL and Planned Parenthood.

I recall reading the data and then thanking God for *Maafa21*. If only I could persuade more Americans to watch this two and a half hour documentary on DVD or YouTube because because all unborn babies' lives matter.

This is the way. Walk in it. The day is coming when our nation demands, "Away with you, NARAL, Planned Parenthood and pro-choice politicians. Your assembly line slaughter of America's children is finished. Begone!"

" . . . the dead babies were in a big white freezer full of dozens of jars, all full of baby parts, little tiny hands, feet, and faces visible through the jars, frozen in blood. The abortion clinics personnel always referred to the dismembered babies as 'tissue'."

From Norma McCorvey, formerly known as Jane Roe of the 1973 *Roe v. Wade* case, in her 2003 affidavit (Section 20) to the Supreme Court of the United States requesting a hearing to reverse the *Roe v. Wade* decision which stripped unborn babies of all rights and protections. SCOTUS refused to hear her case. (Appendix E)

"Today, Planned Parenthood is continuing [Margaret Sanger's] crusade against the Church. In its advertisements, in its literature, in its programs, and in its politics, the organization makes every attempt to mock, belittle, and undermine Biblical Christianity. Bad seed brings forth bitter harvest. The legacy continues."

George Grant
Killer Angel, Highland Books, 2001

For further study:

BlackGenocide.org
www.blackgenocide.org

Issues 4 Life Foundation
www.issues4life.org

CHAPTER TWENTY-FOUR
The Prison and Priest

"I required not a cure, but healing."

Bernard N. Nathanson, M.D., *The Hand of God*

What If We've Been Wrong?

All of the self-help books, finest booze, tranquilizers, and psychiatric sessions couldn't draw Dr. Nathanson from the shadows of depression. He felt seized "... by an unremitting black despair."[63] He reflected, "It wanted all of me ..." For a while he contemplated suicide, telling himself it had worked for his grandfather and sister. But on the other hand he fancied himself with the notion that his obstetrical patients needed him too much; he just couldn't pull the trigger or swallow the pills.

For ten years he relentlessly tried to ease himself of the burgeoning guilt. Nothing seemed to help. "I would awaken each morning at four or five o'clock, staring into the darkness and hoping ... for a message to flare forth acquitting me before some invisible jury. After a suitable period of thwarted anticipation, I would once again turn on my bedside lamp, pick up the literature of sin (by this time I had accumulated a substantial store of it), and reread passages ..."[64] As he faced the absolute barbarism and evil of what he had unleashed, he thought no one person could possibly have this amount of blood on his hands. He compared it to the Nazi Holocaust when the Germans regarded the Jews as less than human and disposable. Despite his Jewish heritage, he had arranged the same fate for millions of babies. In the shadows of Dr. Nathanson's captivity, the black despair held him hostage in the trial of his heart and in the prison of his mind. The charges would repeat over and over again ... two of his children ... seventy-five thousand babies ... *Roe v. Wade* ... *Doe v. Bolton* ... a culture of death ... the fetal-body-parts industry ... the Barbaric Age.

No jail cell was necessary. He felt trapped.

While his emotional state was in turmoil, his pro-life conversion did not go unnoticed by the media. Dr. Nathanson had become the "subject of ridicule and satire in comic strips and news commentary and the butt of jokes [for] television comedians for his change ..."[65] Nevertheless, he pressed on with his scientific, secular pro-life position and was frequently the keynote speaker at pro-life events. Unwavering in his atheism, he was usually immersed in circles of Christ followers who seemed to lead the pro-life cause, and he remained rigidly stiff as they prayed outside abortion facilities or at rallies and fund-raising galas.

He started noticing, though, some common threads among pro-life activists. A watershed moment happened in January 1989, at the biggest Operation Rescue event at which the doors were blocked to a Planned Parenthood facility on 22nd and 2nd Streets in Manhattan, New York, with peaceful people praying for the end of abortion. According to Chris Slattery, one of the major organizers of the sit-in and a friend to Dr. Nathanson, twelve hundred peaceful Americans used the "necessity defense" that day to save children's lives from abortion. Traffic was blocked and the media swarmed over the event, but what was so striking to Dr. Nathanson was the non-violence and the altruistic dedication to saving the lives of little people who have no voice.

Chris said that, "Dr. Nathanson cautiously observed the event that day." The doctor later wrote how amazed he was that the Operation Rescue volunteers prayed for everyone, but not for themselves. He heard them pray for the medical staff and workers at Planned Parenthood, for the media and for the police. They prayed for the pregnant mothers and for their children. Dr. Nathanson would later contemplate, "How can these people give of themselves for a constituency that is (and always will be) mute, invisible, and unable to thank them?"[66] He told me in the interview, "They radiated joy and warmth. Having spent years around angry feminists and self-serving abortionists, not to mention the years I spent as a child in a loveless home, I was not accustomed to experiencing these feelings." Science had changed his mind about abortion, but the *love* that radiated from the peaceful protestors' faces began to chisel away at his stone-cold, hollow core, which he thought was impenetrable. He hungered for the *source* of their joy; he just didn't know where to find it.

According to Chris, the police came and began dragging away a few leaders who were hauled into a metal pen near the demonstration. When the police came for Chris, Dr. Nathanson — who had originally come to the event as a cautious, observant bystander who wanted information for an article about the ethics of this type of demonstration — chose to fall limp as well. Together, they were dragged into the pen and arrested. Chris explained *this* was Dr. Nathanson's pivotal moment when he "embraced the holy crusade" *and* simultaneously desired the source of the demonstrators' joy and peace.

Because of this rescue, Dr. Nathanson, Chris and seven others were sued and served papers in 1990. The federal lawsuit, brought ironically by Betty Friedan's organization, was called *NOW v. Terry* which went on for fifteen years. In the end, Dr. Nathanson settled out of court, Chris was fined $50,000, and Randall Terry, the founder of Operation Rescue, had over $250,000 seized through the courts by NOW and NARAL.

As NARAL's war on women and their children raged on, Dr. Nathanson decided to explore spiritual answers for the depression that kept seizing him. He met a man who promised he could teach him the way of forgiveness, healing, peace and salvation. He was a young, friendly Catholic priest named Fr. C. J. McCloskey, who also lived in New York City. Neither man could remember where they initially met, but what Dr. Nathanson found in this astute clergyman was a confidant, a scholar and someone who valued the rich world of literature as much as he did.

The priest knew that in order to heal the physician's heart he would have to reach him through his intellect. He and the doctor began a five-year journey reading literature and exploring the works of such great thinkers as Hilaire Belloc, C.S. Lewis, G.K. Chesterton, Thomas Merton and John Henry Newman. In addition, they studied the Bible and the Catechism of the Catholic Church. Rev. McCloskey welcomed the doctor's questions and relentless doubts concerning the possibility of Jesus forgiving him. Both men valued their in-depth discussions.

Coincidentally, Dr. Nathanson's favorite book was *Pillar of Fire* written by Dr. Karl Stern, his college psychiatry professor, who had converted to Catholicism at the same time that Bernard was stepping into the abyss of abortion. If only he had known back then, he could have had lengthy discussions with Professor Stern. Bernard's life, America, and the world might have turned out quite differently!

As Fr. McCloskey and Dr. Nathanson explored the mystery of faith together, Dr. Nathanson stopped thinking about suicide. The thoughts disappeared while a tiny seedling of faith, a bud of hope, and a deeper understanding of the meaning of enduring love began to blossom inside of him. The prospect of finding forgiveness for his incalculable sins against humanity seemed more likely as he studied *"... the church of the living God, the pillar and foundation of truth."* 1 Timothy 3:13 (NCAB)

The physician now knew what was ailing him, and the despair that had threatened to take his life was gradually defeated by an overwhelming infusion of wisdom and knowledge. Daily, Dr. Nathanson continued to grow in courage and understanding, and a new sense of loyalty developed, along with his passion to learn more about Jesus Christ and His infinite mercy. Diminishing were the nightmares and early morning suffocation.

The former Abortion King and founder of NARAL was slowly being made new through the love and mercy of Jesus Christ. Interestingly, Chris Slattery would be by Dr. Nathanson's side when the doctor surrendered his life again to authority six years later. This time, though, it would not be to the New York City Police.

In another twist of irony, as Dr. Nathanson spent countless hours in spiritual guidance with Fr. McCloskey and drew closer to the source of the Operation Rescue volunteers' joy, *Catholic* Ted Kennedy patroned a destructive bill. It was the "Freedom of Access to Clinic Entrances Act of 1993" which made it *illegal* for prayerful, peaceful sit-ins to block the entrance of abortion mills. NARAL had won again with a Catholic politician leading the way.

NARAL's war on women and their unborn children raged on.

"While the manners of the abortionists and the uncleanliness of the facilities greatly shocked me, the lack of counseling provided the women was also a tragedy. Early in my abortion career, it became evident that the 'counselor' and the abortionists were there for only one reason – to sell abortions."

From Norma McCorvey, formerly known as Jane Roe of the 1973 *Roe v. Wade* case, in her 2003 affidavit (Section 22) to the Supreme Court of the United States requesting a hearing to reverse the *Roe v. Wade* decision which stripped unborn babies of all rights and protections. SCOTUS refused to hear her case. (Appendix E)

"I call heaven and earth as witnesses today against you, that I have set before you life and death, blessing and cursing; therefore choose life, that both you and your descendants may live . . ."

Deuteronomy 30:19 (NKJV)

To help restore righteousness in America:

The American Prayer Initiative
www.americanprayerinitiative.org

To help end abortion in America:

40 Days for Life
www.40daysforlife.com

CareNet
www.care-net.org

Heartbeat International
www.heartbeatinternational.org

Human Coalition
www.humancoalition.org

National Right to Life Committee
www.nrlc.org

Save the Storks
www.savethestorks.com

To help Chris Slattery save children from abortion in New York City:

Expectant Mother Care Frontline
www.emcfrontline.org

What If We've Been Wrong?

CHAPTER TWENTY-FIVE
The Battlefield

*"I believe the abortion ethic is fatally and forever flawed
by the immorality of the means of its victory. A political victory
achieved by such odious tactics is at best an unstable tyranny
spawned by an unscrupulous and unprincipled minority."*

Bernard N. Nathanson, M.D., *The Abortion Papers*

What If We've Been Wrong?

"Excuse me, sir, would you like to know your senator's voting record on protecting parental rights?"

This was the question my team of volunteers and I asked hundreds of times at the 2011 Independence Day celebration on the historic Civil War Battlefield of Spotsylvania Court House near Fredericksburg — upwards of thirty thousand people attended. It was also the same battlefield in which Senator Houck engaged his constituency all day long in an effort to win his eighth reelection just three months away. A tactical battle emerged between my promise to the cofounder of NARAL and the powerful senator. His ammunition was smiles, handshakes, and hugs; mine was six thousand copies of his voting record.

I had collaborated with Virginia Christian Alliance's political action arm, Virginia Christian Action. Volunteers manned the booth at the local celebration. One of the details for which I thanked the Lord was that we were assigned a location in the children's ride area — perfect! All day long and into the evening parents waited in long, hot lines for the kiddie rides. With not much else to do except read the flyers, hundreds learned how their senator had risked the safety of Virginia's girls by voting to aggressively undermine parental rights. I was overjoyed with parents' responses: "Are you serious? Let me read that again! Whoever is running against my senator will have my vote! I had no idea his voting record was this bad!"

Finally, I had found them! Fathers and mothers who had supported the senator, not knowing he had failed to protect them from abortion special-interest groups. They were a perfect cross-section of people too — white, black, Hispanic, young, middle-aged, grandparents, Christian, and non-Christian. Their reactions were nearly all the same, but the fathers' and "pro-choice" women's responses were what most amazed me.

While holding the hands of their little girls, fathers would calmly ask what they could do to help me and if they could have ten to twenty flyers. They provided their names and contact information. Men told me they had repeatedly voted for Senator Houck with a sort of political blindness and devotion to political party labels. They now understood how their *lack of knowledge* was destructive to families. Much to my surprise, one black man even said that he thought he had been born into a certain political party, but he realized the devastating consequences of such thinking and vowed to become a more informed voter.

On the grounds of this historic battlefield, it was as if fathers had become enlisted infantrymen in a battle for their families. They would do what was necessary to free the district from the snare of aggressive lobbyists. The fathers agreed to share Senator Houck's voting record with family and friends. There was a lot to share, too: the senator's most egregious votes filled four typewritten pages.

Women seemed to respond in a more emotional way. The idea that their trusted senator had voted repeatedly to take away their parental rights incited anger and sometimes even tears. I actually met women who were pro-abortion but confided that they would switch their vote to the other candidate, regardless of his pro-life position. They, too, agreed that their children were more important than protecting a politician's victory or a political party. It was an exciting afternoon discovering that many people will respond to the truth and forgo politics in favor of protecting family values — when provided the truth.

Dusk was approaching, and the children's ride area was nearly empty as thousands of families had gathered onto the green to prepare to watch the fireworks. Exhausted, my team looked at the crowd and our remaining four thousand flyers. Mustering some energy, we set out to distribute them. Within forty-five minutes, there was a sea of yellow paper in the hands of two thousand constituents, and many people were reading the shocking data.

We still had two thousand flyers remaining so we went to the gate where hundreds of people were entering. As if we were handing out ten-dollar bills, citizens eagerly reached for them. Within minutes our box was emptied. I was told that Senator Houck's face turned red again, and he moved to a different area of the event.

As darkness fell, the fireworks exploded over the far end of the battlefield. I thought of the dads and moms nestled with their children on blankets, and how so many of these good parents repeatedly vote for incumbents who vote to usurp parental rights by advancing the abortion industry's goals. Maybe I was just tired, but I could feel the tears slide down my face, just as Rev. Turner's tears did when he watched *Maafa21* for the first time.

Later, I learned that this Civil War battlefield was the same hallowed ground on which Rev. Turner reenacts with the 23rd Infantry Regiment of the United States Colored Troops, who were instrumental in winning the war. As a historian reenactor, he shows what it was like to be a black Union soldier who helped set free his brothers and sisters in the South from the accursed yoke of human bondage when their humanity was not recognized. Having survived abortion and been chosen to defend praying in the name of Jesus in the U.S. courts, Rev. Turner had also become an infantryman in the battle to protect unborn children and their parents from the accursed yoke of decriminalized abortion. I couldn't ignore the parallels or coincidences.

I don't remember the ride back up the former Confederate ridge. I was too tired to pray in the Wilberforce Garden. Once home, I collapsed into bed, too tired to dream.

"No one ever explained that there were psychological and physical risks to harm the mother. There was never time for the mother to reflect or to consult with anyone who could offer help or an alternative. There was no informed consent."

From Norma McCorvey, formerly known as Jane Roe of the 1973 *Roe v. Wade* case, in her 2003 affidavit (Section 22) to the Supreme Court of the United States requesting a hearing to reverse the *Roe v. Wade* decision which stripped unborn babies of all rights and protections. SCOTUS refused to hear her case. (Appendix E)

"The wicked flee when none pursue; but the just, like a lion, are confident."

Proverbs 28:1 (NCAB)

For further study on how to elect pro-life candidates:

National Right to Life PAC

www.nrlpac.org

Susan B. Anthony List

www.sba-list.org

TeenPact

www.teenpact.com

What If We've Been Wrong?

CHAPTER TWENTY-SIX

The Rebirth

"I have been holding lengthy conversations with a priest of Opus Dei, Father John McCloskey, for the past five years ... I am no longer alone."

Bernard N. Nathanson, M.D., *The Hand of God*

What If We've Been Wrong?

"I am ready."

In the fifth year of spiritually mentoring the cofounder of NARAL, Fr. McCloskey heard those precious words spoken. The priest attributes Dr. Nathanson's conversion to the work of the Holy Spirit. Dr. Nathanson, though, depicted Fr. McCloskey as being "... like a knight in shining armor" who used "... the skill and the unerring accuracy of a cardiac surgeon ..."[67] to guide him along his arduous faith journey.

Fr. McCloskey described that special day:

> *December 8, 1996, on a Monday at 7:30 a.m. on the [S]olemnity of the Immaculate Conception of Mary in the crypt chapel of the Cathedral of St. Patrick's in New York City, the City of Man, Dr. Bernard Nathanson became a son of God, incorporated into the Mystical Body of Christ in his One Church ... Among the concelebrants were some of his friends, all well-known spokesmen for life both nationally and internationally ... Standing out among the various persons — most of them close friends, that Dr. Nathanson had invited — was a stranger, a man Dr. Nathanson had never met, Chuck Colson. He traveled a long way to be there, in many senses. He is very well known in the United States as a major figure in the Watergate scandal of the 1970s, for which he spent several years in prison. There he had a conversion to evangelical Christianity and began pastoral work with incarcerated men. Today [1996] he is perhaps the best known Evangelical Protestant leader in the United States, with a radio show and many books to his credit ...[68]*

Sometime later Chuck Colson shared on his radio program his impression of Dr. Nathanson's baptism:

> *This week I saw fresh and powerful evidence that the Savior born two thousand years ago in a stable continues to transform the world. Last Monday, I was invited to witness a baptism in a chapel of St. Patrick's Cathedral in New York City. The candidate for baptism was none other than Bernard Nathanson, at one time one of the abortion industry's greatest leaders, a man who personally presided over some seventy-five thousand abortions, including the abortion of his own child ... I watched as Nathanson walked to the altar. What a moment. Just like the first century – a Jewish convert coming forward in the catacombs to meet Christ. And his sponsor was Joan Andrews. Ironies abound. Joan is one of the pro-life movement's most outspoken warriors, a woman who spent five years in prison for her pro-life activities. It was a sight that burned into my consciousness, because just above Cardinal O'Connor was a cross ... I looked at the cross and realized again that what the Gospel teaches is true;* **in Christ is the victory.** (emphasis added) *He has overcome the world, and the gates of hell cannot prevail against his Church ... And this is the way the abortion war will be won, through Jesus Christ changing hearts, one by one. No amount of political force, no government, no laws, no army of Planned Parenthood workers can ever stop that. It is the one thing that is absolutely invincible. That simple baptism, held without fanfare in the basement of a great cathedral, is a reminder that a holy Baby, born in a stable twenty centuries ago, defies the wisdom of man. [Christ] cannot be defeated.*[69]

Amen.

Fr. McCloskey continues his description:

> But what was the reaction of Dr. Nathanson himself as he received the Sacraments of initiation into his new life as a Christian? 'It was a very difficult moment. I was in a real whirlpool of emotion. And then there was this healing, cooling water on me, and soft voices, and an inexpressible sense of peace. I had found a safe place ... For so many years I was agitated, nervous, intense. My emotional metabolism was way up. Now I've achieved a sense of peace.' At the end of the Mass, Cardinal O'Connor, in a comment that brought gentle laughter to the congregation, said to him, 'There, now you're as Catholic as I am!' After the ceremony Dr. Nathanson's reaction, understandably, was one of gratitude. 'I can't tell you how grateful I am, what an unrequitable debt I have to those who prayed for me all those years when I was publicly announcing my atheism and lack of faith. They stubbornly, lovingly, prayed for me. I am convinced beyond any doubt that those prayers were heard. It brought tears to my eyes.'
>
> On the prayer card handed out at the Mass of his reception, Dr. Nathanson had one quote from Sacred Scripture, 'God, who is rich in mercy' (Ephesians 2:4), the very same phrase that the Holy Father used as the title for his encyclical on God the Father, Deis in Misericordia. It certainly reflects his attitude as he faces his new life as Catholic: 'I'm confident about the future, whatever it may hold, because I've turned my life over to Christ. I don't have control anymore, and I don't want control. I made a mess of it; nobody could do worse than I did. I'm just in God's hands.' [70]

And in God's hands he remained.

Dr. Bernard Nathanson meeting Pope John Paul II

Courtesy of Christine Reisner-Nathanson

Dr. Bernard Nathanson meeting Mother Teresa (middle person unidentified)

Courtesy of Christine Reisner-Nathanson

"No one ever explained that there were options to abortion, that financial help was available, or that the child was unique and irreplaceable."

From Norma McCorvey, formerly known as Jane Roe of the 1973 *Roe v. Wade* case, in her 2003 affidavit (Section 22) to the Supreme Court of the United States requesting a hearing to <u>reverse</u> the *Roe v. Wade* decision which stripped unborn babies of all rights and protections. SCOTUS <u>refused</u> to hear her case. (Appendix E)

"For whatsoever is born of God, overcometh the world: and this is the victory which overcometh the world, our faith."

1 John 5:4 (DRA1899)

"I am not ashamed of the Gospel, because it is the power of God. The salvation of everyone who believes."

Romans 1:16 (KJV)

For contemplation on matters of faith and family:

American Family Association
www.afa.net

The Faith and Reason Institute
www.faithandreason.com

What If We've Been Wrong?

CHAPTER TWENTY-SEVEN

The Shift and the African's Dream

"I have no doubt that the pro-life cause will prevail . . ."

Bernard N. Nathanson, M.D., *The Abortion Papers*

A major shift occurred on August 23, 2011, and it seemed to foreshadow what could happen on the national scale. I had just finished having lunch with one of the most highly respected and influential black ministers in Fredericksburg. He was known for having a big heart and for helping families, and he had just agreed to introduce the pro-life, pro-family candidate to people in his community. He knew it was a risky thing to do with all sorts of political backlash, but, like Rev. Turner, this pastor had not known how extreme Senator Houck's voting record had been against the family unit until I had shared the information. I felt confident that with this honorable man's support, along with Rev. Turner's and that of other pastors, the highlighting of three issues — the sanctity of life, exposing Sanger's "Negro Project," and the protection of parental rights from the abortion industry — could *shift* the election in a monumental way. Then, something unusual happened.

I was on my way home thinking about this political *shift* when the last sermon Pastor John Bibbens gave right before I moved to Fredericksburg came to mind; it was titled "GET READY FOR THE SHIFT." I arrived home, and just a few minutes later, a 5.8 magnitude earthquake hit as the tectonic plates *shifted*. It was the East Coast's largest earthquake in a hundred years and its epicenter was in Senator Houck's district. Ironically, the tremors cracked the Washington Monument seventy-one miles away sending bricks and mortar to the ground. Literally and figuratively, a *shift* had taken place.

I stood on the shaking ground in the Wilberforce Garden wondering if this was just mere coincidence, but believing God had spoken in His magnificent way.

Over the next couple of months, I would frequently pray in the garden asking for God's help to defeat the senator and pave a way to fulfill my promise. God must have known I needed encouragement. He used an evangelical missionary from Africa to deliver a very important message just two weeks before the election. My friend Angela and I were attending a meeting with another Fredericksburg minister who pastored a large minority congregation. At this meeting we discussed the parting message of Dr. Nathanson and the way in which Christians could impact the upcoming election by voting to protect life and family values and by letting go of political party labels.

This pastor was open to the idea of allowing the church to be used as a venue to show the *Maafa21* film, and he invited me to promote the viewing at the following Sunday's service. As Angela and I were leaving the meeting, her phone rang. It was a missionary who had moved to America from Ghana. With a strong accent he excitedly told her about a dream his wife had had the night before: "My wife dreamt last night that Americans had awakened and begun to impact the world of politics for Christ. In her vision she saw hundreds of politicians walking in a long line carrying babies — live babies — and setting them at the feet of the Apostles. The politicians were releasing their political stronghold over the womb and repenting for the millions of lives lost since the *Roe v. Wade* decision!"

It was another surreal moment. I knew God could have arranged that phone call, but it was still astonishing that it had occurred at *that* very moment. My friend and I looked at each other, believing that God was turning the pages of this story again with His resounding message that the shedding of innocent blood *must* stop in the United States of America.

A week later Rev. Turner opened the movie presentation with his personal story of surviving abortion. I told of Dr. Nathanson's saga and his parting message. Feeling certain that people now understood how to help rectify this wrong on election day, I prayed that by exposing a broader understanding of history and the impact of social policies, the election would turn upside down, *setting a new course in American politics.*

"In my opinion, the only thing the abortion doctors and clinics cared about was making money."

From Norma McCorvey, formerly known as Jane Roe of the 1973 *Roe v. Wade* case, in her 2003 affidavit (Section 22) to the Supreme Court of the United States requesting a hearing to <u>reverse</u> the *Roe v. Wade* decision which stripped unborn babies of all rights and protections. SCOTUS <u>refused</u> to hear her case. (Appendix E)

"The LORD responded by shifting the wind, and the strong west wind blew the locusts into the Red Sea. Not a single locust remained in all the land of Egypt."

Exodus 10:19 (NLT)

For further study:

Pro-life Answers to Pro-Choice Arguments
by Randy Alcorn
Multnomah Publisher, 2000

Signs and Wonders for Our Times
www.sign.org

CHAPTER TWENTY-EIGHT

The Prophet

*"The decimation of four thousand innocent lives daily
imposes a crushing urgency upon us to find a solution now."*

Bernard N. Nathanson, M.D., *The Abortion Papers*

What If We've Been Wrong?

Few people understand the depth and breadth of Dr. Bernard Nathanson's pro-life conversion. Fr. McCloskey is one of the few. In *The Hand of God* "Afterword," he describes how Dr. Nathanson forewarned of the unintended consequences of legalized abortion.

> *Several years after his Baptism, Dr. Nathanson retired from his flourishing medical practice in order to dedicate himself more fully to the cause of life. He has intensified his pro-life work throughout the world by means of writings, lectures, and expert witness testimony in court and in legislatures both here and abroad. But he has not restricted himself to fighting the continuing tragedy of legal abortion.*
>
> *For Dr. Nathanson is not just an activist; he is a prophet.*
>
> *As long ago as 1988 – before he was a theist, much less a Catholic – Dr. Nathanson gave the keynote speech at an important Symposium on the Twentieth Anniversary of the Encyclical* Humanae Vitae *held at Princeton University. To a rapt and somewhat astonished audience, he spoke of what was soon to come as a result of the misuse of science and lack of respect for the sacredness of human life: genetic manipulation, sex selection, surrogate motherhood, frozen embryos, cloning, stem cell research, and the sale and use of body parts. All of his predictions have been borne out as the struggle between the Cultures of Life and Death continues. No one at that Princeton conference would have imagined that only ten years later the university's prize chair of Ethics would be held by Dr. Peter Singer, an advocate of all of the above and much worse. We can be sure that Dr. Nathanson will continue to use his professional expertise and his newfound faith to defend the sacredness of human life, as Pope John Paul II puts it, 'from conception to natural death.*[71]

I agree with Father McCloskey. Dr. Nathanson was a prophet.

His warnings have come true and have now been captured on undercover videos by Live Action and The Center for Medical Progress, which document what goes on behind closed doors of the tax-funded abortion giant, Planned Parenthood. (See end of chapter for video links.) As we now know, there is an entire industry in which women are lied to, manipulated, and hurt; laws are broken; and little babies are repositioned in their mothers' wombs prior to abortion so as to decrease the chance of damaging their organs. Purchasers want unblemished organs, not damaged merchandise. Intact babies' organs are traded like commodities while their lives are deemed worthless by people who have lost their consciences. As has been captured on video, they choose Lamborghinis over protecting babies' lives.[72]

America has truly become merciless and our government now pushes population control on a global scale. Indisputably, we are living in the future that Pope Paul VI, Pope John Paul II and Dr. Bernard Nathanson prophetically warned about — a Culture of Death. But God made a promise: *"... if my people, who are called by My name, will humble themselves and pray and seek My face and turn from their wicked ways, then I will hear from heaven, and I will forgive their sin and will heal their land."* 2 Chronicles 7:14 (NKJV) NARAL's cofounder knew what it meant to be humble; he knew what it was like to actively seek God's forgiveness; and he desperately wanted America to *turn* from its wicked ways, so our nation could be healed.

Dr. Nathanson knew that the U.S. Supreme Court Justices should try answering his lingering question, *"And what if we've been wrong?"* He also realized we would *all* be accountable one day for what he unleashed onto America because God's word says so:

> *Rescue those being led away to death; hold back those staggering toward slaughter. If you say, 'But we knew nothing about this,' does not he who weighs the heart perceive it? Does not he who guards your life know it? Will he not repay everyone according to what they have done?* Proverbs 24:10-12 (NIV)

"No abortion clinic cared about the women involved. As far as I could tell, every woman had the name Jane Roe."

From Norma McCorvey, formerly known as Jane Roe of the 1973 *Roe v. Wade* case, in her 2003 affidavit (Section 22) to the Supreme Court of the United States requesting a hearing to reverse the *Roe v. Wade* decision which stripped unborn babies of all rights and protections. SCOTUS refused to hear her case. (Appendix E)

"Render therefore unto Caesar the things that are Caesar's, and unto God the things that are God's."

Matthew 22:21 (KJV)

For further study, watch undercover videos exposing Planned Parenthood's corrupt business:

Baby Body Parts Trafficking

www.stopbabypartstrafficking.org

Center for Medical Progress

Undercover videos of the fetal body parts industry

www.centerformedicalprogress.org

Live Action

Undercover videos of Planned Parenthood exploiting women

www.liveaction.org

www.abortionprocedures.com

CHAPTER TWENTY-NINE

The Worst Virginian in the World

"I believe that an America which permits a junta of moral thugs to foist an evil of incalculable dimensions upon it, and continues to permit that evil to flower, creates for itself a deadly legacy: a millennium of shame."

Bernard N. Nathanson, M.D., *The Abortion Papers*

What If We've Been Wrong?

I was flying to Rome on November 8, 2011, Election Day, to attend the Springtime of Faith Conference. I would not know if Senator Houck had been defeated or had won his eighth term until I checked into the hotel, but the flight over gave me plenty of time to reflect on the previous year and a half.

I recalled not wanting to speak about politics to Pastor Bibbens and then hearing his profound response — that he would never again support a pro-choice candidate. I reflected on how I had wanted to move to Williamsburg, but my family had voted for Fredericksburg, which just happened to be a national pro-life hub and headquarters for 40 Days for Life, American Life League, The Prayer Furnace, and eventually Students for Life. It was also the home of Mothers on the Rock, a group of women who gather to pray on the same boulder upon which Mary Washington would frequently sit and pray for her son, George, while he fought in the Revolutionary War. Mothers on the Rock pray for the restoration of the United States of America beginning with ending abortion. Could it have been just another coincidence, or did God choose Fredericksburg as the setting for my story?

As I headed toward Italy, I thought of how God had orchestrated my meeting so many people who helped move the promise forward, including the ex-offender who couldn't even vote and the prayer warriors who wailed. Four radio programs had allowed me to share with their listeners the Senator's voting record and the editor of the regional paper did what he had promised by publishing the editorial; a liberal blogger had "honored" me with *The Worst Virginian in the World Award* [73] and a conservative blogger shot back with the *The Greatest Impact Award*. [74] It all seemed a little crazy, but none of the mini-victories would have been possible without the collaborative effort of many people desiring to protect parental rights and stand firm on the fact that *all unborn lives matter.*

I realized I had no choice but to continue carrying the message because the pro-life candidate would only speak of jobs and the economy. The parental rights issue was left on the table. He was influenced by his misguided political consultants, who feared tackling moral-social issues. I couldn't persuade him to talk boldly about parental rights during the campaign; however, to the candidate's credit, when I met with him months earlier, he made his pro-life position very clear to me. I felt confident that he would never vote in favor of NARAL or Planned Parenthood.

Regardless of the hoopla, I prayed for two things to happen: that my commitment to Dr. Nathanson would bear fruit and that enough voters would understand that we must first honor God by honoring the gift of life in the voting booth.

When I landed in Rome I felt ill with the thought that, if the incumbent won, I would catch the blame for the other candidate's defeat by bringing "social issues" into the political fray. I nervously logged into the election results with my stomach churning. NARAL and Planned Parenthood's favorite senator had lost by 87 votes on the first count. By the second count, he was in the hole by 227!

I knew what that vote tally really meant.

Considering the fact that the senator had won for *seven* terms by 5,000 – 6,000 votes, he, in a sense, had lost by 5,227 votes. My hypothesis had proven true: given the information, many mothers and fathers will choose to preserve their *fundamental* and *unalienable right* to guide and protect their children over any politician or political party. The problem is that most people just don't know what this industry is doing, and good candidates listen to the wrong consultants — "men with empty chests" who fear failure more than the wrath of God. They would rather have their candidate state his or her "pro-life" position and then not do a thing about it. Their hunger for power blinds them from recognizing that these issues — when fought for properly — lead to victory for God and country. The family unit and life *must* be protected from powerful politicians and corrupt laws.

Reading the election results, I felt encouraged. The false narrative of the "War on Women" mantra was now penetrable using the legacy of NARAL, Dr. Nathanson's testimony and Frederick Douglass's values! I felt confident God would, at some point in the future, do something with this evidence. Maybe, just maybe, a presidential candidate would unequivocally stand up for life and, in a sense, partner with Dr. Nathanson to move the hearts of American voters to honor the *right to life* once again. Maybe he or she would help deliver Dr. Nathanson's parting message. I lay quietly on my bed in Rome as the verse resonated again, *"This is the way. Walk in it . . ."* and I thought how strange it was to end the political campaign on the other side of the Atlantic Ocean and just minutes away from the "headquarters" of what has been and must always remain the abortion industry's greatest adversary — the two-thousand-year-old Catholic Church and its Magisterium that declares the dignity of all human life.

I was in for another surprise. Also on this trip was Dr. Richard Land, then president of Southern Baptist Convention on Ethics and Religious Liberty Commission. His pastime was politics and befriending U.S. presidents. He had actually been following the Virginia Senate race from his home in Tennessee ever since *The Washington Post* ran the story about the flyer I gave to Wilson and his community. He enjoyed hearing about my promise to Dr. Nathanson. Dr. Land has since interviewed me on his radio show and invited me to participate on a Family Research Council podcast, in addition to speaking at the National Conference on Christian Apologetics.

Sitting across from me at the weeklong event was Janet Morana, who cofounded Silent No More and is an executive director for Priests for Life. Beside her was Teresa Tomeo, a well-known EWTN Catholic radio commentator with a worldwide audience. I was hopeful that one day they would be interested in learning more about Dr. Nathanson's parting message.

I went to enjoy some quiet time at St. Peter's Basilica. My goal was to see Michelangelo's famous *Pieta*, the massive marble sculpture of the

Virgin Mary holding her son, capturing the minutes following removal of his body from the Crucifixion cross. I wanted to observe what selfless love looked like carved in marble for all of mankind to see: Mary, the Mother of the Savior, "the one who accepted 'Life' in the name of all and for the sake of all."[75]

This five-hundred-year-old statue protected behind bullet-proof glass was of the ultimate feminist, whose strength was her humility, tenacity and perseverance. It seemed that Michelangelo had sculpted more peace and tenderness on her face than pain, and I could only surmise he intended it that way. The Mother of Christ, *whom all generations will call blessed,* held the Way, the Truth and the Life across her lap in keeping with the divine plan.

Amidst the throng of visitors, I found a space to be still. Admiring the *Pieta,* I recalled the famous quote from Mother Teresa: *"Jesus died on the Cross because that is what it took for Him to do good to us — to save us from our selfishness in sin ... to show us that we, too, must be willing to give up everything to do God's will ..."* My eyes drifted toward Mary. I pondered this young woman who brought Life to the world. Mary could have been stoned to death for her "crisis pregnancy," but she totally trusted God. She *is* the example of sacrificial Motherhood that the world hungers for today. This special woman played a vital role in the doctor's salvation. Because of her — a woman — Dr. Nathanson found what he had always been looking for: unconditional love, unimaginable mercy and peace. He had found Jesus Christ.

"In all the clinics where I worked, the employees are forbidden to say anything that might talk the mother out of an abortion."

From Norma McCorvey, formerly known as Jane Roe of the 1973 *Roe v. Wade* case, in her 2003 affidavit (Section 25) to the Supreme Court of the United States requesting a hearing to reverse the *Roe v. Wade* decision which stripped unborn babies of all rights and protections. SCOTUS refused to hear her case. (Appendix E)

"Mary, who is the Virgin most pure, is also the refuge of sinners. She knows what sin is – not by the experience of its fall, not by tasting its bitter regrets, but by seeing what it did to her Divine Son."

Archbishop Fulton J. Sheen
Victory Over Vice, Sophia Institute Press, 1939

To mobilize young people to spread a culture of love and life:

Students for Life
www.sfl.org

For facts about the abortion – birth control – breast cancer connection:

Breast Cancer Prevention Institute
www.bcpinstitute.org

For video presentation of Dr. Angela Lanfranchi explaining the science of how and why abortion increases the likelihood of breast cancer:

Hosea Initiative
www.hosea4you.org/videos
beginning at minute 14:45

To foster God's plan for Love, Chastity, Marriage and Children:

One More Soul
www.onemoresoul.com

CHAPTER THIRTY

The Answered Prayers

"... it has been my experience – based on seventy-five thousand abortions – that a great many pregnant women remain in doubt even to the door of the abortion clinic."

Bernard N. Nathanson, M.D., *The Hand of God*

What If We've Been Wrong?

January 2012-2015

After returning from Rome, I realized how exhausted I was and how
I had not treated my body kindly during the political campaign — too
much coffee and way too much stress. One morning I awakened to my
fingers in a frozen state, jaw locked shut, and my feet throbbing. I had
developed severe rheumatoid arthritis and thought, "Senator Houck got
defeated and I got arthritis. Something is not right here." It hurt to move.

In addition to healing my physical illness, I desperately wanted God to
release me from my promise to Dr. Nathanson. As the months went by,
I tried justifying why I should be excused. One morning in the winter of
2013, I was praying and asking to be set free from my promise to
Dr. Nathanson. The quiet voice spoke again. It was the same persistent
voice I had heard tell me to interview the doctor. I simply heard in
response to my request, "No, there's going to be a movie." I did not rejoice.
In fact, I wept. I so wanted to be done. I begged to be let go from
this obligation, but like the interview instruction in 2009, I knew I had
already lost the argument.

I called Mrs. Nathanson with whom I had not spoken in nearly two years.
I had, however, sent her a note when I heard that Dr. Nathanson had died
a year earlier. She had replied and sent me a prayer card with a photo of
him from his funeral Mass. It had remained on my desk for nearly a year.
She welcomed me back to Manhattan to speak with her and several
other people who had known her late husband quite well. She also
referred me to Fr. McCloskey, who now lived in Chicago. This began the
next leg of my journey in some very unexpected ways.

After meeting with the priest, I made my first attempt at writing this book.
It was a complete failure. Months later, I tried again and deleted it
from my computer. Periodically, I would call Fr. McCloskey, who always
encouraged me not to give up. He would say, "America needs

Dr. Nathanson's parting message." In fact, he said my story should probably be translated into Spanish as well, since Planned Parenthood had made huge inroads into the once-solid, pro-life Hispanic community. The abortion giant had exported their population control ideas to most South American countries. So I wrote a third draft that I was somewhat pleased with, but I felt devoid of any ideas on how to draw closure to the story; something substantial was missing. Months and months later, and after a lot of prayer, the Lord answered.

January 21, 2015

I was on the way to my seventh March for Life in Washington, D.C. This is the nation's largest pro-life event with hundreds of thousands of Americans marching up Constitution Avenue to the U.S. Supreme Court building to protest the 1973 *Roe v. Wade* decision and memorialize the millions of babies who have died through abortion. I was planning to attend the Law of Life Conference hosted by Americans United for Life the day before the March, knowing many of the national pro-life leaders would be there. I entered the crowded conference room feeling a little intimidated. "Lord, please connect me with the person you want me to meet." My prayers would be answered within the next three hours.

I listened to an excellent presentation by a Notre Dame University professor. He explained how Justice Kennedy — a Catholic — is most likely the swing vote who could reverse the Court's *Roe, Doe* and *Casey* decisions in a case properly brought before the Supreme Court. I daydreamed that Justice Kennedy would learn about Dr. Nathanson's scientific pro-life conversion and the courage and humility it required of him to publicly change his mind. I thought if the "Abortion King" could change his mind based on science, so could Catholic Justice Kennedy.

Tired of sitting, I moved to the back of the room. When the next conference speaker finished, I introduced myself to the gentleman standing next to me. His name was Samuel Casey. He asked my name and what I do, probably thinking I was an attorney. I told him about my promise to Dr. Nathanson and I shared my hope of meeting an attorney who was qualified to write an easy-to-understand summary for my book regarding what went wrong in the *Roe* case.

Mr. Casey said that he had known Dr. Nathanson and was good friends with Allan Parker, the attorney who had represented Norma McCorvey in her 2003 case against the federal government petitioning it to *reverse* the *Roe v. Wade* decision. (Ms. McCorvey is the "Roe" of *Roe v. Wade,* whom activist lawyers deceived and used to strike down anti-abortion laws in all fifty states. She admits to being coerced into the *Roe* lawsuit, and she, like Dr. Nathanson, deeply regrets her involvement in decriminalizing abortion. As it turned out, Mr. Casey had written an amicus brief for her lawsuit to *reverse* the *Roe* decision. The U.S. Supreme Court declined to hear her case. (Her must-read affidavit appears in Appendix E.)

I asked him if he would be interested in writing the appendix to my book, and he happily agreed right there on the spot! In fact, he suggested that Allan Parker might agree to co-write it with him. It seemed God had just answered my prayer to connect me with the person He wanted me to meet. Since then, they wrote *Roe v. Wade: A Failed Exercise in "Assumicide,"* published in Appendix C — a well-documented resource to understand in detail the six assumptions made in the *Roe* case which have all proven erroneous.

In summary, the *first* assumption the Court made was that *"we can't know what a human being is and when its life begins."* Science now recognizes that a new human has come into being at the moment of conception. This is no longer in dispute; it is a proven medical fact.

The *second* assumption was that *"abortion is healthcare involving a normal healthy physician-patient relationship."* This is inaccurate because the vast majority of women seeking abortions make the decision to have the surgery without any physician consultation. There is no doctor-patient relationship; they are strangers in a sense.

The *third* assumption was that *"motherhood and child-rearing forces upon the woman a distressful life and future"* prohibiting the pregnant woman from working or furthering her education. So many advances have been made in women's employment, social, and legal rights that if "... *Roe* were to be reversed, these rights would not be lost because their legal and social existence are entirely independent of *Roe*." In addition, all fifty states now have Safe Haven laws, also known as "Baby Moses" laws, which allow a parent to abandon a child to the State anytime during the first year of life without any civil or criminal responsibility making the "distressful life and future" argument <u>false</u>.

The *fourth* assumption the U.S. Supreme Court made in the *Roe* case was that the decision to have an abortion would be *"truly voluntary and informed."* Not so. Four decades of decriminalized abortion have proven otherwise. The Justice Foundation has collected more than *five thousand two hundred* declarations from women testifying how abortion has hurt them psychologically, physically, or both, including the testimony of Norma McCorvey. Many of the women admit to being coerced to abort by husbands, boyfriends or parents. Many testify that abortions have hurt them psychologically because they were told "it" — the baby — was just a mass of tissue, only to later discover that the baby had arms, legs, and a beating heart. These mothers were *not* fully informed.

The *fifth* assumption was that *"abortion is safe and the mortality risk is less than pregnancy."* Decriminalizing abortion did not decrease the chances for uterine perforation, scar tissue, and cervical trauma.[76] The Court did not take into consideration the long-term effects of abortion — it increases the risk of pre-term birth, infertility, as well as depression.[77] In addition, the justices had no way of knowing what scientific research would reveal in the next couple of decades (conveniently compiled for readers at Breast Cancer Prevention Institute www.bcpi.org). Many documented, statistically significant studies show that when a woman chooses abortion, it increases "her risk [of developing breast cancer] in four ways: she creates in her breasts more places for cancers to start, which is the 'independent effect'; she loses the protective effect that a full-term pregnancy would have afforded her; she increases the risk of premature delivery of future pregnancies; and she lengthens her susceptibility window. . ."[78]

Lastly, the court made a *sixth* assumption that *"women face significant difficulties as a result of a cultural stigma of unwed motherhood."* This is no longer the case. In fact, single motherhood is glamorized and quite prevalent in certain circles.[79]

Many erroneous assumptions (see Appendix C: *Roe v. Wade – An Exercise in "Assumicide"*) — led the U.S. Supreme Court to condone violence, which has injured countless women and men and killed over sixty million people — a number every American should pause and think about. Equally bizarre is to think that so few abortion advocates, particularly millennials, are aware that Norma McCorvey would continue to desire that the Supreme Court *overturn* its 1973 decision. Her passionate plea to ask the United States Supreme Court to hear her 2003 petition for reversal was rejected. (See Appendix E: The *Roe* Affidavit.)

As I left the Law of Life Conference quite elated for having met Mr. Casey, something else happened, which should cause *anyone* of little or no faith to at least pause and reconsider their worldview. This long-awaited answer to my petition for a closing story is a gentle reminder to rejoice in the living God we serve because He hears our petitions; He feels our pain; and He loves our praise of Him. My friend Leslie called, urging me to come to the hotel lobby right away to meet her Silent No More friends. They were eager to hear about my interview with Dr. Nathanson.

I agreed, but I wasn't sure what to expect. As I approached, each woman was holding an *"I Regret My Abortion"* sign. They were cheerful and welcoming, but something even more profound struck me as I observed their interactions. It was their affinity for one another. They were a tightly connected kinship of women, a sort of sisterhood of strength, who profoundly understood the deepest wounds and pains a mother can possibly bear — the loss of a child. They were helping each other heal, paving the way for other mothers in need to seek alternatives rather than killing their babies.

We pulled some chairs together in the busy lobby where thousands of March for Life attendees were passing through. I shared my odyssey and answered their questions. They thanked me for my steadfastness in trying to fulfill my promise.

Afterwards, one of the ladies came close and sat beside me. She seemed very pensive as she asked me more questions about Dr. Nathanson. I asked her why she was so interested in him and her response astounded me. She shared that she had an abortion at seventeen in 1972 at the C.R.A.S.H. facility in New York City, the last year Dr. Nathanson served as medical director. For twenty-five years the abortion had nearly ruined her life, and in an effort to bring a deeper level of personal healing, she attended the doctor's funeral on February 28, 2011, at St. Patrick's Cathedral.

I realized immediately that her story might help bring closure to mine and that our meeting was likely not a mere coincidence. Even her name held significance: *Mary.*

She described suffering in silence and denial for years. Mary's self-protection had been a hard, cold exterior. After the abortion she was broken, always running from the truth and what was good. Eventually she married and started a family. While seeing her unborn child on an ultrasound image, Mary was emotionally awakened because she recognized the humanity of her baby. Nervously hoping she was worthy enough to be a mother, she began a long journey into recovery with a desire to put together all of the pieces that had led her to Dr. Nathanson's abortion facility. She needed to retrace her steps to be able to put closure on the death she had not yet grieved. She began the process of asking forgiveness from all those whom she had hurt along the way during her years of angry denial. Her family and her friends came first, and then she began to seek knowledge of all the memories of her experience of that day.

Mary retraced her steps to the C.R.A.S.H. abortion facility, which was no longer there. She searched the Internet for information about the staff and doctor who performed her abortion. What Mary found was Dr. Nathanson's testimony and conversion story. She was amazed at the way in which God was able to enter Dr. Nathanson's heart and profoundly change it, giving him the strength to speak out and ask for forgiveness from those he had hurt with his lies, propaganda campaign and arrogance. She spent the next year not only reading Dr. Nathanson's autobiography, *The Hand of God,* but also listening to his recorded speeches and reading his published articles.

As Mary entered St. Patrick's Cathedral on the day of Dr. Nathanson's funeral, she entered for reconciliation and restoration — another step in healing. She sat alone, separated from the congregation to avoid anyone she might have known.

A large procession of Catholic priests entered, including Archbishop Timothy Dolan and Fr. McCloskey. A Scripture reading followed, one in which St. Paul encouraged, *"Bearing with one another and forgiving one another, if one has a complaint against another; even as the Lord hath forgiven you, so you do also."* Colossians 3:13 (DRA) Then she heard the Gospel message, which she had prayed so many times before:

"Come to me, all you who labor and are burdened, and I will refresh you."
Matthew 11:28 (DRA) The Rev. Gerald E. Murray gave a homily and
attorney Thomas A. Moore shared a special eulogy for his dear friend.
Mary said that the love and peace of Christ filled the sanctuary.

Something else did, as well, before the end of the funeral Mass: the
voice of someone who felt honored to have known, loved and shared
married life with Dr. Nathanson. Christine Reisner-Nathanson offered,
as a tribute to her husband, her recording of a song called "Proud."
It had been Dr. Nathanson's favorite among the songs recorded on her
first album, and her lovely voice resonated throughout the Church.
The lyrics spoke of love for her husband:

> *Proud of my love for you.*
> *I am proud that you loved me too.*
> *And now if you'll stand with me*
> *for the world to see,*
> *I'd be proud.*
>
> *Though some may say it's wrong*
> *still I know that a love this strong*
> *will live till the sea runs dry*
> *till the day I die.*
> *That is why I am proud.*[80]

As the Mass drew to a close, the tremendous cathedral doors opened.
The rain had stopped and light was streaming down as it had on
Dr. Nathanson's life. The procession exited in front of Our Lady of
Guadalupe chapel, where the beautiful tilma replica of Mother Mary's
apparition hangs high in honor of her ending human sacrifice in the Aztec
Empire in the 1500s and converting millions to faith in Christ Jesus.

In the opposite direction stood the other Mary, who whispered the
powerful words, *"Rest in peace Dr. Nathanson. I forgive you."*

When I heard Mary say *"I forgive you,"* it seemed as if she spoke for *all* Americans because we have *all* been impacted by this immoral law. Not one person has remained untouched from the exploitation of women and their children. It has cost our country dearly. It seemed odd to be sitting in Washington, D.C. listening to Mary's story knowing this was the same city in which Rev. Hashmel Turner had survived a criminal abortion; where U.S. Supreme Court Justices in 1973 had stripped the unborn child from all rights and protections; where the National Black Caucus continues to ignore Margaret Sanger's well-documented "Negro Project" and the dismal Bureau of Vital Statistics data that abortion is the number one killer of black Americans; where some U.S. presidents have endorsed Planned Parenthood and ignored the genocide; where some of the most powerful Catholics in the U.S. Senate and House of Representatives grind America down with NARAL's nearly five-decade-old "Catholic Strategy." The white steps of the Supreme Court of the United States is where NARAL Pro-Choice America celebrates victory by using Dr. Nathanson's old propaganda. So victorious is the killing industry, abortionists would soon win another Supreme Court decision which removes a basic standard of care — abortionists no longer are required to have admitting privileges at a local hospital. *(Whole Woman's Health v. Hellerstedt 2016)*

Everything seemed upside down in a culture that *pretends* to demand justice.

My eyes brimmed with tears of joy for:

— the Marys of America, who will be able to forgive;

— for the Leslies, who discover that Christ can remove their cinder blocks;

— for the Tricias, who acknowledge that abortion destroys human life, not blobs of tissue;

— for the Glorias, who pray for their daughters as feminists
   continue devaluing the virtue of chastity;

— for the Wilsons, who have temporarily lost their right to vote,
   but not their voice for protecting human life;

— for pastors like Pastor Bibbens, who share *Maafa21* with their
   congregations and transform the world of politics for the good
   of mankind;

— for the Reverend Turners, who survive abortion and grow up
   to do great things for the Lord;

— for the clergy, like Fr. McCloskey, who lead people to the pillar
   and foundation of truth.

My tears were also for Dr. Nathanson and his magnificent story of
personal redemption. In my mind he was no longer America's
"Abortion King," "The Keeper of the Abortion Industry Keys," or
"The Father of the Modern Abortion Industry." He was Bernard
Nathanson, a sinner, just like me, who found unimaginable mercy,
forgiveness and peace in his Savior, Jesus.

He was Bernie, *a child of God,* who left a great vision for America
— to become a civilization of life and love, not violence. His restored
vision for our country can create a national paradigm shift in cultural
conscience, helping Americans understand that there is a much better
way to live. We do not need to support violence and pagan practices.
Because America would have the full story and Dr. Nathanson's parting
message, WE THE PEOPLE could choose to honor God by choosing life
once again — in the voting booth and in caring for the well-being of
our neighbors. He predicted the day would come when the Supreme
Court overturns its bad decisions *(Roe, Doe and Casey),* which, in effect,
would return the issue of abortion to the states to decide. Most likely

an informed public in every state would make the right decision for protecting the right to life. As for Planned Parenthood and NARAL, they could be dismembered, defunded and destroyed and looked upon as selfish and wicked as the slave industry. These organizations grounded in secular humanism would become a shameful thing of the past as more Americans come to the realization that worldviews really do matter and have real consequences.

Lastly, my tears were for people like me, who once thought *"What does abortion have to do with me?"* How wrong I was, and yes, like Dr. Nathanson, I had to humble myself and let go of pride to admit the error of my apathetic ways. My silence and my lack of knowledge had made me an accomplice to millions of deaths that have deformed our nation.

I turned my attention back to the lobby, where I sat looking at people arrive from every state across America for the March for Life the following day. I noticed the joy and energy among the marchers. They crisscrossed the lobby getting ready for the next day's march, arming themselves with signs: We Are the Pro-life Generation, Defend Life, Choose Life, Adoption is the Option, Silent No More and Save the Storks. I quietly thought to myself, "It's the movement Dr. Nathanson referenced so articulately. These are the people."

This movement is the only movement I know of, in which if it is successful, those of you who worked in it will get no thanks from anybody because there are no voices to thank you. It's the most altruistic movement of all time. More than the abolition movement because at least the slaves, once freed, could thank their emancipators. Here, the little voices are lost and all you get out of it is the feeling and the knowledge that you have done an immeasurable good and I salute you and I love you for it.

Bernard N. Nathanson, M.D., *speaking at the Human Life International World Conference*

"After I saw all the deception going on at the abortion facilities, and after all the things that my supervisors told me to tell women, I became very angry. I saw women being lied to, openly, and I was a part of it. There's no telling how many children I helped kill while their mothers dug their nails into me and listened to my warning, 'Whatever you do, don't move!'"

From Norma McCorvey, formerly known as Jane Roe of the 1973 *Roe v. Wade* case, in her 2003 affidavit (Section 26) to the Supreme Court of the United States requesting a hearing to reverse the *Roe v. Wade* decision which stripped unborn babies of all rights and protections. SCOTUS refused to hear her case. (Appendix E)

"I [urge] you, by all that is dear, by all that is honorable, by all that is sacred, not only that ye pray but that ye act." [8]

Address of **John Hancock** in 1774
in the Old South Church on the Boston Massacre of 1770

To support life-affirming women's healthcare and education:

Divine Mercy Care
www.divinemercycare.org

John Paul II Life Center
www.jpiilifecenter.org

CHAPTER THIRTY-ONE
The Mantle

*"That was a millennium ago scientifically;
no ultrasound, no electronic fetal heart monitoring, no concept
of the unborn as our second patient."*

Bernard N. Nathanson, M.D., *Blessed are the Barren*

What If We've Been Wrong?

"Dr. Nathanson, I know you are too sick to travel getting your message out. *If* you have something to tell America, I promise I will carry it across our nation for you."

Pausing to contemplate, he spoke a deliberate and carefully worded response in a soft, tired voice.

> *Yes. Yes, I do. Continue teaching the strategy of how I deceived America, but also deliver this special message. Tell America that the cofounder of NARAL says to: Love one another. Abortion is <u>not</u> love. Stop the killing. The world needs more love. I'm all about love now.*

With his tender eyes looking up at me, I contemplated the clarity, simplicity, and power of his personal parting message. In lieu of the former dictatorial relativism of his "Choice" propaganda, his parting message to love one another was beautiful, good, and true.

Choose love, *not* violence. He should know better than anyone — abortion is not love.

As I reached to shake his hand, I sincerely told him,

> *I promise, Dr. Nathanson, I will carry your message and teach Americans your deceptive strategy until it becomes common knowledge or until the* Roe v. Wade *decision is overturned, whichever comes first."*

I thought I saw in his eyes a glimmer of hope for a better tomorrow, hope for our nation that will admit its errors before it is too late.

As I left his apartment, Mrs. Nathanson bid me well and best wishes on keeping my promise. I thanked her again and the door slowly closed. I stared momentarily at the door just thinking of the magnitude of what I had just promised this dear old man with my handshake and my heart.

I would soon move to Fredericksburg and take quiet walks along the knoll and into the Wilberforce Garden, a sanctuary in which I would frequently pray that God would make a way to fulfill my promise because I could not do this alone. Thousands of yellow buttercups grew along the grassy knoll and into the garden. I kneeled down in prayer with my elbows in the grass. The perfectly shaped little buttercups seemed to stare back at me. Each one was beautiful and intricately designed. I knew that for each flower, ten thousand lives could be saved, providing ten thousand more opportunities to love someone and become pencils in God's hand.

And then He began answering my prayers.

"A new command I give you: Love one another.
As I have loved you, so you must love one another."

Jesus Christ
John 13:34 (NIV)

CHAPTER THIRTY-TWO

The Rest of the Story

*"For the sake of His sorrowful Passion,
have mercy on us and on the whole world."*

From the Chaplet of Divine Mercy

What If We've Been Wrong?

2016

After making Dr. Nathanson the promise, I never felt like I was operating on my own timeline. It began with prayer and then it led me into politics. I tried launching efforts to get his message told in other ways that I thought I was supposed to, but most of those seemed to fail. It was quite frustrating. I would try again, always remembering the babies who had violently lost their lives, while I seemed to flounder. With each passing year at least a million more lives were lost. The pressure to fulfill this promise mounted.

I also got dragged into the school-of-hard-knocks for which I am grateful because it taught me how injured post-abortive women and men are who haven't been healed yet. As for the book manuscript, it took much longer to write than I had anticipated. Periodically I would have writing breakthroughs, and then I would shut down as if it wasn't the right time to be finished with the story. In addition, I knew I had "heard" movie, but it did not even remotely seem possible.

I was slowly learning that my timeline is not God's timeline. I had to wait for Him to move, and when He did, a torrent of blessings would flow, like this one.

Two weeks before the March for Life 2016, nearly a year after meeting Mary, who had attended Dr. Nathanson's funeral, a friend of mine called to tell me she had finished reading the manuscript. She passionately urged me to send it to her friend who is a movie producer from Los Angeles and who worked in Hollywood for a number of years. He was now living in Virginia. In lieu of mailing it to him, the producer and I arranged to meet for dinner just two days before the March for Life.

I shared my seven-year odyssey and he seemed quite interested. And then came my surprise. It turned out that he had been on at least five men's spiritual retreats with Dr. Nathanson. This producer had sat for hours with the doctor and had listened and comforted him as he lamented his grievous errors. In addition, he had managed thousands of hours of television documentaries including *National Geographic's "In the Womb,"* a breakout hit and one of its largest selling videos of its era. Not only that, but Fr. McCloskey had been this man's spiritual advisor for twenty years. We are currently collaborating on a film based on this book. This blessing happened during a thirty-three day retreat as I consecrated myself to Our Blessed Mother Mary.

God never ceases to amaze me!

Something else happened. The following evening I attended a dinner gathering with attorney Allan Parker, who had represented Norma McCorvey in her suit to overturn *Roe v. Wade*. At this small gathering was a couple from the Netherlands who had flown to America to attend the March. They run a radio station and strongly encouraged me to continue with the mission. They had met with Dr. Nathanson years ago and were confident that his parting message would help turn the heart of America back to God and be a catalyst to end abortion. They asked for a copy of my book once it is published. It felt like the beginning of my sending Dr. Nathanson's parting message around the world.

Then, the spunky lady sitting to my right invited me to meet Dick Simmons, founder of a ministry called Men4Nations. This prayer ministry reaches from the East Coast to West Coast. Back in the 1980s, Dick Simmons organized a national prayer movement for a period of time asking the Lord to do something significant to help end abortion. A short time later, Dr. Nathanson released *The Silent Scream*. Men4Nations considered this an answer to their prayers. As I met with Mr. Simmons and shared my journey, I felt confident that Dr. Nathanson, had he still been alive and in good health, would have visited

Men4Nations in person and joined with Mr. Simmons in prayer.
He would invite me back within a few months to share my story with
some of his prayer warriors who had come to Washington, D.C. to pray.
I have never been in the presence of such passionate prayer led my men
who understand that the the Lord *hates* the shedding of innocent blood
and He will punish nations that turn against the Word.

Lastly, I met Sister Rose. She is a nun from Kenya who works in
Washington, D.C. Well aware of the population-control and eugenics
measures of the International Planned Parenthood Federation,
Sister Rose informed me that the abortion giant is working hard to
decriminalize abortion in her home country. As if killing three hundred
thousand American babies annually isn't enough blood shed for
Planned Parenthood, it wants the black Kenyan children too. Sister Rose
and I prayed fervently for this story to travel nationwide and to ignite
a movement of mercy to love our neighbor and to end violence against
humanity. She wants Americans to know that many Kenyans are
fighting to keep Planned Parenthood out of their country. They don't
want the culture of death to spread there too as it has already been
exported to many developing countries.

Sister Rose implores Americans to fund the secondary school she
started in Kenya, Africa, called Mother of Mercy Girls School in the
Njoro district of Nakuru County. Sister Rose said, "Kenyan girls simply
need education, *not abortion.* Tell Bill Gates, Warren Buffet and the other
supporters of Planned Parenthood, including taxpayers, to stop funding
the abortion giant and destroy it. And when you vote, vote pro-life."

In June 2016, the United States Supreme Court released another
destructive opinion entitled *Whole Woman's Health v. Hellerstedt,
Commissioner,* which struck down a Texas Law requiring medical
doctors who perform abortions to have medical privileges at a local

hospital and that abortion facilities have the same standards of care as outpatient surgical centers. These two requirements were

> ... *the express will of the people of Texas. They were commonsense health and safety regulations, in the event of an emergency arising out of surgical abortions. The rejection of these restrictions by the Supreme Court rips the veneer off of the Court's pretense to impartiality. The sophistry found in the judicial opinions following Roe and Doe, which purport to allow States to pass reasonable restrictions of abortion, are now proven to have been a subterfuge ... The ruling is a disaster for mothers and children in the womb.*[82]

Justice Kennedy was the swing vote on this case again which tipped the ruling in the abortion industry's favor. The beat goes on. Why? Because a vote for a "pro-choice" elected official is essentially a "vote" for a U.S. Supreme Court justice who will undoubtedly favor the abortion industry's exploitation of women and disregard a baby's right to life. Period.

Before I close, I ask readers of *What If We've Been Wrong?* to understand a fundamental principle of righteousness that Dr. Nathanson ultimately embraced as a Messianic Jewish man: If righteousness exalts a nation,

> *[the] issues that the Bible identifies as directly impacting national righteousness should be foremost in Biblical 'voters' minds as they select a President. Dozens of Bible passages, Deuteronomy 28, I Chronicles 21, I Kings 18 (NKJV) affirm that a nation's righteousness is determined by its public policies and how well they conform to God's standards; only God-honoring policies that lead to God-honoring actions can exalt a nation.*[83] *These righteous policies*

... are the result of God-honoring public officials enacting those policies. Therefore, if righteousness (God-honoring policy) is to exalt a nation, then a nation must have leaders like ... David ... not Jezebel ... In America, the only way there will be God-honoring public officials is if God-honoring citizens elect them ... Therefore, the first and foremost consideration in choosing a President is whether that individual will advance policies upholding biblical standards of righteousness and oppose policies that encourage what the bible defines as sin or unrighteous behavior. – i.e. Biblical rights and wrongs — must always take precedence over economic, environmental, healthcare, energy, and other issues. These other issues are important, but...Jesus told His disciples that if they would make the pursuit of righteousness their primary emphasis, then everything else would be provided. Matthew 6:33 (NKJV) However, if economic (or other) issues become the primary focus for voters, the nation usually ends up attaining neither the economic prosperity voters desired nor the national righteousness that should have been their primary concern in the first first place.[84]

If American voters make a bold stand for upholding the dignity of human life, this ugly chapter of national deception will be closed forever — just like the chapter on slavery. If not, violence, public turmoil and the breakdown of family will increase, just like Dr. Nathanson predicted. In fact, just yesterday (July 7, 2016) in Dallas, Texas, the same city where Norma McCorvey's *Roe v. Wade* case originated, fourteen police officers were shot and five died. Public turmoil indeed. There was a time when American culture was not this violent, but immoral laws *(Roe, Doe, Casey)* and legalized homicide *beget* immoral people and more homicide.

As I have been penning this closure, a beautiful, large rainbow appears in the field next to my home as if another confirmation that America needs Dr. Nathanson's message. Trying to fulfill my promise to Dr. Nathanson has let me experience one thing for sure — the Kingdom of God *is* at hand and in Jesus Christ *is* the victory. His Kingdom of love is more powerful than presidents, political party bondage, racism and all of the weapons of mass destruction — including the abortion-population control industry. We can change the world for good and it begins by first uniting on the gift that God gave the human family —the unalienable right to life and the ability to love one another.

"Love one another.
Abortion is not love.
Stop the killing.
The world needs more love.
I'm all about love now."

Bernard N. Nathanson, Child of God

Dr. Bernard Nathanson, Christine Reisner-Nathanson and Hillie

Courtesy of Christine Reisner-Nathanson

A cheerful time with Dr. Bernard Nathanson, his wife Christine Reisner-Nathanson
and their dog, Hillie

Courtesy of Christine Reisner-Nathanson

Dr. Bernard Nathanson with Hillie on his lap

Courtesy of Christine Reisner-Nathanson

Epilogue

By Deacon Keith Fournier

Because you are reading this Epilogue, I know we share a great blessing, we have all read *What If We've Been Wrong? Keeping my promise to America's "Abortion King."*

I am confident that, like me, you were moved in the place which the Bible and Christian teaching refers to as the heart. The heart, in the words of the Catholic Catechism, is the "seat of moral personality," the place where we make our deep and lasting choices.

Our choices not only change the world around us, they change us. This is the core of Christian moral teaching. We need men and women who have truthfully informed their conscience concerning the great human rights issue of our age, the fundamental human right to life, and will make the choices required to live in a morally coherent manner in a culture which has forgotten God and, as a result, is losing its soul. We need people who will courageously struggle to restore human rights protection to our first neighbors in the womb and face the fury of the enemy of life, unafraid.

I hope this book, and the movie it inspires, will change millions of hearts. Then, that all who have been changed as a result will choose to band together and work to transform the current culture of death into a culture of life and civilization of love. Every procured abortion is the taking of innocent human life and is therefore intrinsically immoral. This is not simply a "religious" position. It is revealed in the natural law and undeniable to honest men and women. In addition, without the right to life there are no other rights and the very infrastructure of rights is thrown into jeopardy.

Our failure to recognize that our first neighbors in the womb have a right to be born and live a full life in our community undermines any claim to favor a compassionate society. All the talk about compassion for the poor rings hollow when we fail to hear the cry of the ones whom Teresa of Calcutta rightly called the "poorest of the poor." Medical science confirms what our conscience long told us. We are taking the lives of our children. We now routinely operate upon them in the womb. We send 3 and 4D ultrasound photos of him or her as they grow in that first home of the whole human race.

These children are members of our human family and we have no excuse for what we do in every procured abortion. It is evil, plain and simple. The words of the great Hebrew prophet Isaiah cry out in our day, *"Woe to those who call evil good and good evil, who put darkness for light and light for darkness, who put bitter for sweet and sweet for bitter!"* (Isaiah 5:20)

Terry Beatley is a passionate, tireless advocate for the Right to Life. She is also an example of what Pope St. John Paul II called a "new feminism." In a letter entitled *"The Gospel of Life"* he wrote, "In transforming culture so that it supports life, women occupy a place, in thought and action, which is unique and decisive. It depends on them to promote a "new feminism" which rejects the temptation of imitating models of 'male domination' in order to acknowledge and affirm the true genius of women in every aspect of the life of society, and overcome all discrimination, violence and exploitation."

In another letter addressed to women entitled *On the Dignity of Women,* he wrote, *"The moral and spiritual strength of a woman is joined to her awareness that God entrusts the human being to her in a special way. Of course, God entrusts every human being to each and every other human being. But this entrusting concerns women in a special way — precisely by reason of their femininity — and this in a particular way determines their vocation."*

Terry has that *"feminine genius"* and she takes to heart the vocation which lies at the root of it. She is a courageous, faithful, feminine woman, who is answering the prophetic call of this urgent hour in our history, both as a Church and a Nation. She has a vocation to defend life and she lives it! Her love and passion for the Lord informs her whole way of life. She does not separate the moral, spiritual, economic or political issues; she is morally coherent. She is a spiritual and cultural warrior in a new missionary age and this book is one of her responses to that call. I am honored to recommend it to everyone.

I met Bernie Nathanson at a Christian retreat, many years ago. It was sponsored by the personal prelature of *Opus Dei.* I will never forget the moment I first saw him. He was kneeling in the chapel, obviously deep in prayer. He seemed profoundly burdened. I had known *of* him for many years, especially because of my work as a Constitutional lawyer dedicated to the defense of life, liberty and family.

However, on that weekend, and for many years to come, I really came to *know* him – and in receiving the gift of his friendship I was forever changed. I cherished our enduring friendship and valued his wisdom, courageous witness, humor, warmth, and persevering, prophetic faith.

I still miss him deeply, but I know his work continues and this book
is a part of it.

In 1996, Bernie was baptized into Jesus Christ and His Church by
Cardinal John O'Connor in New York's St. Patrick's Cathedral, he also
received the Sacraments of Confirmation (Chrismation in the East)
and Holy Eucharist. He was fully initiated into the Body of Jesus Christ,
the Church and born anew. He wrote concerning that experience,
*"I was in a real whirlpool of emotion, and then there was this healing,
cooling water on me, and soft voices, and an inexpressible sense
of peace. I had found a safe place."*

My friend Bernie died as a friend of Jesus Christ, the author of life.
I watched the Holy Spirit make Bernie into a humble, loving, modern day
apostle, a new creation. It reminded me of the transformation of the
Apostle Paul. Bernie, in his self-deprecating manner, would never accept
the analogy. He became a humble man, a true follower of the One who
poured Himself out for all of us on that tree on the Hill of Calvary.

I know that Bernie has now found the safest and happiest of places,
in the heart of the communion of God's love for all eternity. But his story
and the witness of his new life in the Lord must continue to be told.
There is so much work to be done! His witness of continuing response
to the Lord can inspire millions.

His lifetime of choices for Life, once his eyes were opened to the truth,
sets the standard for the responses which will be required in the work
which lies ahead. My prayer is that through this book, and the movie it
generates — the story of Bernie Nathanson — will be shouted from
the housetops!

Deacon Keith Fournier is Editor in Chief at Catholic Online, *a Constitutional lawyer
and Founder of* The Common Good Foundation.

Divine Mercy Chaplet

O Blood and Water, which gushed forth from the Heart of Jesus
as a fountain of Mercy for us, I trust in You!

Eternal Father, I offer you the Body and Blood, Soul
and Divinity of Your Dearly Beloved Son,

Our Lord, Jesus Christ, in atonement for our sins
and those of the whole world.

For the sake of His sorrowful Passion, have mercy on us
and on the whole world.

Eternal God, in whom mercy is endless and the treasury
of compassion is inexhaustible, look kindly upon us and increase
Your mercy in us, that in difficult moments we might not despair
nor become despondent, but with great confidence
submit ourselves to Your holy will, which is Love and Mercy itself.

What If We've Been Wrong?

APPENDIX A

In Gratitude

The gift of thirty years of marriage made this book possible. Without my supportive spouse, I would not have been able to work toward fulfilling my promise to Dr. Nathanson. My husband's patience is boundless and he exemplifies what marriage is supposed to be — a team effort with personal sacrifices. Many lives will be saved because of him. Thank you Kenny Beatley.

I also thank my daughters, McAyla and Kirsten, for their patience and growing support. I pray I have shown them an example of perseverance and how loving others by sharing the truth honors Jesus Christ. Truth helps restore our nation to a biblical worldview — the only way that leads to peace and justice.

I am also thankful for the support of Mrs. Christine Reisner-Nathanson, who could have easily declined my request to interview her husband. Her motivation to honor his legacy and her generosity in sharing private photographs and writings have boosted my confidence that Americans will want to read this true story.

There is someone who probably thought I would never finish this manuscript — Fr. C. J. McCloskey III. He encouraged me to keep my commitment to getting this story completed. I appreciate his prayers in more ways than I can say. He introduced me to the Eucharist which brought fullness and joy to my life. Many thanks also to Pastor John Bibbens, who agreed to a three-hour meeting — his response proved to me that the racial and political divide in America can be minimized by honoring God first, not political parties. I am grateful to Pastors Marvin and Renee Johnson for their color-blind love and friendship, Dianne Sexton for her prayers and for sharing her father's vision, Neal and Tish Rothenbach for housing, The Church of the Nazarene for blessing this endeavor, and Rev. Hashmel Turner for standing up for life. I am also grateful to Pastor Michael Hirsch for introducing me to many minority ministers, Bishop Joseph Henderson for his courage, Dale Swanson and her team for feeding nearly three hundred people breakfast, Teri Buck for office space, Pastors Angela Kittrell, Charles Ervin and James Arkord for their friendship, Dr. Alveda King for speaking at my press conference, as well as Wayne and Gloria Whitley for encouragement and for sharing their story. Many thanks also to Tom White of Virginia Right blog who gave my events coverage, and Ponch K. McPhee of FM Talk Radio, and Rob Schilling of The Schilling Show, who provided radio publicity. Additionally, I would like to thank *The Free Lance Star* for publishing my guest editorial exposing Senator Houck's attack on parental rights, Tom McDevitt, Chairman of *The Washington Times,* for sharing part of my story in The Power of Prayer supplement, Dr. Richard Land for interviewing me on his radio shows, Jim Sedlak of American Life League for recommending *Grand Illusions* book and The Fredericksburg Prayer Furnace for helpers and prayers. In addition, Don Blake and Greene Hollowell of Virginia Christian Alliance deserve tremendous credit for helping me bring awareness of the threat against parental rights, as does Bishop Eugene Reeves, for encouraging me to help the disenfranchised. The dividends were enormous. I am also appreciative for the Family Foundation Action's General Assembly Report Card and for Virginia Delegate Robert (Bob) Marshall for coauthoring an excellent resource about Planned Parenthood's legacy called *Blessed Are the Barren,* along with Chuck Donovan.

Many thanks, also, to the Hosea Initiative team — Andrea DelVecchio, Tricia Powell, Leslie Blackwell and Kathleen Johnson — for your "threats" to hold me accountable to finish the manuscript. Your support and friendship mean so much to me. In addition, there were people who committed to praying regularly and stuck with it. The ones I know of are Carlie Dixon, Ken Ferguson, Craig Hudgins, Jimmy Berkon, Liz Crnkovich and Lisa Turner — all of whom helped me understand "M Power." Also, Nancy Schulze, Sharon Turner, Sharon Maulding, Bernadette Barber and Mickie Teetor, I thank you for your consistent prayers.

A big shout-out goes to Mark Almas for designing the beautiful book cover, buttercups, and for laying out the contents of the book. Thank you for sharing your talent and dealing with my many "final drafts!"

I also appreciate the advice from Harry Crocker, Vice President of Regnery Publishing, which published Dr. Nathanson's autobiography, *The Hand of God.* The advice and insight from Thomas Moore, Chris Slattery, Joan Andrews Bell and Deacon Keith Fournier — all friends of Dr. Nathanson's — was also truly a blessing.

I am grateful to Samuel Casey, J.D., and Allan Parker, J.D., for writing the bonus section: *Roe v. Wade: A Failed Exercise in "Assumicide."* You are an answer to prayer! In addition, I thank Norma McCorvey for her years of speaking up in *defense* of preborn children, for sharing her story of being deceived by activist lawyers, and for her quest for justice in the Supreme Court which refused to hear her case to reverse *Roe v. Wade.* May my story be a catalyst to getting her message told to millennials who hunger for justice.

There are other people who helped in various ways. You know who you are. I thank you!

Lastly, I thank the Lord for setting me about this task. It has been a blessing in many ways, particularly experiencing how God made Himself visible in so many invisible ways.

APPENDIX B

The Teenage Victims

**This is a partial list of American teenagers who have died
as a result of abortion surgery complications.**

Deanna B. — IL, Age 13	Denise M. — TX, Age 15
Teresa C. — GA, Age 17	Germaine N. — NJ, Age 14
Patricia C. — CA, Age 16	Sara N. — GA, Age 15
Sharon D. — NM, Age 17	Katrina P. — FL, Age 16
Laniece D. — CA, Age 17	Dawndalea R. — NY, Age 13
Gwendolyn D. — CA, Age 15	Erica R. — MD, Age 16
Christella F. — MI, Age 16	Sharonda R. — DC, Age 17
Janice G. — IL, Age 17	Tamiia R. — MI, Age 15
Gracealynn H. — DE, Age 19	Jan S. — CA, Age 16
Wilma H. — DC, Age 17	Deloris S. — GA, Age 15
Barbara H. — CA, Age 16	Jennifer S. — CA, Age 17
Debra L. — NJ, Age 17	Latachie V. — TX, Age 17
Sophie M. — NY, Age 17	Cheryl V. — CA, Age 17
Rita M. — DC, Age 16	Chivon W. — MI, Age 17
Natalie M. — CA, Age 16	

Courtesy of Life Dynamics.

APPENDIX C

Roe v. Wade: A Failed Exercise in "Assumicide"

Samuel B. Casey, J.D. and Allan Parker, J.D.[85]

"The two cases, *Roe v. Wade* (and its companion case, *Doe v. Bolton,* decided January 22, 1973) and *Planned Parenthood v. Casey* (1992), in combination, created an essentially unqualified constitutional right of pregnant women to abortion—the right to kill their children, gestating in their wombs, up to the point of birth. After [more than] four decades, *Roe's* human death toll stands at nearly sixty million human lives, a total exceeding the Nazi Holocaust, Stalin's purges, Pol Pot's killing fields, and the Rwandan genocide combined. Over the past [forty-three] years, one-sixth of the American population has been killed by abortion. One in four African-Americans is killed before birth. Abortion is the leading cause of (unnatural) death in America."[86]

Professor Michael Stokes Paulsen
University Chair & Professor of Law,
University of St. Thomas, School of Law

INTRODUCTION

"Assumicide" can rightly be termed to be an assumption that proves fatal to ourselves or others, like the 'assumption' that an entranced cobra won't strike; or that the 'light' at the end of the tunnel is daylight not an oncoming train engine's headlight; or that the "Titanic" is unsinkable. In the case of elective abortion the 'assumicide' committed by America's Supreme Court in legalizing this practice has been extremely fatal to tens of millions of America's unborn children and their physically or psychologically injured mothers drawn in by its numerous false assumptions unproven in the record before it and subsequently disproven by the evidence the Court seemingly ignored then and we ought not doubt now.

Why? Because on January 22, 1973 in its companion decisions: *Roe v. Wade*, 410 U.S. 113 (1973) and *Doe v. Bolton*, 410 U.S. 179 (1973), which the Court then held "are to be read together," the United States Supreme Court usurped the democratic process, removed the ultimate regulation of abortion from the political branches of government and delegated to itself the plenary role of determining to what extent, if any, any state may absolutely prohibit, selectively ban, or even regulate elective abortion without violating the Due Process Clause of the 14th Amendment to the United States Constitution.

The crew on the HMS Titanic, realizing the ship had fallen prey to the "assumicide" that she was unsinkable, obeyed one sacrificial yet inspiring order by their ill-fated Captain Smith on that desperate night as hopes of a quick rescue sank: SAVE THE WOMEN & CHILDREN FIRST.[87] Sadly, this exceptionally brave practice has not been the practice of America's abortion industry who since 1973, if not "murder", have gotten away with constitutionally-excused homicide based upon the Court's "assumicide" that we can't know when human life begins and women can't live equally and safely in this country unless they can terminate their pregnancies at any time for any reason or no reason at all.

As you read this article, appended to Terry Beatley's telling pro-life conversion story of one of the abortion industry's founders, Dr. Bernard Nathanson (1926-2011), let's begin with United States Supreme Court Justice Louis Brandeis' advice that "the life of the law is in the facts."[88] So what are the facts? What should we think of the American pro-life movement to date? The answer is tragically clear: For all the minds and hearts it has changed, the mothers and children it has rescued from abortion,[89] and the American elections it has and still influences, America' pro-life movement has still has not yet achieved its ultimate political objective: *"An America in which every unborn child is protected in law and welcomed in life."* [90]

To achieve this objective, it is necessary but not sufficient under the existing legal circumstances for at least five justices of the Supreme Court to decide based upon the facts and challenged law of record in a case properly before it to reverse the central holding in *Roe* subsequently upheld in its *Casey* decision by showing that *Roe* and its progeny have not been good for women and is not needed as a back-up for failed contraception for women to enjoy equal opportunity in America.

Such a judicial reversal will not be sufficient because, as American United for Life's Senior Counsel, Clarke Forsythe, reminds us: *"If* Roe *were overturned today, abortion would still be legal in at least forty-one states tomorrow, perhaps all fifty...Returning the issue to the people would result in virtually no immediate change because fewer than ten states would have an enforceable [abortion] prohibition on the books ... Overturning* Roe *means that the issue will return to the democratic process."* [91] Ultimately, this means that the "assumicide" that the *Roe* Court justified in its opinion by "the demands of the profound problems of the present day" (*Roe*, 410 U.S. at 165) will have to be rectified, *or not,* by *each* state legislature. So, because the long-term legality of abortion ultimately depends on public opinion, the pro-life movement must tirelessly work for a "culture of life" and the restoration of the political possibility of an open, even-handed state legislative debate about abortion, a public evaluation of the results of each abortion reform and regular accountability to the people for such reforms. Obviously, to get from today to that great day, much remains to be done.

In many states, abortion is effectively legal for all nine months for any reason or no reason at all, including sex selection and disability (*e.g.* Down Syndrome children fatally experience more than an estimated 65% abortion rate).[92]

Despite popular opposition, America's abortion laws remain the laxest on planet Earth — far less protective of unborn life than the laws in most countries. In fact, the United States is one of only seven nations worldwide that permits elective abortion after 20 weeks, according to a report recently released by the Charlotte Lozier Institute, the education and research arm of the Susan B. Anthony List.[93] The report—which examined gestational limits and abortion laws in 198 countries, independent states, and semi-autonomous regions with populations of more than 1 million—found both the United States and Canada rank alongside known human rights abusers North Korea, Vietnam, and China as countries with the world's most permissive abortion laws. In the United States, this means constitutionally allowing abortion on demand, with no substantially burdensome restrictions, up to the point of fetal viability, usually placed at 24 weeks.[94]

Abortion is being effectively subsidized by the health care fees and premiums authorized by the Affordable Care Act ("Obamacare").[95] Seventeen states fund all or most medically necessary abortions; while 32 states fund abortion only in cases involving life endangerment, rape and incest.[96] Well-intended restrictions on abortion after "viability" most often include "life AND health of the mother"— exceptions any doctor could drive a truck through—and laws against partial birth abortion only ban one method of destroying unborn children, out of many late-term abortion methods.[97]

The abortion industry's largest practitioner, Planned Parenthood, is not only responsible for almost one-third of America's abortions (at least 300,000 per year) for which, conservatively estimated, it charges patient fees in excess of $144 million dollars per year, it annually receives federal funding in excess of $500 million dollars for its alleged non-abortion "reproductive health" services, which Americans have most recently learned include "financial reimbursement" from Planned Parenthood's clients for the provision of dead aborted baby parts for medical research.[98] As a consequence of these "revelations" about Planned Parenthood's "business practices", on March 26, 2016, Florida became the 12th state to block state taxpayer dollars from going to any group who operates or is affiliated with any licensed abortion facility, including Planned Parenthood.

These are the facts: without any evidence to explain it or sufficient notice to avoid it, the United States Constitution was severely "gashed" by the U.S. Supreme Court's breathtaking decision in *Roe v. Wade* in 1973. Consequently, close to sixty million Americans have died without a legal "lifeboat" in the freezing waters of the abortion license created by the *Roe* Court to sink any state law that challenges or seeks to distinguish its central holding.

As still surviving pro-life advocates, our job – an advocacy job that may take yet another entire lifetime – is to use whatever legal "lifeboats" we can find to save the women and children first. Whether and when the "sunken titanic" of the American Constitution's 14th Amendment can ever be raised and repaired will depend on a multitude of legal, economic, political and cultural factors about which this book, *What If We've Been Wrong?*, has been written.

Of course, the *Titanic* ran into that iceberg because she was moving too fast arrogantly operating under the assumption that she was unsinkable. The *Roe* case and its legal progeny similarly suffers from such "assumicide". Just as Dr. Bernard Nathanson humbly asked *"what if we've been wrong?"* in his letter of resignation as the Executive Director of the National Abortion Rights Action League shortly after he saw his first ultrasound of an abortion, let us now turn to the six factual "assumptions" the Court relied upon in *Roe* and *Doe* that has led to such loss of life, national heartache and social division to see how wrong each of these assumptions is.

THE "FACTS" *ROE* GOT WRONG

As has been discussed or commented upon by many law professors, including most notably Professor Michael Paulsen, *Roe v. Wade* is not only ill-conceived constitutional law unfounded in the text and legal traditions of this country, it is also in our legal opinions a failed exercise in what we call "assumicide.'[99] As explained below, the Supreme Court's infamous *Roe v. Wade* decision is specifically based upon six different misplaced *assumptions of fact* (never established by any admissible evidence in the case) that were critical to the *Roe* Court's holding that the states lacked an interest sufficiently compelling to prohibit or meaningfully regulate ("substantially burden") the woman's "liberty interest" in being able to lawfully consent ("gain access") to her abortion procedure.[100]

We can list these six judicially misplaced factual "assumptions" briefly as:

- **We can't know what a 'human being' is and when its life begins.**

- **Abortion is 'health care' involving a normal 'responsible' doctor-patient relationship.**

- **Motherhood and child-rearing force upon the woman 'a distressful life and future.'**

- **An abortion decision is truly voluntary and fully informed.**

- **The risk to the women's health and life was 'far greater in carrying the child to full term' than in having an abortion.**

- **A woman faces significant difficulties as a result of a cultural stigma of unwed motherhood.**

As was concluded and first completely documented in the South Dakota Task Force Report on Abortion (2005),[101] as well as further verified by subsequent developments in science, medicine and law, each of these six assumptions if not wrong then are surely arguable if not completely wrong now:

> As a result of the advances in modern science and
> medicine, and particularly because of information derived
> from the practice of abortion since its legalization,
> the Task Force finds that each of these assumptions has
> been entirely or largely disproved. The new understanding
> about these facts, and the new information not previously
> known concerning them, are important in understanding
> how abortion affects the lives, rights, interests,
> and health of women.

Let's briefly address each of these assumptions one at a time and discuss why each of them is arguable if not completely wrong today:

1. The Unborn Child is Not a Living Human Being

First, the Supreme Court *assumed* that it could not determine the answer to the question of when the life of a human being begins: Thus, the Court neither affirmed nor denied that the "unborn child" (what embryologists call the "embryo" or "fetus") is a living human being:

> When those trained in the respective disciplines of
> medicine, philosophy, and theology are unable to arrive
> at any consensus, the judiciary, at this point in the

development of man's knowledge, is not in a position to
speculate as to the answer. (Roe v. Wade, 410 U.S. at 159)
(Emphasis added).

To understand this point, it is important to distinguish three separate questions. The first question is a scientific one: is the human being, from the moment of conception, a whole separate living member of the species Homo Sapiens in the biological sense? The second question is a moral question: assuming that the answer to the first question is yes, should the life of that human being be accorded the same value, worth, and dignity at all stages of development, *i.e.*, as a blastocyst, embryo, fetus, child, adolescent, and adult? And the third question is a legal one: does the Constitution of the United States protect the rights of human beings at all stages of development before birth (is a human being a "person" as that term is used in the 14th Amendment)?

In *Roe v. Wade,* the Supreme Court expressly declined to answer the scientific or moral questions. With regard to the scientific question, the Supreme Court said that at this "point in the development of man's knowledge" it could not say whether a human embryo or fetus is or is not a human being. Science, as more recently acknowledged by the United States District Court of Appeals for the Eighth Circuit *en banc* in *Planned Parenthood v. Rounds,* agrees that the life of a human being begins at fertilization and it is not untrue or misleading to require an abortion doctor to inform a mother prior to the abortion of her pregnancy "[t]hat the abortion will terminate the life of a whole, separate, unique, living human being." 530 F.3d 724, 735-36 (8th Cir. 2008).

In addition to announcing that it was in no position to speculate as to when life began, the Court in *Roe* went on to state (again based upon the state of medical science at that time) *"that conception is a 'process' over time, rather than an event." Roe,* 410 U.S., at 161 (emphasis added). In the 42 years since *Roe* was decided, and based upon the substantial uncontested evidence presented by the State of North Dakota in *MKB Management Corp. v Burdick,*[102] it can no longer be denied that human life begins at conception. As testified by Dr. Obritsch, M.D., FACOG, board-certified obstetrician/gynecologist, in that case: *"Human development is a continuous process that begins (being conception) when an oocyte (ovum) from a female is fertilized by a sperm (spermatozoon) from a male."* Moore, *et al., The Developing Human 9E, Clinically Oriented Embryology,* 9th edition, 2013, Chapter 1, Introduction to the Developing Human, page 1.[103]

Thus, when the Court in *Roe v. Wade* said that conception is a process over time, the Court was medically incorrect. Rather, it is *human development* that is a process over time. Conception takes place as a singular event, at a specific time, and is complete at that moment. Thereafter, human development occurs and continues until the heart stops beating (one of the long used measurements of death). Indeed, one can look at a newly delivered infant, and compare it to what that infant will be like 5 years later, 10 years later, 20 years later, and so forth until death, and one can see the process of that continued human development all put in motion by the singular event of conception.

In support of the medical conclusion that an unborn child should be deemed viable from the point of conception, it is also now well-documented in the uncontradicted evidence submitted in the *MKB Management Corp.* case that "viability in Obstetrics and Human Reproduction has vastly changed over the past decades. Viability was once thought to mean or be defined (as also assumed by the *Roe* Court) as only the ability of the unborn child to survive outside the uterus, albeit under the sophisticated care of the Neonatologist in the highly complex medical environment of the Neonatal Intensive Care unit (NICU). In modern and current medical and clinical practice, the embryo is able to survive as a human being independently at conception. This occurred for the first time in 1978 with the successful birth of Louise Brown and was known as the 'test tube baby.' Dr. Robert G. Edwards, the physiologist who developed the technology to successfully achieve this goal, was awarded the Nobel Prize in Medicine in 2010. Today *In Vitro* Fertilization (IVF) is commonly practiced and actually, Reproductive Endocrinology and Infertility (REI) has evolved into a well-recognized sub-specialty of the field of Obstetrics and Gynecology. The development of Reproductive Technology has caused and allowed an embryonic unborn child to live outside the human uterus (womb) for 2-6 days after conception – which is viability as defined by the United States Supreme Court and in the North Dakota statutes because this embryonic unborn child is not just potentially but is in fact living outside the woman's womb, albeit through artificial means."[104]

Moreover, as Dr. Alexander Tsiaras' famous TED talk, "Conception to Birth – Visualized,"[105] shows, the heartbeat is detectable in an unborn child within the womb at about 45 days from conception. Thereafter, there exists a medically recognized 98% rate of survival and live birth, and this medically recognized rate of survival and live birth drops slightly to 82% when the woman has a history of recurrent pregnancy loss (being three or more consecutive spontaneous losses of an unborn child).[106]

While the Eighth Court of Appeals in its *MKB Management* decision rejected Dr. Obritsch's *medical* definition of viability as being inconsistent with the *legal* definition of viability "assumed" by the *Roe* Court, the Court of Appeals went on to state that "good reasons exist for the [Supreme] Court to now reevaluate its [abortion] jurisprudence":

> *To begin, the Court's viability standard has proven unsatisfactory because it gives too little consideration to the "substantial state interest in potential life throughout pregnancy." Casey, 505 U.S., at 876 (plurality opinion). By deeming viability "the point at which the balance of interests tips," id. at 861, the Court has tied a state's interest in unborn children to developments in obstetrics,*

not to developments in the unborn. This leads to troubling consequences for states seeking to protect unborn children. For example, although "states in the 1970s lacked the power to ban an abortion of a 24-week-old-fetus because that fetus would not have satisfied the viability standard of that time, [t]oday … that same fetus would be considered viable, and states would have the power to restrict [such] abortions." Edwards, 786 F.3d at 1118 (final alteration in original) (citation and internal quotation marks omitted). How it is consistent with a state's interest in protecting unborn children that the same fetus would be deserving of state protection in one year but undeserving of state protection in another is not clear. The Supreme Court has posited there are "logical and biological justifications" for choosing viability as the critical point. Roe, 410 U.S. at 163. But this choice is better left to the states, which might find their interest in protecting unborn children better served by a more consistent and certain marker than viability. Here, the North Dakota legislature has determined that the critical point for asserting its interest in potential life is the point at which an unborn child possesses a detectable heartbeat. "To substitute its own preference to that of the legislature in this area is not the proper role of a court." Edwards, 786 F.3d at 1119 [emphasis in original].

By taking this decision away from the states, the Court has also removed the states' ability to account for "advances in medical and scientific technology [that] have greatly expanded our knowledge of prenatal life," Hamilton v. Scott, 97 So.3d 728, 742 (Ala.2012) (Parker, J., concurring specially), including that "a baby develops sensitivity to external stimuli and to pain much earlier than was …

believed [when Roe *was decided]."* McCorvey v. Hill,
385 F.3d 846, 852 (5th Cir.2004) (Jones, J., concurring).
"[B]ecause the Court's rulings have rendered basic abortion
policy beyond the power of our legislative bodies, the
arms of representative government may not meaningfully
debate" medical and scientific advances. Id. (Jones, J.,
concurring). Thus the Court's viability standard fails to fulfill
Roe's *"promise that the State has an interest in protecting*
fetal life or potential life." Casey, *505 U.S. at 876, 112 S.Ct.*
2791 (plurality opinion).

Medical and scientific advances further show that the
concept of viability is itself subject to change. The Court
has already acknowledged that viability continues to
occur earlier in pregnancy. See Casey, *505 U.S. at 860,*
112 S.Ct. 2791. When the Court decided Roe *in 1973,*
viability generally occurred at 28 weeks. Roe, *410 U.S. at*
160, 93 S.Ct. 705. In 1992, viability "sometimes" occurred
at 23 to 24 weeks. Casey, *505 U.S. at 860, 112 S. Ct. 2791.*
Today, viability generally occurs at 24 weeks, but it may
occur weeks earlier. See Matthew A. Rysavy, B.S., et al.,
Between–Hospital Variation in Treatment and Outcomes in
Extremely Preterm Infants, 372 New England Journal of
Medicine 1801 (2015) (documenting survival of 775 rates of
infants born at 22 weeks); see also Edwards, *786 F.3d*
at 1119 (discussing the case of Amillia Taylor, who survived
after being born at 21 weeks). Dr. Obritsch's declaration,
although insufficient to create a genuine dispute of fact
in the face of the Supreme Court's current definition of
viability, shows the concept of viability may be attacked
from the point of conception forward, as well. As IVF and
similar technologies improve, we can reasonably expect
the amount of time an "embryonic unborn child" may

survive outside the womb will only increase. The viability standard will prove even less workable in the future.[107]

2. Abortion is Healthcare Involving a Normal Healthy Physician-Patient Relationship

Second, the *Roe* Court assumed that there would be a normal healthy physician-patient relationship in which the doctor would impart pertinent information, and that decisions would be made through consultation between the physician and patient. "All these are factors the woman and her responsible physician necessarily will consider in consultation." (*Roe v. Wade,* 410 U.S. at 153) (Emphasis added). In fact, it is indisputable that a normal healthy physician-patient relationship is rarely, if ever, established in a typical abortion clinic with any "client" seeking an abortion.

While the citable examples are legion, former abortionist Dr. Robert Siudmack, M.D., explains the lack of doctor/patient relationship in an abortion clinic, as follows:

> *I would like to believe all doctors share a genuine concern for the health and well-being of their patients. The doctor-patient relationship is unique one that is started on the first visit and develops over the course of time. In an abortion clinic, there is no doctor-patient relationship. The doctor enters the room, there's a brief introduction. The patient is already on the table ready to have the procedure done. There is no sort of opportunity for any sort of meaningful relationship to develop.*[108]

In the most definitive state-wide study of the matter, based upon the testimony of the then current abortion providers in South Dakota, the State of South Dakota concluded:

> We find that the process which results in the pregnant mother signing the consent form and making her decision before ever seeing or speaking to an abortion doctor is incompatible with the principles of a doctor's duty to see that the patient's decision is informed before she consents to an operative procedure. We find that there is no true physician-patient relationship in this process, and once the decision has been made, the woman is seeing the doctor, not for counseling, consultation, or help in reaching a decision, but rather, to submit to the medical procedure that she has already committed to, whether or not it was informed.[109]

3. Motherhood and Child-Rearing Forces "Upon the Woman a Distressful Life and Future"

Third, the *Roe* Court assumed that motherhood and child-rearing forced "upon the woman a distressful life and future" and that child-rearing could cause "mental and physical" health problems and "distress" of such a nature that abortion had to be available, and that the absence of legalized abortion was a detriment imposed upon the women by the state. (*Roe v. Wade*, 410 U.S. at 153.) In *Planned Parenthood v. Casey*, the Court reiterated that the woman's right to an abortion was predicated upon the fact *"that the inability to provide for the nurture and care of the infant is a cruelty to the child and an anguish to the parent."* *Casey*, 505 U.S., at 853.

During the oral arguments in *Roe* the justices were told that Texas' abortion prohibition prevented pregnant women from continuing her schooling or from holding a job.[110] Cited legal disabilities included education discrimination, hiring discrimination, loss of job security or chance of rehire and lack of provision for maternity leave, unemployment compensation or welfare.

Since then, these disabilities have been lifted, but not because of *Roe*. *Roe* is rarely cited as precedent for women's rights in any area other than abortion. Virtually all progress in women's legal, social and employment rights since *Roe* has come about wholly unrelated to and not because of *Roe*. If *Roe* were reversed, these rights would not be lost because their legal and social existence are entirely independent of *Roe*.

Perhaps, the most significant legal change in all 50 states since *Roe* has been the enactment of so-called Safe Haven (also known as *"Baby Moses"*) laws which effectively relieve all motherhood and child-rearing responsibilities from the mother for up to a year from the birth of her child. With the advent of Safe Haven laws throughout the country, society as a whole has assumed the responsibility and expense of raising unwanted children, no longer placing that burden on pregnant women. Safe Haven laws provide a mechanism for an unwanted child to be confidentially abandoned to the State without any civil or criminal responsibility imposed on the parents of the unwanted child. Consequently, the central underlying justification given for abortion by the Court in *Roe* and *Casey* is no longer applicable. Every state now has such laws.[111]

This remarkable social evolution completely eliminates any need for legal abortion or abortion as a constitutional right. This new legal reality, transferring child care responsibility from mother to the State, means there is no "undue burden" because there is no longer any need for abortion to relieve pregnant women from unwanted child care obligations. Every child in America is now legally "wanted" and abortion of "unwanted" children is no longer necessary. Every woman who feels trapped and alone, desperate for help, can now confidentially transfer that burden to the State as a matter of right, no questions asked.

Contrariwise, nowhere in the *Roe* decision did the Court mention the distress due to the pregnant mother losing her child to abortion. In fact, there is no mention of the great benefit and joys that the mother-child relationship brings to the mother, or the devastating loss and distress incurred by the mother who loses her child to abortion. The absence of mention of the nature of this loss and this profound distress is, in all likelihood, attributable to the fact that in 1973 there had not yet been adequate experience with the after-effects of abortion.

Science has now documented extensively that abortion has serious adverse psychological consequences. For example, the 8th Circuit held after an extensive trial, that adequate scientific evidence exists, despite non-unanimity, to support the statutorily required pre-abortion disclosure to the mother that abortion increases a woman's risk for suicide and suicidal ideation.[112] As summarized by psychiatrist Dr. Martha Shuping, M.D., one the expert witnesses in the *MKB Management* case:

> *Abortion has a profound and significant adverse effect upon the mental health, emotional and psychological well-being of women. In my opinion, to a reasonable degree of medical and scientific certainty, the overwhelming preponderance of scientific and medical evidence demonstrates abortion is a substantial contributing factor and cause of increasing the risk of mental health, emotional and psychological problems for women that have had an abortion, and in turn abortion has a profound and significant adverse effect on women's mental health, emotional and psychological well-being."* (Emphasis added)[113]

As even recognized by the Court in 1992 in its *Casey* decision, 505 U.S., at 852:

> *Abortion ... is an act fraught with consequences for others: for the woman who must live with the implications of her decision; for the persons who perform and assist in the procedure; for the spouse, family, and society which must confront the knowledge that these procedures exist, procedures some deem nothing short of an act of violence against innocent human life; and, depending on one's beliefs, for the life or potential life that is aborted.*

As further acknowledged by the Court in 2007 its *Gonzales* decision, 550 U.S., at 159 *et seq.:*

> *While we find no reliable data to measure the phenomenon, it seems unexceptionable to conclude some women come to regret their choice to abort the infant life they once created and sustained. See Brief for* Sandra Cano et al. as Amici Curiae *in No. 05–380, pp. 22–24 [citing the testimony of post-abortive women regarding the harm they suffered from their abortions]. Severe depression and loss of esteem can follow.* See ibid.

> *In a decision so fraught with emotional consequence some doctors may prefer not to disclose precise details of the means that will be used, confining themselves to the required statement of risks the procedure entails. From one standpoint this ought not to be surprising. Any number of patients facing imminent surgical procedures would prefer not to hear all details, lest the usual anxiety preceding invasive medical procedures become the more intense. This is likely the case with the abortion procedures here in issue.*

*It is, however, precisely this lack of information concerning
the way in which the fetus will be killed that is
of legitimate concern to the State.* Casey, supra, at 873
*(plurality opinion) ("States are free to enact laws to provide
a reasonable framework for a woman to make a decision
that has such profound and lasting meaning"). The State
has an interest in ensuring so grave a choice is well
informed. It is self-evident that a mother who comes to
regret her choice to abort must struggle with grief more
anguished and sorrow more profound when she learns,
only after the event, what she once did not know: that she
allowed a doctor to pierce the skull and vacuum the fast
developing brain of her unborn child, a child assuming the
human form.*

*The State's interest in respect for life is advanced by the
dialogue that better informs the political and legal systems,
the medical profession, expectant mothers, and society as
a whole of the consequences that follow from a decision
to elect a late-term abortion.*

Likewise, the *Roe* Court never mentioned nor considered the fact that
the pregnant mother possesses a constitutionally-protected relationship
with her unborn child or the fact that this relationship, protected as a
fundamental right, is terminated by the abortion procedure. However,
in 2011, the Eight Circuit Court of Appeals, in *Planned Parenthood v.
Rounds,* 653 F.3d 662 (2011), over the South Dakota abortion industry's
objections after reviewing substantial written evidence, found that the
State of South Dakota may constitutionally mandate that abortionists
provide the following pre-abortion advisory disclosures to their clients
because they are truthful, non-misleading statements of fact that will
assist a pregnant mother make a voluntary, fully informed decision
whether or not to terminate her pregnancy with an elective abortion:

(1) That the abortion will terminate the life of a whole, separate, unique, living human being [the human being advisory]; (2) That [the patient] has an existing relationship with that unborn human being and that the relationship enjoys protection under the United States Constitution and under the laws of South Dakota; (3) That by having an abortion, her existing relationship and her existing constitutional rights with regards to that relationship will be terminated.

In fact, it well-documented that *Roe* has not solved any of the problems the Court supposed its decision might solve or at least alleviate. As the murder prosecution of Kermit Gosnell illustrated, women today still run the gamut of fear, inadequate information and substandard medical conditions in abortion clinics.[114] Child abuse rates have increased, not decreased, since 1973. The illegitimacy rate in the United States has increased since *Roe*, 33% of all children are born out of wedlock in the United States today.[115]

4. The Decision to Have an Abortion Would be Truly Voluntary and Informed.

Fourth, the *Roe* Court's opinion assumed that a decision to have an abortion would be truly voluntary and informed. In fact, all sides agree that coercion in abortion decision-making is highly predictive of an adverse psychological outcome and costs. Furthermore, when a woman's decision is not her own, she cannot freely provide her informed consent.

While we do not know how many women are coerced into obtaining an abortion, the studies identify a range of 11-64%.[116] Women undergoing an abortion are 3 times more likely to be victims of interpersonal violence. Women with multiple abortions are more likely than those women with one abortion to report that the person responsible for the current pregnancy was abusive. Approximately 40% of women obtaining an abortion are likely to have abuse in their history. Coercion, abortion and abuse are all correlated, interrelated and highly prevalent. Anyone counseling a woman with a crisis pregnancy certainly needs to screen for coercion and abuse and, if indicated, provide appropriate referrals.

The 2005 REPORT ON ABORTION IN THE STATE OF SOUTH DAKOTA concluded that the *Roe* Court incorrectly assumed that the abortion decision is truly voluntary and informed:

> *We received and reviewed the testimony of more than 1,940 women who have had abortions. This stunning and heart-wrenching testimony reveals that there are common experiences with abortions. Women were not told the truth about abortion, were misled into thinking that nothing but "tissue" was being removed, and relate that they would not have had an abortion if they were told the truth. They relate that they were coerced into having the abortion by the father of the child or a parent, and that the abortion clinics also apply pressure to have the abortion. They almost uniformly express anger toward the abortion providers, their baby's father, or society in general, which promote abortion as a great right, the exercise of which is good for women. They almost invariably state that they were encouraged to have an abortion by the mere fact that it was legal. They are stunned by their grief and the negative impact it has had on their lives. Many of these women are angered by grief at the loss of a child they were told never existed. One woman testified before the Task Force about three abortions she was misled into having, only to find that she was rendered infertile by the vacuum aspiration that damaged her fallopian tubes. She was distraught at having to explain to her new husband*

*why they could never have children. Each of these
women's stories is powerful. The overwhelming majority
of women testified that they would never have considered
an abortion if it were not legal. Their testimony revealed
that they feel that the legalization of abortion simply gave
a license to others to pressure them into a decision they
otherwise would not have made. Most of the women
stated that abortion should not be legal.*[117]

5. Abortion is Safe and Mortality Risk is Less Than Pregnancy

Fifth, the *Roe* Court assumed that the abortion procedure was safe and
that the risk to the women's health and life was far greater in carrying
the child to full term than in having an abortion. See, *e.g. Roe v. Wade,*
at 149 *("consequently, any interest of the state in protecting the woman
from an inherently hazardous procedure... has largely disappeared").*

The *Roe* Court did not consider long-term risks from abortion before
making its assumption that abortion is safer than childbirth.[118] Since the
Court's decision in *Casey,* though, dozens of studies have been published
in international medical journals documenting the existence of several
long-term risks from abortion, especially the increased risk of pre-term
birth after abortion. For example, in a major landmark analysis published
in 2002, the researchers concluded: *"that informed consent before
induced abortion should include information about the subsequent risk
of preterm delivery and depression. Although it remains uncertain
whether elective abortion increases subsequent breast cancer, it is clear
that a decision to abort and delay pregnancy culminates in a loss of
protection with the net effect being an increased risk."*[119] In 2009,
three systematic-evidence reviews demonstrating the increased risk
of pre-term birth after abortion were also published.[120]

More significantly, in the most recent peer-reviewed meta-analysis of
the relevant studies, Dr. John M. Thorp, M.D.,[121] one of America's most

distinguished women's healthcare experts, questions the *Roe* Court's
maternal mortality assumptions casting "doubt on [its] claim that
the TOP [termination of pregnancy through elective abortion] is safer
than pregnancy continuation":[122]

> *Termination of Pregnancy (TOP) epidemiologists lump all
> deaths together across the full spectrum of gestational
> age despite the well-known fact that TOP morbidity and
> mortality increase with advancing gestational age. The fact
> that TOP most often occurs in the first trimester in the US
> skews the aggregated mortality numbers used in most
> comparisons toward the time in pregnancy where TOP
> procedures are relatively safer. The risk of death associated
> with TOP increases from one death for every one million
> TOPs at less than 9 weeks to three per one hundred
> thousand TOPs at 16–20 weeks to 10 per one hundred
> thousand at 21 or more weeks in the US [References omitted].
> Reardon and Coleman just published an article which
> looked at maternal mortality for an epoch of 25 years using
> Danish birth and death records. Their cohort consisted of
> 463,473 women and they used TOP in the first pregnancy
> as the exposure of interest, controlling for pregnancy
> outcomes in subsequent gestations. For women having
> TOP at <12 weeks, cumulative mortality rates were higher
> from 180 days to 10 years from the index pregnancy.
> The association between TOP and cumulative mortality
> was similar but stronger for TOP>12 weeks gestation.
> The comparison group was women who delivered after
> 20 weeks gestation. While far from definitely answering
> the question, the linkage study does cast doubt on the
> claim that TOP is safer than pregnancy continuation.*

Another problem inherent in comparing aggregated deaths for TOP and pregnancy is the failure to control for important confounders other than gestational age when the TOP is performed. Women seeking TOP in the US are younger and presumably healthier, although they are more likely to be single and of lower socioeconomic status which have negative health effects. Thus, failure to control for important confounders makes direct comparisons of crude rates even less accurate. [References omitted].

In terms of lives lost, current TOP epidemiologic approaches assume that the embryo or fetus has a null moral status and that the loss of a potential human being (which is the stated goal of every TOP procedure) should not be considered. This failure to account for the impact of losing a future citizen has had profound demographic consequences in countries with unrestricted access to TOP, such as the US.

In a horrible twist reminiscent of the eugenics movements of the 20th century, some US states have even lowered barriers to TOP with the stated intent of lowering the number of individuals needing social support or mental health services. These losses are not captured in mortality statistics that solely value the life of the mother. Despite the inherent absurdity in comparing death rates from TOP to childbirth, such comparisons continue to be done by prominent clinicians and various advocacy groups. Comparisons are inherently biased and those biases may confuse women considering whether to have a TOP or continue their pregnancy. Differences in ascertainment of deaths, duration of susceptibility to mortality, lack of accounting for gestational age, and choice of appropriate comparison group make these comparisons a fool's errand.

As pointed out by Dr. Thorp, the U.S. has no national health registry identifying and linking all individual healthcare interventions, diagnoses, hospitalizations, births, deaths and other vital statistics, unlike Scandinavian countries. Accordingly, epidemiological studies using these national data sets from abroad are methodologically superior to U.S. data. In a recently published study of 463,473 women using Danish linked birth and death registry records for an epoch of 25 years, when compared to women who delivered, women with TOP < 12 weeks gestation had higher cumulative mortality rates from 180 days to 10 years later.[123] In a second study using the same national registries, the researchers again found increased risks of death for women electing abortion compared to childbirth.[124] Record linkage studies of the population of Finland and of low income women in California have also reported higher death rates associated with abortion than childbirth.[125] Other large-scale studies based on data linkage from the US, Britain, Denmark and Finland, have shown that women who undergo induced abortion have a sharply increased death rate compared to women who give birth. Having an induced abortion also greatly increases a woman's chance of later attempting or committing suicide, while carrying a baby to term greatly reduces that likelihood. As two recent researchers write, "pregnant women considering their options deserve accurate information about comparative risks."[126]

In short, the *Roe* Court's assumption that induced abortion is safer than childbirth could likely only be validated today based on faulty scientific methodologies and incomplete data, and is in any case limited to the period immediately after childbirth or termination of pregnancy. It completely ignores four data-linkage studies, which are based on a far more objective and neutral methodology, as well as complete and reliable data. Those and other studies effectively explode the myth that abortion is safer for a woman than childbirth. Moreover, any reduction in maternal mortality rates have not been reduced by abortion, but due to antibiotics, women's health education and other medical advancements.

"The data suggest that there have been as many maternal deaths in the United States annually from legal abortion (estimates range from 15-35 per year) as there were maternal deaths from illegal abortions in the years immediately before *Roe v. Wade* was decided."[127]

6. Woman Face Significant Difficulties as a Result of a Cultural Stigma of Unwed Motherhood

Sixth, the Supreme Court in *Roe* assumed that the woman faced significant difficulties as a result of a cultural stigma of unwed motherhood. A stigma that obviously no longer exists as unwed motherhood is celebrated in the popular culture and is more prevalent than wed motherhood in some social circles.

Roe 2.0: How *Planned Parenthood v. Casey* Changed *Roe v. Wade*[128]

Under normal circumstances, unclouded by what some social commentators have cynically labeled the federal judiciary's "abortion distortion,"[129] one would think that the U.S. Supreme Court, confronted with the extensive scholarly criticism of its *Roe* decision[130] and the "changed circumstances" that, as described above, have revealed the incorrectness of each the major factual assumptions upon which *Roe* rests, would by now have simply reversed its decision in *Roe* and returned the jurisdiction over abortion prohibition and/or regulation to the several states for independent legislative decision. However, when provided with just such an opportunity to do so, the Court in *Planned Parenthood v. Casey,* 505 U.S. 833 (1992), decided instead to modify its constitutional rationale for continuing abortion on demand in America.

In *Casey,* Justice Kennedy writing for a plurality of the Court said that *Roe* should not be overturned merely because its original rationale might have been wrong.[131] Instead, the Court held that more was needed to justify overturning *Roe* because women had come to "rely" upon abortion as a backup to failed contraception. In other words,

Roe must be reaffirmed because of women's "reliance interest" in elective abortion.[132] The recognition of the "reliance interest" changed the manner in which the Court maintained control over the abortion issue, as well as how abortion proponents advanced their abortion cause in the name of democracy and "reproductive health."[133]

Without understanding that *Roe* was significantly modified by the Supreme Court's 1992 decision in *Planned Parenthood v. Casey,* there can be no effective strategy to overturn *Roe v. Wade.* Twenty years after *Roe*, the Court in Casey substantially changed *Roe* and the Court's justification for upholding *Roe.*[134] There is no majority of the Court today that defends a historical right to abortion or that believes that an abortion right is deeply rooted in American law or tradition. Nor is there a majority that holds to *Roe* or *Casey* because of a lack of information about fetal development or the fetus' status as a person. The woman's "reliance interest" rationale set forth in *Casey* is the glue that now holds together a majority of the Justices in support of *Roe v. Wade.*

Consequently, historical arguments that *Roe* was wrong as an original matter of constitutional interpretation will always be necessary, but insufficient. Likewise, establishing and focusing on the humanity of the unborn child from conception will always be necessary, but insufficient. There is an intimate biological and psychological relationship between mother and child in pregnancy which is uniquely manifested in the contemporary debate over the "reliance interest" and the myth of legal abortion as a "necessary evil."

This means that focusing on the unborn child alone will not effectively counter the support for legal abortion in the courts (and lead the Court to overturn *Roe* or *Casey*) or decisively change public opinion. The impact of abortion on the mother will always be an equally important public concern.

Some might ask how the "reliance interest" rationale maintains its power if two of the three Justices who wrote the plurality opinion in *Casey* (Justices Souter and O'Connor) are no longer on the Court. The "reliance interest" rationale retains its power in the person of Justice Kennedy—the third author of the plurality opinion in *Casey*—and, more importantly, in the general pragmatic cast of American legal culture. The "reliance interests" rationale is mirrored in public opinion that legal abortion, at least to some degree is a "necessary evil."[135]

Stripped of its arcane legal terminology, the "reliance interest" rationale of *Casey* is simply defined by "good results." Has the Court's management of the abortion issue yielded good results? Are women's lives better with the Court in control of the abortion issue? Any public perception that the answer to these questions is "yes" must be countered with data about the negative impact of abortion on women.

As Nicholas DiFonzo, a professor of psychology at Rochester Institute of Technology explained in the November 2011 issue of FIRST THINGS, specifics about the negative impact of abortion and the practical impact of abortion policies are critical to changing minds.[136] Educating about the negative impact of abortion on women includes both rebutting the medical mantra that "abortion is safer than childbirth" and increasing public awareness of the long-term risks of abortion to women. This is necessary to convert a "necessary evil" in the public mind into an "evil," pure and simple.

THE WAY FORWARD

The pro-life gains made since *Roe* was decided in 1973 are the result of prudential steps that will continue to generate future momentum. Based on the gains made and the foundation that already exists, the legal-legislative-political-educational dynamic must be pushed as aggressively in the days and years ahead:

- The target of law and policy is not simply *Roe,* but Roe 2.0: *Planned Parenthood v. Casey* and the "reliance interest" rationale. Pro-life efforts need to focus on rebutting the "reliance interest," because that is the real target of opportunity in the courts, not the original underpinnings of *Roe.* If effective, these efforts will serve the dual purpose of rebutting the "reliance interest" and eradicating the public myth of abortion as a "necessary evil." Rebutting both will shore up public opinion, increase public skepticism of abortion as good for women, and raise support for increasing limits and restrictions on abortion.

- The negative impact of abortion on women must be highlighted. This includes highlighting the substandard conditions in abortion clinics and the medical risks to women through both education and legislation.

- Political developments, relieving or creating obstacles, will inevitably shape the steps forward. Elections and changing demographics will shape the opportunities or the obstacles and the timetable for overturning *Roe.*

- Legal protection for the unborn outside the context of abortion must be advanced. Legal protection for the unborn child was not comprehensive before *Roe* and must continue to grow and evolve in the years ahead.

- Criticism of *Roe* in popular and scholarly education must continue. The American public must better understand the legal scope of *Roe,* its negative impact, and its continuing relevance.

- Abortion must be constrained and limited by state legislation. The more than 30 percent drop in abortions between 1992 and 2014 shows the impact of state abortion-related laws. The enactment and enforcement of more life-affirming legislation, along with other factors, including the effectiveness of our adoption and safe haven laws, will likely cause the abortion rate to continue to drop.[137]

- Abortion providers must be defunded. State and federal funding for abortion providers, like Planned Parenthood, not only subsidizes abortion, but it also funds those who oppose a revitalized culture of life.

- The right President and Senate must be elected to change the Supreme Court. A Supreme Court decision can only be overturned through a constitutional amendment or through the Court reversing its own decision. The latter requires (1) changing the Justices; and (2) the right test case requesting the right remedy.

CONCLUSION

As observed by Justice O'Connor in *Planned Parenthood v. Casey*, 505 U.S., at 864:

> *In constitutional adjudication as elsewhere in life, changed circumstances may impose new obligations, and the thoughtful part of the Nation could accept each decision to overrule a prior case as a response to the Court's constitutional duty.*

Given the fact that none of the factual assumptions that undergird *Roe* are correct today the Court must ultimately reevaluate its abortion jurisprudence in light of extensive evidence in the record of cases before it of 1) new scientific advances on viability, 2) increasing evidence of the devastating physical and psychological consequences of abortion, and 3) society's willingness to remove from pregnant women all burdens of child care for every unwanted child through the Safe Haven laws that now exist in all 50 states.

Roe can be overturned. But it will take 'champions' of all types working in every state. The opportunity for a direct assault on *Roe* and *Doe* may come in the next five years or in the next decade. In the meantime, the progress made in creating political momentum through the legal-legislative-political-educational dynamic created by the champions of this cause will provide the necessary foundation to not only successfully challenge *Roe* but ultimately create an America where every child, born or unborn, is protected in law and welcomed in life.

As we do so, let us be encouraged by Dr. Nathanson's last thoughts on the subject that he asked the author of this book to convey to America:

> *Tell America that the co-founder of NARAL Pro-Choice America says to "Love one another. Abortion is not love. Stop the killing. The world needs more love. I'm all about love now.*

*Endnotes to Appendix C may be found on page 367 and following.

APPENDIX D
Personhood Proclamation

January 14, 1988
By the President of the United States of America
A Proclamation

America has given a great gift to the world, a gift that drew upon the accumulated wisdom derived from centuries of experiments in self-government, a gift that has irrevocably changed humanity's future. Our gift is twofold: the declaration, as a cardinal principle of all just law, of the God-given, unalienable rights possessed by every human being; and the example of our determination to secure those rights and to defend them against every challenge through the generations. Our declaration and defense of our rights have made us and kept us free and have sent a tide of hope and inspiration around the globe.

One of those unalienable rights, as the Declaration of Independence affirms so eloquently, is the right to life. In the 15 years since the Supreme Court's decision in *Roe v. Wade,* however, America's unborn have been denied their right to life. Among the tragic and unspeakable results in the past decade and a half have been the loss of life of 22 million infants before birth; the pressure and anguish of countless women and girls who are driven to abortion; and a cheapening of our respect for the human person and the sanctity of human life.

We are told that we may not interfere with abortion. We are told that we may not "impose our morality" on those who wish to allow or participate in the taking of the life of infants before birth; yet no one calls it "imposing morality" to prohibit the taking of life after people are born. We are told as well that there exists a "right" to end the lives of unborn children; yet no one can explain how such a right can exist in stark contradiction of each person's fundamental right to life.

That right to life belongs equally to babies in the womb, babies born handicapped, and the elderly or infirm. That we have killed the unborn for 15 years does not nullify this right, nor could any number of killings ever do so. The unalienable right to life is found not only in the Declaration of Independence but also in the Constitution that every President is sworn to preserve, protect, and defend. Both the Fifth and Fourteenth Amendments guarantee that no person shall be deprived of life without due process of law.

All medical and scientific evidence increasingly affirms that children before birth share all the basic attributes of human personality — that they in fact are persons. Modern medicine treats unborn children as patients. Yet, as the Supreme Court itself has noted, the decision in *Roe v. Wade* rested upon an earlier state of medical technology. The law of the land in 1988 should recognize all of the medical evidence.

Our nation cannot continue down the path of abortion, so radically at odds with our history, our heritage, and our concepts of justice. This sacred legacy, and the well-being and the future of our country, demand that protection of the innocents must be guaranteed and that the personhood of the unborn be declared and defended throughout our land. In legislation introduced at my request in the First Session of the 100th Congress, I have asked the Legislative branch to declare the "humanity of the unborn child and the compelling interest of the several states to protect the life of each person before birth." This duty to declare on so fundamental a matter falls to the Executive as well. By this Proclamation I hereby do so.

NOW, THEREFORE, I, Ronald Reagan, President of the United States of America, by virtue of the authority vested in me by the Constitution and the laws of the United States, do hereby proclaim and declare the unalienable personhood of every American, from the moment of conception until natural death, and I do proclaim, ordain, and declare that I will take care that the Constitution and laws of the United States are faithfully executed for the protection of America's unborn children. Upon this act, sincerely believed to be an act of justice, warranted by the Constitution, I invoke the considerate judgment of mankind and the gracious favor of Almighty God. I also proclaim Sunday, January 17, 1988, as National Sanctity of Human Life Day. I call upon the citizens of this blessed land to gather on that day in their homes and places of worship to give thanks for the gift of life they enjoy and to reaffirm their commitment to the dignity of every human being and the sanctity of every human life.

IN WITNESS WHEREOF, I have hereunto set my hand this fourteenth day of January, in the year of our Lord nineteen hundred and eighty-eight, and of the Independence of the United States of America the two hundred and twelfth.

President Ronald Reagan

What If We've Been Wrong?

APPENDIX E

Norma McCorvey's Affidavit Requesting Reversal of the *Roe v. Wade* Decision

The Most Exploited Woman in America

Author's note:

Every American should read this sworn affidavit from Norma McCorvey, formerly known as Jane Roe. Herein lies the truth of how a young, pregnant woman was *used* by activist lawyers and certain judges on the U.S. Supreme Court. Combined with Dr. Nathanson's deceptive propaganda campaign, as of 2016 over 60,000,000 children were murdered and almost twice as many women and men wounded because of the *Roe v. Wade* decision.

**IN THE UNITED STATES DISTRICT COURT
FOR THE NORTHERN DISTRICT OF TEXAS
DALLAS DIVISION
Norma McCorvey, formerly known as
JANE ROE**

   Plaintiff,

VS.

**HENRY WADE, Through His Official Successor in Office, William
"Bill" Hill, Dallas County District Attorney,
Defendant.
CIVIL ACTION NO. 3-3690-B and NO.3-3691-C.
AFFIDAVIT OF NORMA MCCORVEY**

BEFORE ME, the undersigned authority on this day personally appeared
NORMA MCCORVEY, who after being duly sworn upon her oath
deposed and said as follows:

1. My name is Norma McCorvey and I reside in Dallas, Texas.
   I am competent to make this affidavit. The facts stated in this
   affidavit are within my personal knowledge and are true
   and correct.

2. Thirty-three years ago, I came before the United States District
   Court Northern District of Texas Dallas Division as the Plaintiff
   "Jane Roe", the young woman whose case legalized abortion
   in the United States, *Roe v. Wade*. At that time, I was an
   uninformed young woman. Today I am a fifty-five-year old
   woman who knows the tragedy that arose from my
   unsuspecting acquiescence in allowing my life to be used to
   legalize abortion.

3. In 1970, I told this court in the form of an affidavit that
   I desired to obtain an abortion never really understanding
   the ramifications. Today, I once again appear before this

court in the form of an affidavit to present evidence never presented in my earlier case, but today I come with a complete understanding of what my participation *Roe v. Wade* has brought to this country. My personal experience with this three-decade-abortion-experiment has compelled me to come forward, not only for myself and the women I represented then, but for those women whom I now represent. It is my participation in this case that began the tragedy, and it is with great hope that I now seek to end the tragedy I began.

4. Because of my role in *Roe v. Wade* and my subsequent experience with abortion, this Court will be provided with information and a perspective unavailable from other source. Previously, the courts, without looking into my true circumstances or taking the time to decide the real impact abortion would have upon women, used me, my life, and my circumstances to justify abortion. Those judges who made the earlier decisions never had the advantage of the real facts to base their decision because the entire basis for *Roe v. Wade* was built upon false assumptions. Consequently, the decision was rendered in a vacuum totally devoid of findings of facts and solely based upon what abortion advocates wanted [for] women. Because the courts allowed my case to proceed without my testimony, without ever explaining to me the reality of abortion, without being cross-examined on my erroneous perception of abortion, a tragic mistake was made — a mistake that this Court has the opportunity to remedy.

5. The years following the *Roe. v. Wade* decision have been very difficult, in a number of respects, but my life was never easy. Prior to my pregnancy with the "Roe" baby, I gave birth to two other children. My first, a daughter, was adopted by my mother. It was difficult to part with my child, yet I have always been comforted by the fact that my daughter is alive.

My second daughter was raised by her father, a young intern at Baylor Methodist Medical School. He wanted to get married and make a home, but I wasn't ready for that kind of commitment. Later, when I became pregnant with the "Roe" baby, I was really in a predicament. My mother expressed her disapproval and told me how irresponsible I had been. She made it clear that she was not going to take care of another baby.

6. Although I knew I was pregnant, I waited for a while before I went to the doctor. While I was waiting to be examined, I questioned the some of ladies in the waiting room about whether they knew where a woman could go have an abortion. A lady told me where an illegal clinic was located and told me that it would cost $250.00. Following our discussion, I told the doctor that I wanted to have an abortion, but he refused stating that abortion was illegal. He didn't believe in abortion and gave me the phone number of an adoption attorney.

7. When I had saved about $200.00, I took a cross-town bus to the illegal clinic, which turned out to be a dentist's office that had been closed down the previous week. For some reason, I felt relieved yet angry at the same time. All my emotions were peaking; first, I was angry, then I was happy, and then I'd cry. From the abortion clinic, I took the bus to my dad's apartment and decided to speak with the adoption attorney. The attorney set up the meeting and referred me to Sarah Weddington, the attorney who represented me in *Roe v. Wade*.

8. Following the adoption attorney's introduction, Weddington invited me out to dinner. Although Weddington and I were about the same age, our lives were quite different. She was a young attorney, and I was homeless and lived in a park. Unconcerned about politics, I sold flowers and the underground newspaper

that describe the types and availability of illegal narcotics.
At the time, I simply sought to survive. During our initial meeting,
I met with Sarah Weddington and her friend, Linda Coffee.
Both Weddington and Coffee had recently finished law school,
and they wanted to bring a class-action suit against the State
of Texas to legalize abortion.

9. During our meeting, they question me, "Norma, don't you think
that abortion should be legal?" Unsure, I responded that I did
not know. In fact, I did not know what the term "abortion"
really meant. Back in 1970, no one discussed abortion. It was
taboo, and so too was the subject of abortion. The only thing I
knew about the word was in the context of war movies.
I had heard the word "abort" when John Wayne was flying his
plane and order the others to "abort" the mission. I knew "abort"
meant that they were going back. "Abortion", to me,
meant "going back" to the condition of not being pregnant.
I never looked up the word in the dictionary until after I had
already signed the affidavit. I was very naïve. For their part,
my lawyers lied to me about the nature of abortion.
Weddington convinced me, "It's just a piece of tissue. You just
missed your period." I didn't know during the *Roe v. Wade* case
that the life of a human being was terminated.

10. That evening, the two female lawyers and I discussed the case
over a few pitchers of beer and pizza at a small restaurant
in Dallas. Weddington, Coffee, and I were drinking beer and
trying to come up with a pseudonym for me. I had heard that
whenever women were having illegal abortions, they wouldn't
carry any identification with them. An unidentifiable woman
was often referred to as Jane Doe. So we were trying to come
up with something that would rhyme with "Doe". After three
or four pictures of beer, we started with the letter "a" and
eventually we reached "r" and agreed on "Roe." Then I asked,

"What about Jane for the first name?" Janie used to be my imaginary friend as a child. I told them about her and how she always wanted to do good things for people, and it was decided — I became Jane Roe, by the stroke of a pen.

11. These young lawyers told me they had spoken with two or three other women about being in the case, but they didn't fit their criteria. Although I did not know what "criteria" meant, I asked them if I had what it took to be in their suit. They replied, "Yes. You're white. You're young, pregnant, and you want an abortion." At that time, I didn't know their full intent. Only that they wanted to make abortion legal, and they thought I'd be a good plaintiff. I came for the food, and they led me to believe that they could help me get an abortion.

12. After our meeting, I went to my father's apartment and began to drink alcohol heavily. I was depressed with my plight in life. I tried to drown my troubles in alcohol. Shortly thereafter I even attempted suicide by slitting my wrists. When my father questioned me about what was troubling me, I responded that I was pregnant again. When he asked me what I was going to do, I responded that I was thinking about having an abortion. He inquired, "What is that?" I said, "I don't know. I haven't looked it up yet."

13. Later, Weddington and Coffee presented the affidavit for my signature at Coffee's office. I told them that I trusted them and that I did not need to read the affidavit before I signed it. I never read the affidavit before signing it and do not, to this very day, know what is written in the affidavit. Both Weddington and Coffee were aware that I did not read the affidavit before I signed it. At no time did they tell me that I had to read it before they accepted my signature. I told them that I trusted them. We called ourselves "the three musketeers." I know now that

is one place where I went wrong. I should have sat down and I should have read the affidavit. I may not have understood everything in the affidavit and I would have probably signed it anyway. I trusted the lawyers.

14. My lawyers never discussed what an abortion is, other than to make the misrepresentation that "it's only tissue." I never understood that the child was already in existence. I never understood that the child was a complete separate human being. I was under the false impression that abortion somehow reversed the process and prevented the child from coming into existence. In the two or three years during the case, no one, including my lawyers, told me that an abortion is actually terminating the life of an actual human being. The courts never took any testimony about this, and I heard nothing which shed light on what abortion really was.

15. In 1972, Sarah Weddington argued in the courts, presumptuously on my behalf, that women should be allowed to obtain a legal abortion. The courts did not ask whether I knew what I was asking for. The abortion decision that destroyed every state law protecting the rights of women and their unborn babies was based on a fundamental misrepresentation. I had never read the affidavit, and I did not know what an abortion was. Weddington and the other supporters of abortion used me and my circumstance to urge the courts to legalize abortion without any meaningful trial which addressed the humanity of the baby, and what abortion would do to women. At that time, I was a street person. I lived, worked, and panhandled out on the streets. My totally powerless circumstance made it easy for them to use me. My presence was a necessary evil. My real interests were not their concern.

16. As the class action plaintiff in the most controversial U.S. Supreme Court case of the twentieth century, I only met with the attorneys twice. Once over pizza and beer, when I was told that my baby was only "tissue" and at another time at Coffee's office to sign the affidavit. I had no other personal contacts. I was never invited into the court. I never testified. I was never present before any court on any level, and I was never at any hearing on my case. The entire case was an abstraction. The facts about abortion were never heard. Totally excluded from every aspect and every issue of the case, I found out about the decision from the newspaper just like the rest of the country.

17. In a way, my exclusion, and the exclusion of real meaningful findings of fact in *Roe v. Wade*, is symbolic of the way in which the women of the nation and their experiences with abortion have been ignored in a national debate by the abortion industry. The view that is presented is the view of what the abortion industry thinks is good for women. The reality of women's experiences is never presented.

18. I never had an abortion and gave the baby up for adoption. It was only later in life that I was confronted with the reality of abortion. Being unskilled and uneducated, with alcohol and drug problems, finding and holding a job was always a problem for me. But with my notoriety from *Roe v. Wade*, abortion facilities, usually paying a dollar an hour more than minimum wage, we're always willing to add "Jane Roe" to their ranks.

19. In 1992, I began working in abortion facilities where I was always in control. I could either make a woman stay or help her leave. My duties were similar to those of a LVN or an RN, such as taking patient's blood pressure and pulse and administering oxygen, although I never took any statistics or

temperatures. Basically, I would stand inside the procedure room, hold the woman's hands, and say things to distract them by saying, "What is the most exciting, or happiest period of your life?" Meanwhile, the abortionist was performing what is represented as a "painless" procedure and the women were digging their nails into me in an effort to endure the pain.

20. I worked for several abortion facilities over the years. In fact, I even worked at two facilities at the same time. They were all the same with respect to the condition of the facilities and the "counseling" the women receive. One clinic where I worked in 1995 was typical: Light fixtures and plaster falling from the ceiling; rat droppings over the sinks; backed up sinks; and blood splattered on the walls. But, the most distressing room in the facility was the "parts room". Aborted babies were stored here. There were dead babies and baby parts stacked like cordwood. Some of the babies made it into buckets and others did not, and because of its disgusting features, no one ever cleaned the room. The stench was horrible. Plastic bags full of baby parts that were swimming in blood were tied up, stored in the room and picked up once a week. At another clinic, the dead babies were in a big white freezer full of dozens of jars, all full of baby parts, little tiny hands, feet, and faces visible through the jars, frozen in blood. The abortion clinics personnel always referred to the dismembered babies as "tissue."

21. While all the facilities were much the same, the abortion doctors in the various clinics where I work were very representative of abortionists in general. The abortionists I knew were usually of foreign descent with the perception that the lax abortion laws in the United States presents a fertile money-making opportunity. One abortionist, in particular, would sometimes operate bare chested,

and sometimes shoeless with his shirt off, and earned a six-figure income. He did not have to worry about his bedside manner, learning to speak English, or building a clientele.

22. While the manners of the abortionists and the uncleanliness of the facilities greatly shocked me, the lack of counseling provided the women was also a tragedy. Early in my abortion career, it became evident that the "counselors" and the abortionists were there for only one reason — to sell abortions. The extent of the abortionists' counseling was, "Do you want an abortion? OK, you sign here and we give you abortion." Then he would direct me, "You go get me another one." There was nothing more. There was never an explanation of the procedure. No one even explained to the mother that the child already existed and the life of a human was being terminated. No one ever explained that there were options to abortion, that financial help was available, or that the child was a unique and irreplaceable. No one ever explained that there were psychological and physical risks of harm to the mother. There was never a time for the mother to reflect or to consult with anyone who could offer her help or an alternative. There was no informed consent. In my opinion, the only thing the abortion doctors and clinic workers cared about was making money. No abortion clinic cared about the women involved. As far as I could tell, every woman had the name of Jane Roe.

23. Typically, most of the women would cry as soon as the suction machine was shut off, or, at some point. Sometimes, I thought that they realized what had been done to their babies. Once, I heard a woman call her mother and say, "I just killed my baby. I'm so glad you never killed me!"

24. The doctors always hid the truth from the mothers. I would say about eighty-percent of the women would try to look down during the abortion and try to see what was happening. This is the reason the doctors would start with the scalpel: to make sure there was just blood and torn up "tissue" for the women to see. Specifically, I remember one woman who came in for an abortion, a pretty, sweet young woman about eighteen years old, with a teddy bear. During the procedure she looked down and saw the baby's hand fall into the doctor's hand. She gasped and passed out. When she awoke and asked about what she saw, I lied to her and told her it didn't happen. But she insisted that she had seen part of her baby. A few weeks later, when she returned for her follow-up exam, she was a changed person: her sweetness had died and had been replaced with an indescribable hardness. I could not look her in the eye. It took quite a few beers that night to make that particular day go away.

25. In all of the clinics where I worked, the employees were forbidden to say anything that might talk the mother out of an abortion. While the abortionists' counseling was nonexistent, my counselor technique gradually became different depending on my mood and the stage of my career. The experience of abortion began to take its toll on me. In later years, I would sometimes take all the instruments that were used in an abortion procedure and purposely leave a little of the blood on some of the instruments. Laying the instruments out on the little table in front of the woman, I would tell her, this is the first instrument that is going to be inserted into your vaginal area." It would have just had a little smudge a blood, and I thought it was very dramatic. In retrospect, I don't even know why I was doing these things. It was as if I was trying to talk these women out of the abortion — something we were forbidden

to do. In other counseling sessions, I would demonstrate the position and warn her that the instruments were sharp, and that if she moved the doctor might slip, and puncture her uterus, and she would bleed to death. In other situations, when a woman asked me how much it cost, I asked her in response how much she wanted to pay to kill her baby. She replied, "They told me it wasn't a baby." I responded, "What do you think it is inside you, a fish?" Other times, I would comfort them after the abortion by saying, "It wasn't a baby. It was only a missed period." Sometimes when I managed to make the women unsure, I would offer to refund their money except for the ultrasound.

26. After I saw all of the deception going on in the abortion facilities, and after all of the things that my supervisors told me to tell the women, I became very angry. I saw women being lied to, openly, and I was part of it. There was no telling how many children I helped kill while their mothers dug their nails into me and listened to my warning, "Whatever you do, don't move!" Because I was drunk or stoned much of the time, I was able to continue this work for a long time, probably much longer than most clinic workers. It is a high turnover job, because of the true nature of the business. The abortion business is inherently a dehumanizing one. A person has to let her heart and soul die or go numb to stay in practice. The clinic workers suffer, the women suffer, and the babies die. I can assure the Court that the interests of these mothers is not a concern of abortion providers. I obviously advocated legalized abortion for many years following *Roe v. Wade*. But, working in the abortion clinics forced me to except what abortion really is: It is a violent act which kills human beings and destroys the peace and the real interest of the mothers involved.

Norma McCorvey a.k.a. Jane Roe of
Roe v. Wade
SWORN TO AND SUBSCRIBED BEFORE ME, the undersigned
authority, on this day of 6-11- 2003.
RAYMOND J. SEXTON
Notary Public
STATE OF TEXAS

What If We've Been Wrong?

APPENDIX F

Dr. Bernard Nathanson's Photo with "Doe" and "Roe"

All three became pro-life leaders.

Sandra Cano, (left) formerly known as Mary Doe of *Doe v. Bolton,* was used by activist lawyers, similar to Norma McCorvey (right), to decriminalize abortion. *Doe v. Bolton* defined "health" as all factors – physical, emotional, psychological, familial, and the woman's age which meant that a woman could have an abortion for any reason and simply claim it was for her "health." Like Norma McCorvey, Cano wanted to see her case overturned, as well.

(Photographer unknown; image from Google Images)

What If We've Been Wrong?

APPENDIX G

Excerpts from *Humanae Vitae*

ENCYCLICAL LETTER OF HIS HOLINESS POPE PAUL VI

To the Venerable Patriarchs, Archbishops, Bishops and other local Ordinaries in Peace and Communion with the Apostolic See, to Priests, the Faithful and all Men of Good Will

14. In conformity with these landmarks in the human and Christian vision of marriage, we must once again declare that the direct interruption of the generative process already begun, and, above all, directly willed and procured abortion, even if for therapeutic reasons, are to be absolutely excluded as licit means of regulating birth.

   Equally to be excluded, as the teaching authority of the Church has frequently declared, is direct sterilization, whether perpetual or temporary, whether of the man or of the woman. Similarly excluded is every action which, either in anticipation of the conjugal act, or in its accomplishment, or in the development of its natural consequences, proposes, whether as an end or as a means, to render procreation impossible.

To justify conjugal acts made intentionally infecund, one cannot invoke as valid reasons the lesser evil, or the fact that such acts would constitute a whole together with the fecund acts already performed or to follow later, and hence would share in one and the same moral goodness. In truth, if it is sometimes licit to tolerate a lesser evil in order to avoid a greater evil or to promote a greater good, it is not licit, even for the gravest reasons, to do evil so that good may follow therefrom, ...

17. Upright men can even better convince themselves of the solid grounds on which the teaching of the Church in this field is based, if they care to reflect upon the consequences of methods of artificial birth control. Let them consider, first of all, how wide and easy a road would thus be opened up towards conjugal infidelity and the general lowering of morality. Not much experience is needed in order to know human weakness, and to understand that men-especially the young, who are so vulnerable on this point-have need of encouragement to be faithful to the moral law, so that they must not be offered some easy means of eluding its observance. It is also to be feared that the man, growing used to the employment of anticonceptive practices, may finally lose respect for the woman and, no longer caring for her physical and psychological equilibrium, may come to the point of considering her as a mere instrument of selfish enjoyment, and no longer as his respected and beloved companion.

Let it be considered also that a dangerous weapon would thus be placed in the hands of those public authorities who take no heed of moral exigencies. Who could blame a government for applying to the solution of the problems of the community those means acknowledged to be licit for married couples in the solution of a family problem? Who will stop rulers from favoring, from even imposing upon their peoples, if they were to consider it necessary, the method of contraception which they judge to be most efficacious? In such a way men, wishing to avoid individual, family, or social difficulties encountered in the observance of the divine law, would reach the point of placing at the mercy of the intervention of public authorities the most personal and most reserved sector of conjugal intimacy.

Consequently, if the mission of generating life is not to be exposed to the arbitrary will of men, one must necessarily recognize unsurmountable limits to the possibility of man's domination over his own body and its functions; limits which no man, whether a private individual or one invested with authority, may licitly surpass. And such limits cannot be determined otherwise than by the respect due to the integrity of the human organism and its functions,...

18. It can be foreseen that this teaching will perhaps not be easily received by all: Too numerous are those voices-amplified by the modern means of propaganda-which are contrary to the voice of the Church. To tell the truth, the Church is not surprised to be made, like her divine founder, a "sign of contradiction," yet she does not because of this cease to proclaim with humble firmness the entire moral law, both natural and evangelical. Of such laws the Church was not the author, nor consequently can she be their arbiter; she is only their depositary and their interpreter, without ever being able to declare to be licit that which is not so by reason of its intimate and unchangeable opposition to the true good of man.

In defending conjugal morals in their integral wholeness, the Church knows that she contributes towards the establishment of a truly human civilization; she engages man not to abdicate from his own responsibility in order to rely on technical means; by that very fact she defends the dignity of man and wife. Faithful to both the teaching and the example of the Savior, she shows herself to be the sincere and disinterested friend of men, whom she wishes to help, even during their earthly sojourn, "to share as sons in the life of the living God, the Father of all men."

Endnote Citations

1   Bernard N. Nathanson, *The Abortion Papers: Inside the Abortion Mentality* (New York: Frederick Fell Publisher, Inc., 1983), 209.

2   Robert Marshall and Charles Donovan, *Blessed are the Barren* (San Francisco: Ignatius, 1991), 17.

3   https://www.liveaction.org/research/margaret-sanger-quotes-history-and-biography/

4   George Grant, *Grand Illusions* (Highland Books, Third Edition), 37.

5   Marjorie Dannenfelser, President Susan B. Anthony List, May 18, 2016.

6   http://www.centerformedicalprogress.org

7   Bernard N. Nathanson, M.D., *The Abortion Papers: Inside the Abortion Mentality,* 209.

8   http://www.naralva.org/in-our-state/judicialbypass2012.shtml

9 Bernard N. Nathanson, M.D., *Aborting America* (New York: DOUBLEDAY &COMPANY, INC., 1979), 16-17.

10 Marshall and Donovan, *Blessed are the Barren,* 17-22.

11 Nathanson, *The Abortion Papers: Inside the Abortion Mentality,* 5.

12 Bernard N. Nathanson, M.D., *The Hand of God* (Washington, D.C.: REGNERY PUBLISHING, INC., 1996), 129.

13 Margaret Sanger, "America Needs a Code for Babies" (March 27, 1934).

14 http://lapurisima.org/documents/2017/2/Paul%20VI%20%20-%20Humanae%20Vitae%20Contraception%20-%20A%20Challenge%20to%20Love%20by%20Dr.%20Janet%20Smith-1.pdf

15 https://parentalrights.org/understand_the_issue/

16 http://fathersforlife.org/feminism/truth_a_la_friedan.htm

17 Sue Ellen Browder, *Subverted* (San Francisco: Ignatius Press, 2015), 54.

18 Browder, 70.

19 Browder, 70.

20 Nathanson, *The Hand of God,* 86.

21 Nathanson, *Aborting America,* 36.

22 Nathanson, *The Abortion Papers,* 199.

23 Nathanson, *The Abortion Papers,* 198.

24 Nathanson, *The Abortion Papers,* 189.

25 http://www.varight.com/?s=terry+beatley+wins+virginia+right&x=0&y=0

26 http://libertymessengerusa.org/

27 http://patrickmadrid.com/?s=sons+of+perdition

28 Janet Smith, PhD. https://www3.nd.edu/~afreddos/ courses/264/popepaul.htm

29 http://lapurisima.org/documents/2017/2/Paul%20VI%20 %20-%20Humanae%20Vitae%20Contraception%20-%20 A%20Challenge%20to%20Love%20by%20Dr.%20Janet%20 Smith-1.pdf

30 https://www.cdc.gov/std/stats15/std-surveillance-2015-print.pdf

31 Judith A. Reisman, Ph.D., *Sexual Sabotage* (Washington, D.C.: WorldNetDaily, 2010).

32 Reisman, *Sexual Sabotage.*

33 http://lapurisima.org/documents/2017/2/Paul%20VI%20 %20-%20Humanae%20Vitae%20Contraception%20-%20 A%20Challenge%20to%20Love%20by%20Dr.%20Janet%20 Smith-1.pdf

34 Nathanson, *The Hand of God,* 90.

35 Nathanson, *The Abortion Papers,* 16.

36 Nathanson, *The Abortion Papers,* 196.

37 Nathanson, *The Abortion Papers,* 177.

38 Nathanson, *The Abortion Papers,* 196.

39 Nathanson, *The Abortion Papers,* 190.

40 Nathanson, *The Abortion Papers,* 178.

41 Nathanson, *The Abortion Papers,* 180.

42 Nathanson, *The Abortion Papers,* 180-181.

43 Nathanson, *The Abortion Papers,* 198-199.

44 Nathanson, *The Abortion Papers,* 181.

45 Nathanson, *The Abortion Papers,* 196-197.

46 Nathanson, *The Abortion Papers,* 189.

47 Nathanson, *The Abortion Papers,* 185.

48 http://patrickmadrid.com/sons-of-perdition-how-certain-catholic-priests-turned-the-kennedys-pro-abortion/

49 Nathanson, *The Abortion Papers,* 189.

50 Nathanson, *The Hand of God,* 108.

51 Nathanson, *Aborting America,* 72.

52 Nathanson, *The Abortion Papers,* 177.

53 Nathanson, *The Abortion Papers,* 197.

54 Fr. Peter Cameron, Editor in Chief, *Magnificat,* June 2015.

55 David Kupelian, *The Marketing of Evil* (Nashville, TN: Cumberland House Publishing, 2005) 192-193.

56 Bernard Nathanson, M.D., "Deeper into Abortion?", *The New England Journal of Medicine,* (November 1974).

57 Randy Alcorn, *ProLife Answers to ProChoice Arguments,* (Oregon: MULTNOMAH PUBLISHERS, INC., 2000), 114.

58 Randy Alcorn, *ProLife Answers to ProChoice Arguments,* 115.

59 Bernard N. Nathanson, M.D., *Aborting America-The Story of an Ex-Abortionist and Ex-Atheist,* DATE, Denver, Lighthouse Catholic Media CD.

60 Director Jack Duane Dabner, Producer/Writer Donald S. Smith, Narrated by Bernard N. Nathanson, M.D., *The Silent Scream,* 1984, Brunswick, OH, American Portrait Films, DVD.

61 Robert T. Zintl and Carolyn Lesh, "Abortion: New Heat Over an Old Issue", *Time,* (February 4, 1985).

62 Director Bernard Nathanson, Producer Bernard Nathanson/ Adelle Roban Nathanson, Narrator Bernard Nathanson/ Charlton Heston, *Eclipse of Reason*, 1987, Brunswick, OH, American Portrait Films, DVD.

63 Nathanson, *The Hand of God*, 188.

64 Nathanson, *The Hand of God*, 188.

65 Nathanson, *The Hand of God*, 198.

66 Nathanson, *The Hand of God*, 192.

67 Nathanson, *Aborting America - The Story of an Ex-Abortionist and Ex-Atheist*, see note 59.

68 Nathanson, *The Hand of God*, 199.

69 Nathanson, *The Hand of God*, 200-201.

70 Nathanson, *The Hand of God*, 201-202.

71 Nathanson, *The Hand of God*, 202-203.

72 www.centerformedicalprogress.org

73 http://worstvirginians.blogspot.com/search?q=terry+beatley

74 http://www.varight.com/?s=terry+beatley+wins+virginia+right&x=0&y=0

75 *John Paul II Evangelium Vitae, encyclical letter.* (Vatican City, Italy: Libreia Editrice Vaticana, 1995).

76 Angela Lanfranchi, M.D., Prof. Ian Gentles, Elizabeth Ring-Cassidy, *Complications: Abortions Impact on Women* (Ontario, Canada: The deVeber Institute for Bioethics and Social Research, 2013), 183-193.

77 Angela Lanfranchi, M.D., Prof. Ian Gentles, Elizabeth Ring-Cassidy, Complications: *Abortions Impact on Women*, 271-283.

78 http://www.bcpinstitute.org/publishedpapers.htm

79 Samuel B. Casey, J.D and Allan Parker, J.D., *"Roe v Wade: An Exercise in 'Assumicide'"*, *What If We've Been Wrong?*, 2016, Appendix C.

80 Christine Reisner-Nathanson. "Proud." https://www.youtube.com/watch?v=JBRv76fMbpw

81 David Barton, *The Bible, Voters & the 2008 Election,* (Texas: WallBuilder Press, 2008), 45.

82 https://stream.org/whole-womans-health-supreme-court-case-disaster-mothers-children-right-life/

83 David Barton, *The Bible, Voters & the 2008 Election,* 4.

84 David Barton, *The Bible, Voters & the 2008 Election,* 4-5.

Endnotes to Appendix C

85 Mr. Casey is the Managing Director and General Counsel of the Jubilee Campaign's Law of Life Project (www.lawoflifeproject.org). Mr. Parker is founding President of The Justice Foundation (www.http://www.txjf.org/). Mr. Parker was one of the attorneys of record representing the original plaintiffs, Norma McCorvey *(Roe v. Wade)* and Sandra Cano *(Doe v. Bolton)* in subsequent separate federal court actions by each woman publicly expressing regret for their role in their original lawsuits and recanting their submitted testimony in those cases asking the courts in their subsequent cases under Rule 60(b) of the Federal Rules of Civil Procedure "as justice requires" to relieve them from the prospective application of the Court's judgments in *Roe* and *Doe*. The Court refused to do so. Mr. Casey represented "friends of the court" in both of those subsequent cases. See *McCorvey v. Hill,* 385 F.3d 846 (5th Cir 2004), *cert. denied,* 543 U.S. 1154 (2005), and *Cano v. Baker,* 435 F.3d 1337 (11th Cir.2006), *cert. denied,* 549 U.S. 972 (2006).

Messrs. Casey and Parker have each been practicing law for more than 30 years, are members of the Bar of the United States Supreme Court, and have appeared on numerous occasions in cases before the United States Supreme Court either representing parties or "friends of the Court" urging the Court to either further limit, reconsider and reverse the central holding in the *Roe* and *Casey* cases, thereby returning the lawful regulation of abortion to the several states where it exclusively resided under American law before the state's exclusive jurisdiction over abortion regulation was usurped by the federal courts. Such cases pending before the United States Supreme Court in its 2015-16 Term, included: No. 15-627: *Stenehjem v. MKB Management,* 795 F.3d 768 (8th Cir. 2015) (North Dakota regulation banning abortion, with some exceptions, after fetal heartbeat detected); No. 15-448: *Edwards v. Beck,* 786 F.3d 1113 (8th Cir. 2015) (Arkansas regulation banning abortion, with some exceptions, beginning 12 weeks after gestation, where the heartbeat of the unborn child is detected); No. 14-997: *Jackson Women's Health Org., et al. v. Currier, et al.,* 760 F.3d 448 (5th Cir. 2014) (regulation of abortion at all stages of pregnancy); and No. 15-274: *Whole Woman's Health, et al. v. Cole, et al.,* 790 F.3d 563 (5th Cir. 2015) (regulation of abortion at all stages of pregnancy). Ultimately, the Supreme Court decided not to review the *Stenehjem* and *Edwards* cases leaving the decisions below that had found the laws unconstitutional as the law of the land. The Court did grant review in the *Cole* case involving two Texas laws: one requires physicians who perform abortions to have admitting privileges at a hospital no more than thirty miles from the clinic, while the second requires abortion clinics to have facilities equal to an outpatient surgical center. Several Texas abortion clinics are seeking to block the laws. Following oral argument on March 2, 2016, a decision is expected in the *Cole* case before July 1, 2016.

86 Michael Stokes Paulson, *The Unbearable Wrongness of Roe*, PUBLIC DISCOURSE (The Witherspoon Institute, January 23, 2012) at 1. The total number of abortions since *Roe* is an estimate based upon figures through 2011. http://www.lifenews. com/2015/01/21/57762169-abortions-in-america-since-roe-vs- wade-in-1973/

87 Despite the widespread notion that women and children have a better chance at surviving a shipwreck because they will be saved first, a new study finds that that's just wishful thinking. The captain, crew and male passengers are more likely to survive maritime disasters than women and children, finds a new study by economists at Uppsala University in Sweden. When it comes to abandoning ship, "it appears as if it's every man for himself," said lead researcher Mikael Elinder in a statement. Elinder and his colleague studied 18 shipwrecks, including the *Titanic* and *Lusitania,* from 1852 to 2011 that involved more than 15,000 passengers and more than 30 nationalities. They limited their study to disasters that included information on the sex of survivors, that involved at least 100 people, and where at least 5 percent survived and 5 percent died. Their findings run counter to the notion that women and children get priority when escaping a shipwreck. The sinking of the *Titanic* 100 years ago, where three times more women survived than men, popularized this *"unwritten law of the sea,"* because the captain ordered that women and children went into the lifeboats first. But it turns out that this is the *exception* rather than the rule. Study co-author Oscar Erixson grew up on stories of chivalrous men on the *Titanic* who gave their lives for the women and children. "[So] the survival patterns we found [in this study] came as surprise to me,"

the economist wrote in an email to LiveScience. In results published online on July 30, 2012 in the journal Proceedings of the National Academy of Sciences, Erixson and Elinder found that overall, women were about half as likely to survive as men. And they found that crewmembers were about 18.7 percent more likely to survive than passengers, no matter how much time it took a ship to sink. Consistent with this study, *Titanic's* Captain Smith's last words are reported to have been: *"'Well boys, you've done your duty and done it well. I ask no more of you. I release you. You know the rule of the sea. It's every man for himself now, and God bless you."*

88 *See* Mason, Alpheus T., *Brandeis–A Free Man's Life* (Viking Press 1946) 46. Justice Brandeis' quote was likely influenced by his reading of his Harvard Law Professor, Chief Justice Oliver Wendell Holmes, Jr., with whom Brandeis later served on the United States Supreme Court. In the first chapter of his famous book, *The Common Law* (Little Brown & Co., Boston 1881), Justice Holmes wrote: *"The life of the law has not been logic; it has been experience. The felt necessities of the time, the prevalent moral and political theories, intuitions of public policy, avowed or unconscious, even the prejudices which judges share with their fellow-men have had a great deal more to do than the syllogism in determining the rules by which men should be governed."*

89 From 1990, when an estimated 1.6 million children were aborted in the USA until today America's annual number of total elective abortions has been declining to less than an estimated 1.1 million abortions. If these figures are accepted, more than an estimated 7 million more American children are alive today thanks, in part, to the cumulative efforts of the millions of people who comprise America's pro-life movement. *See* http://www.lifenews.com/2015/01/21/57762169-abortions-in-america-since-roe-vs-wade-in-1973/

90 From the co-authors' perspective, this political objective has been the pro-life movement's objective from its beginnings in the mid-1960s. *See generally* Dr. & Mrs. John C. Willkie, *Abortion and the Pro-Life Movement: An Inside View* (Infinity Publishing 2014). Beginning in the 1990s, following the Supreme Court's reaffirmation of its central holding in *Roe v. Wade* on different ground in *Planned Parenthood v. Casey,* 505 U.S. 833 (1992), the reasons supporting the pro-life movement's political objective were well-articulated in THE AMERICA WE SEEK: A STATEMENT OF PRO-LIFE PRINCIPLE AND CONCERN, signed by many of America's pro-life leaders and published in May 1996 in First Things magazine. *See generally* https://www.firstthings.com/article/1996/05/005-the-america-we-seek-a-statement-of-pro-life-principle-and-concern

91 Clarke D. Forsythe, *Abuse of Discretion: An Inside Story of Roe v. Wade* (Encounter Books, New York 2013) at 348-49.

92 As of December 2015, forty-two states had bans on *post-viability* (after 23 weeks gestation) abortions that were not facially unconstitutional under *Roe v. Wade* (i.e. banning all abortions) or enjoined by court order. In addition, the Supreme Court in the case of *Gonzales v. Carhart,* 550 U.S. 124 (2007), ruled that Congress may ban certain late-term abortion techniques, "both pre-viability and post-viability". *See* http://www.kff.org/womens-health-policy/state-indicator/later-term-abortions/?currentTimeframe=0&sortModel=%7B%22colId%22:%22Location%22,%22sort%22:%22asc%22%7D

Pre-viability twenty week abortion bans with varying exceptions have been enacted in 16 states: Alabama, Arizona, Arkansas, Georgia, Idaho, Indiana, Kansas, Louisiana, Mississippi, Nebraska, North Carolina, North Dakota, Oklahoma, Texas, West Virginia and Wisconsin. Laws banning abortion at

20 weeks have been blocked in three states: Arizona, Georgia, and Idaho. As a result of litigation, therefore, a total of 13 such bans were in effect as of January 25, 2016. *See* https://rewire.news/legislative-tracker/law-topic/20-week-bans/. Nine states have enacted laws banning abortion based upon sex-selection. See ARIZ. REV. STAT. § 13-3603.02 (2013); IND CODE § 16-18-218.5 & 16-34-4(K);720 ILL. COMP. STAT. § 510/6-8 (2013); KAN. STAT. § 65-6726 (2013); N.C. GEN. STAT. § 90-21.121 (2013); N.D. CENT. CODE § 14-02.1-04.1 (2013); OKLA. STAT. TIT. 63, § 1-731.2 (2013); 18 PA. CONS. STAT. § 3204 (2013); H.B. 1162, 89th Leg., Reg. Sess. (S.D. 2014) (enacted). On April 1, 2016, Indiana became the ninth state to ban sex-selection, but went even further banning abortion "because of the fetus's race, color, national origin, ancestry, sex, or diagnosis or potential diagnosis of the fetus having Down syndrome or any other disability." In doing so, Indiana became the second state, along with North Dakota, to ban abortion due to diagnosis of a non-lethal disability, like Down Syndrome. *See* Charlotte Lozier Institute's April 21, 2015 study, https://lozierinstitute.org/new-study-abortion-after-prenatal-diagnosis-of-down-syndrome-reduces-down-syndrome-community-by-thirty-percent/. Planned Parenthood of Indiana has filed a federal law suit challenging the Indiana law. Congress and another 20 states have considered banning abortion based upon sex selection, race or disability. *See generally* University of Chicago Law School, CERD SHADOW REPORT, *Sex Selection Abortion Bans in the United States and their Discriminatory Effect on Asian-American Women* (June 2014); Casey, Samuel *et al., No Girls Allowed: Sex Selection Abortion and a Guide to Banning it in the United States,* 5 REGENT J. LAW & PUB. POLICY 111 (2013). Such laws are easily avoided by simply omitting or misstating the true reason for electing abortion.

93 Gallup polling data since at least 1975 show a solid and persistent majority of Americans who support abortion only in "certain circumstances" early in pregnancy. Support for what the court actually did in *Roe* — abortion for any reason, at any time of pregnancy — declined from 12 percent to 7 percent between 2006 and 2009, according to data from the Polling Company. Since 1995, the more liberal Gallup Polling indicates no more than average of about 26% of Americans support the legality of abortion in all circumstances. http://www.gallup.com/poll/1576/abortion.aspx. A more recent CNN poll (September 9, 2015) indicates that a majority of the public thinks that abortion should be illegal under most circumstances. http://www.cnn.com/2015/09/14/politics/abortion-poll-cnn-orc/index.html. One simple reason that abortion is more controversial in the United States than in other countries is that the justices have imposed the views of no more than 26% of the American people on all us since 1973.

94 *See* CHARLOTTE LOZIER INSTITUTE, *Gestational Limits on Abortion in the United States Compared to International Norms* (Angelina Baglini, J.D.) https://lozierinstitute.org/wp-content/uploads/2014/02/American-Report-Series-INTERNATIONAL-ABORTION-NORMS1.pdf

95 *See* WASHINGTON POST (January 26, 2015), *Does Obamacare Provide Federal Subsidies for Elective Abortions,* https://www.washingtonpost.com/news/fact-checker/wp/2015/01/26/does-obamacare-provide-federal-subsidies-for-elective-abortions/?utm_term=.6492ef5ce4dc

96 *See* http://www.kff.org/medicaid/state-indicator/abortion-under-medicaid/?currentTimeframe=0&sortModel=%7B%22coIId%22:%22Location%22,%22sort%22:%22asc%22%7D

97 *Roe v. Wade,* 410 U.S. 113, *"If the state is interested in protecting fetal life after viability, it may go so far to proscribe abortion during that period, except when it is necessary to preserve the life or health of the mother." Id.* at 163-165.

98 On October 7, 2015, the U.S. House of Representatives appointed a fourteen-member SELECT PANEL ON ABORTION AND THE SALE OF ABORTED BABY BODY PARTS, chaired by Rep. Marsha Blackburn (R-TN) that will spend a year thoroughly investigating the Planned Parenthood abortion business amid the scandal revealed by the Center for Medical Progress videos showing Planned Parenthood selling aborted babies and appearing to break multiple federal laws in so doing. *See* https://www.youtube.com/user/centerformedprogress. The Select bi-partisan committee, composed of Democratic and Republican representatives, will investigate: (1) Medical procedures and business practices used by entities involved in fetal tissue procurement; (2) Any other matters with respect to fetal tissue procurement; (3) Federal funding and support for abortion providers; (4) The practices of providers of second and third trimester abortions, including partial birth abortion procedures that may lead to a child born alive as a result of an attempted abortion; (5) Medical procedures for the care of a child born alive as a result of an attempted abortion; and (6) Any changes in law or regulation necessary as a result of any other findings made. The Select Panel consists of eight Republicans and five Democrats, nine of whom are women. Within the next year, following its investigation, the Select Panel will submit a report to Congress with recommendations. The work of this panel will be in addition to the ongoing Planned Parenthood investigations at the Judiciary Committee and Oversight and Government Reform Committee. On October 13, 2015,

Planned Parenthood announced it would terminate the practice of some of its affiliates receiving reimbursement for its cost of providing aborted baby parts for medical research, but said it would still permit the practice of allowing their clients to donate their aborted child's parts for medical research. http://www.wsj.com/articles/planned-parenthood-stops-taking-reimbursements-for-fetal-tissue-1444744800. In addition to these investigations, The Senate voted, 52 to 47, on December 2, 2015, to repeal large portions of Obamacare and defund Planned Parenthood and redirect their funding to other women's health organizations that do not perform abortions. The repeal was wrapped inside a budget reconciliation bill that needed a simple majority of 51 senators to make good on a longstanding promise to voters that a GOP-led Congress would eliminate large portions of Obamacare. But after months of pressure from conservatives, Senate leaders decided to add language to defund Planned Parenthood. As expected, when the House voted favorably on the bill, President Obama vetoed the bill. http://www.lifenews.com/2016/01/08/obama-vetoes-bill-to-de-fund-planned-parenthood-abortion-biz-caught-selling-aborted-baby-parts/

99 *See* Michael Stokes Paulsen, *The Unbearable Wrongness of Roe,* Public Discourse, (Witherspoon Institute, January 23, 2012), http://www.thepublicdiscourse.com/2012/01/4577/. Other legal scholars have been no less harsh in their reception of *Roe.* The decision has frequently been criticized by scholars and commentators, including those who favor legalized abortion. Among the extensive literature, *see, e.g.,* Laurence H. Tribe, *Toward a Model of Roles in the Due Process of Life and Law,* 87 Harv. L. Rev. 1, 7 (1973) (*"One of the most curious things about* Roe *is that, behind its own verbal smokescreen, the substantive judgment on which it rests is nowhere to be*

found"); John Hart Ely, *The Wages of Crying Wolf: A Comment on Roe v. Wade,* 82 Yale L.J. 920, 947 (1973) (*Roe* is a *"very bad decision"* because *"it is bad constitutional law, or rather because it is not constitutional law and gives almost no sense of an obligation to try to be"*); Benjamin Wittes, *Letting Go of Roe,* ATLANTIC MONTHLY 48 (Jan./Feb. 2005) (*"Since its inception* Roe *has had a deep legitimacy problem, stemming from its weakness as a legal opinion."*).

100 Justice Harry Blackmun, the author of *Roe,* said in a 1991 interview that the Court's decision to hear the abortion cases was a "serious mistake" because the justices initially thought they were considering a narrow procedural question of when federal courts should intervene in pending criminal prosecutions. As a result, the justices decided the abortion cases without possessing a factual record about the medical, social and legal effects of various abortion restrictions. As well-documented by legal historian, Clarke D. Forsythe, based upon his review of the Justices' papers, in his book *Abuse of Discretion: The Inside Story of Roe v. Wade* (Encounter Books 2013), this lack of factual record gave a speculative, free-floating quality to the deliberations that resulted in the factual "assumicide" that has chronically undermined the constitutional legitimacy of the Court's analysis and holdings in the abortion cases up until this day.

101 http://www.dakotavoice.com/Docs/South%20Dakota%20Abortion%20Task%20Force%20Report.pdf

102 The *MKB Management Corp* case involved both a state court and a federal court challenge to North Dakota's law (D.C.C. §§ 14-02.1-05.1 and 14-02.1-05.2) that bans abortion after an unborn child's heartbeat is detectable, except in emergency cases or to protect the health or life of the mother, as defined in the statue. After the North Dakota Supreme Court could

not conclude by the required number of votes that the statute was unconstitutional and, therefore, reversed the preliminary injunction by the trial court enjoining the statute, *MKB Management v. Burdick,* 2014 ND 97, 855 N.W.2d 31 (2014), the federal courts found the statute unconstitutional. *MKB Management v. Burdick,* 954 F. Supp. 2d 900 (D.N.D. 2013) [preliminary injunction], 16 F. Supp. 3d 1059 (D.N.D. 2014) [summary injunction]; affirmed sub nom. *MKB Management v. Stenehejm,* 795 F.3d 768 (8th Cir. 2015). North Dakota has filed its petition for certiorari in the U.S. Supreme Court asking the Court *"to reevaluate its abortion jurisprudence in light of extensive evidence in the record of 1) new scientific advances on viability, 2) increasing evidence of the devastating physical and psychological consequences of abortion, and 3) society's willingness to remove from pregnant women the burden of child care for every unwanted child, and uphold the constitutionality of North Dakota's law restricting abortion where there is a detectable human heartbeat?" See Stenehejm v. MKB Management,* _U.S._2015 WL 7180647, USSC Docket No. 15-627 (2015). http://www.aul.org/2012/06/video-auls-legal-symposium-from-planned-parenthood-v-casey-until-the-day-after-roe-caseys-impact-on-abortion-jurisprudence/. On January 25, 2016, the Supreme Court decided not to hear the case.

103 *"[T]he life of a new human being commences at a scientifically well-defined event; the fusion of the plasma membranes of sperm and egg. This conclusion is not a matter of religious belief or societal convention; it is a matter of objective, scientific observation."* Maureen L. Condic, Ph.D., *When Does Human Life Begin? The Scientific Evidence and Terminology Revisited,* UNIVERSITY OF ST. THOMAS J.OF L. & PUB. POLICY, Vol. VIII, No. 1, page 44 (June 2014).

104 *See* STENEHJEM PETITION, *supra* note 19 TO 102.

105 Dr. Alexander Tsiaras, TED TALK, *Conception to Birth Visualized* (December 2010) https://www.ted.com/talks/alexander_tsiaras_conception_to_birth_visualized?language=en

106 *See* Hyer, *et al. Predictive Value of the Presence of an Embryonic Heartbeat for Live Birth: Comparison of Women with and Without Recurrent Pregnancy Loss*, STERILITY AND FERTILITY, Vol. 82, No. 5, November, 2004.

107 *MKB Management v. Stenehejm,* 795 F.3d 768, 773-775 (8th Cir. 2015).

108 http://liveactionnews.org/former-abortionist-abortion-big-business/

109 REPORT OF THE SOUTH DAKOTA TASK FORCE TO STUDY ABORTION SUBMITTED TO THE GOVERNOR AND LEGISLATURE OF SOUTH DAKOTA DECEMBER 2005 at pp. 16-17. [The "SOUTH DAKOTA REPORT"]. http://www.dakotavoice.com/Docs/South%20Dakota%20Abortion%20Task%20Force%20Report.pdf

110 Transcript and audio recording of the arguments are available online via the Oyez project, at http://www.oyez.org/cases/1979-1979/1971/1971_70_18/argument

111 Ala. Code §§ 26-25-1 to -5 (2013); Alaska Stat. §§ 47.10.013, .990 (2013); Ariz. Rev. Stat. Ann. § 13-3623.01 (2013); Ark. Code Ann. §§ 9-34-201, -202 (2013); Cal. Health & Safety Code § 1255.7 (West 2013); Cal. Penal Code § 271.5 (West 2013); Colo. Rev. Stat. § 19-3-304.5 (2013); Conn. Gen. Stat. §§ 17a-57, -58 (2012); Del. Code. Ann. tit. 16, §§ 902, 907-08 (2013); D.C. Code §§ 4-1451.01 to .08 (2013); Fla. Stat. § 383.50 (2013); Ga. Code Ann. §§ 19-10A-2 to -7 (2013) Hawaii Rev. Stat. §§ 587D-1 to -7 (2013); Idaho Code Ann. §§ 39-8201

to -8207(2013); 325 Ill. Comp. Stat. 2/10, 2/15, 2/20, 2/27 (2013); Ind. Code § 31-34-2.5-1 (2013); Iowa Code §§ 233.1, .2 (2014); Kan. Stat. Ann. § 38-2282 (2012); Ky. Rev. Stat. Ann. §§ 216B.190, 405.075 (LexisNexis 2013); La. Child. Code Ann. arts. 1149-53 (2013); Me. Rev. Stat. tits. 17-A, § 553, 22 § 4018 (2013); Md. Code Ann. Cts. & Jud. Proc. § 5-641 (LexisNexis 2013); Mass. Gen. Laws Ch. 119, § 39 1/2 (2013); Mich. Comp. Laws §§ 712.1, .2, .3, .5, .20 (2013); Minn. Stat. §§ 145.902, 260C.139, 609.3785 (2013); Miss. Code Ann. §§ 43-15-201, -203, -207, -209 (2013); Mo. Rev. Stat. § 210.950 (2013); Mont. Code Ann. §§ 40-6-402 to -405 (2013); Neb. Rev. Stat. § 29-121 (2012); Nev. Rev. Stat. §§ 432B.160, .630 (2013); N.H. Rev. Stat. Ann. §§ 132-A:1 to :4 (2013); N.J. Stat. Ann. §§ 30:4C-15.6 to -15.10 (West 2013); N.M. Stat. Ann. §§ 24-22-1.1, -2, -3, -8 (2013); N.Y. Penal Law §§ 260.00, .10 (McKinney 2013); N.Y. Soc. Serv. Law § 372-g (McKinney 2013); 146a N.C. Gen. Stat. § 7B-500 (2012); N.D. Cent. Code §§ 27-20-02, 50-25.1-15 (2013); Ohio Rev. Code Ann. §§ 2151.3515, .3516, .3523 (LexisNexis 2013); Okla. Stat. tit. 10A, § 1-2-109 (2013) Or. Rev. Stat. § 418.017 (2011); 23 Pa. Cons. Stat. §§ 4306, 6502, 6504, 6507 (2013); R.I. Gen. Laws §§ 23-13.1-2, -3 (2012); S.C. Code Ann. § 63-7-40 (2012); S.D. Codified Laws §§ 25-5A-27, -31, -34 (2013); Tenn. Code Ann. §§ 36-1-142, 68-11-255 (2013); Tex. Fam. Code Ann. §§ 262.301, .302 (West 2013); Utah Code Ann. §§ 62A-4a-801, -802 (LexisNexis 2013); Vt. Stat. Ann. tit. 13, § 1303 (2013); Va. Code Ann. §§ 8.01226.5:2, 18.2-371.1, 40.1-103 (2013); Wash. Rev. Code § 13.34.360 (2013); W. Va Code § 49-6E-1 (2013); Wis. Stat. § 48.195 (2013); Wyo. Stat. Ann. §§ 14-11-101,-102,-103,-108 (2013). *See generally* www. nationalsafehavenalliance.org

112 *See Planned Parenthood v. Rounds,* 686 F. 3d. 889 (8th Cir. 2012) *(en banc)* (also contains a well-reasoned analysis of the evidence and counter arguments of the American College of Obstetricians and Gynecologists (ACOG) and other medical groups).The 8th Circuit Court rejected the abortion industry assertion that abortion is not associated with increased risk of suicide.

113 The Stenehejm Petition, at 4. There is consensus among most social and medical science scholars that a minimum of 20% of women who abort suffer from serious, prolonged negative psychological consequences. *See* Bradshaw & Slade, *The effects of induced abortion on emotional experiences and relationships: A critical review of the literature,* Clin. Psychol. Rev., 23, 929-958 (2003).

114 In April 2013, Philadelphia abortionist, Dr. Kermit Gosnell, M.D., was convicted on three counts of murder in the deaths of 3 newborn babies. Gosnell routinely delivered live babies and then ended their lives by severing their spinal cords with scissors. The Grand Jury Report estimates hundreds of babies met similar fates at Gosnell's Philadelphia abortion center. Gosnell preyed on vulnerable women with his abortion business and subjected them to dangerous and unsanitary conditions. One woman named Karnamaya Mongar died at Gosnell's center after an overdose of Demerol. After Mongar's death, a former employee said Gosnell reassured her that she'd done nothing wrong. According to the Grand Jury Report, for political reasons, the PA Department of Health ceased inspections of abortion centers allowing the atrocities to continue for years. *See generally* In re County Investigating Grand Jury *(In re Gosnell,* Misc. No. 0009901-2008, Common Pleas Court, 1st Jud. District, Criminal Trial Division), http://www.nrlc.org/uploads/factsheets/gosnellfactsheet.pdf

115 *See* Forsythe, *supra* note 91, at 311-316.

116 *See* Greg Scandlen, The Federalist (September 18, 2015), *How Many Women are Pressured into Abortions?* http://thefederalist.com/2015/09/18/how-many-women-are-pressured-into-abortions/

117 The South Dakota Report, note 109, at 21.

118 *See, e.g.,* Clarke D. Forsythe & Bradley N. Kehr, *A Road Map Through the Supreme Court's Back Alley,* 57 Vill. L. Rev. 45, 48 (2012).

119 John M. Thorp, Jr., MD, Katherine E. Hartmann, MD, PhD and Elizabeth Shadigian, MD, *Long-Term Physical and Psychological Health Consequences of Induced Abortion: Review of the Evidence,* Vol. 58, No.1 Obst. & Gyn. Survey (2002), found at https://www.debatepolitics.com/abortion/199563-long-road-abortion-some-countrys-poorest-women-2.html

120 P. S. Shah & J. Zao, *Induced Termination of Pregnancy and Low Birthweight and Preterm Birth: A Systematic Review and Meta-analyses,* 116 Brit. J. of Ob. Gyn. 1425 (2009); Hanes M. Swingle, *et al., Abortion and the Risk of Subsequent Preterm Birth: A Systematic Review with Meta-analyses,* 54 J. Reprod. Med. 95 (2009); R. Freak-Poli, *et al., Previous Abortion and Risk of Preterm Birth: A Population Study,* 22 J. of Maternal-Fetal Med. 1 (2009).

121 Dr. Thorp is the Hugh McAllister Distinguished Professor of Obstetrics and Gynecology at the University of North Carolina (Chapel Hill) School of Medicine and the Gillings School of Public Health at the University of North Carolina at Chapel Hill where he serves as the Deputy Director of the Center for Women's Health Research, in the Departments of Obstetrics and Gynecology and Department of Epidemiology,

respectively). Dr. Thorp is a Fellow of the Carolina Population Center and has been the Director of the Biomedical Core of the Carolina Population Center of the University of North Carolina at Chapel Hill. The author of 21 book chapters and a journal referee (reviewer) for 39 different medical journals, including THE NEW ENGLAND JOURNAL OF MEDICINE, MAYO CLINIC PROCEEDINGS, OBSTETRICS & GYNECOLOGY, THE AMERICAN JOURNAL OF OBSTETRICS AND GYNECOLOGY, BRITISH JOURNAL OF OBSTETRICS AND GYNECOLOGY, LANCET, AND THE JOURNAL OF PERINATAL MEDICINE. Dr. Thorp currently serves as the deputy editor-in-chief of the BRITISH JOURNAL OF OBSTETRICS & GYNECOLOGY, an international journal considered one of the most prestigious in the field. Dr. Thorp has served has an expert medical research witness in a number of legal cases involving the state regulation of abortion, including the *MKB Management* case, challenging the constitutionality of North Dakota's abortion prohibition once a heartbeat is detected, currently pending before the U.S. Supreme Court. *See* STENEHEJM PETITION, *supra* note 102, *et seq.*

122 Dr. John Thorp *et al., Public Health Impact of Legal Termination of Pregnancy in the US: 40 Years Later* (SCIENTIFICA, 2012) found at http://www.hindawi.com/journals/scientifica/2012/980812/

123 Reardon, D. & Coleman, P., *Short and Long Term Mortality Rates Associated with First Pregnancy Outcome: Population Register Based Study for Denmark 1980-2004.* MEDICAL SCIENCE MONITOR, 2012, found at: http://www.ncbi.nlm.nih.gov/pmc/articles/PMC3560645/

124 Coleman, P. Reardon, D. & Calhoun, B., *Reproductive History Patterns and Long-term Mortality Rates: A Danish, Population-Based Record Linkage Study.* EUROPEAN J. OF PUB. HEALTH (September 5, 2012), found at http://eurpub.oxfordjournals.org/content/23/4/569

125 Post-pregnancy death rates within one year were nearly 4 times greater among women who had an induced abortion (100.5 per 100,000) compared to women who carried to term (26.7 per 100,000). Gissler, M., *et al. Pregnancy Associated Deaths in Finland 1987-1994: Definition Problems and Benefits of Record Linkage.* 76 A Acta Obstetricia et Gynecologica Scandinavica 1997, 76: 651-7; mortality was significantly lower after a birth (28.2 per 100,000) than after an induced abortion (83.1 per 100,000). Gissler, M. Berg, C., Bouvier-Colle, M. Buekins, P. *Pregnancy-associated mortality after birth, spontaneous abortion, or induced abortion in Finland, 1987-2000.* Am. J. of Obs. and Gyn., 2004, 190: 422-427; women who aborted, when compared to women who delivered, were 62% more likely to die over an 8 year period from any cause after adjustments were made for age. Reardon, D. *et al. Deaths Associated with Pregnancy Outcome: A Record Linkage Study of Low Income Women,* So. Med. J., 2002, 95: 834-841.

126 Raymond, E., Grimes, D., *The Comparative Safety of Legal Induced Abortion and Childbirth in the United States,* Obs. & Gyn. 2012. 119:215-9, pp. 187-91.

127 Dellapenna, Joseph W., *Dispelling the Myths of Abortion History* (Carolina Academic Press 2006) at 702; *see generally* Forsythe, note 91, at 312-314.

128 *See* Clarke D. Forsythe, *Can Roe v Wade Be Overturned after 40 Years?* Defending Life (Americans United for Life, 2013); Forsythe, *supra* note 91.

129 *"It's well known that Democrats generally don't appoint anyone to the federal bench who isn't a reliable supporter of abortion. As Shannen Coffin pointed out in a 2004 article in National Review, this selection bias sometimes leads to 'abortion distortion' — courts twist the law to achieve a result just*

because abortion is involved." Jonathan Keim, "Pamela Harris and 'Abortion Distortion'," *Judicial Crisis Network,* June 7, 2014, https://judicialnetwork.com/pamela-harris-abortion-distortion/

130 *See supra* note 100.

131 505 U.S. 833 (1992).

132 C.D. Forsythe & S.B. Presser, *infra* note 134.

133 The messaging on women and power has been deployed on multiple levels, and has moved in concert with the underlying legal strategy defending abortion rights. The legal rationale for "reproductive freedom" has evolved significantly over time. In the mid-1980s, when pro-life Harvard Law Professor, Mary Ann Glendon, asked the then Dean of the Harvard Law School, Al Sacks, why he "and so many other constitutional lawyers stopped criticizing the Court's abortion decisions after most of them had been so highly critical" of *Roe*, Dean Sacks sighed and spoke for men like himself saying: *"I suppose it was because we had been made to understand that the abortion issue was so important to the women in our lives, and it just did not seem that important to most of us." See* Mary Ann Glendon, *The Women of Roe v. Wade,* First Things (June, 2003), https://www.firstthings.com/article/2003/06/the-women-of-roe-v-wade. In its 1992 decision, *Planned Parenthood v. Casey,* Justice Kennedy writing for the Court asserted that we must tolerate abortion because of a "reliance interest" – women have come to rely on abortion to maintain their position and advancement in society: *"[F]or two decades of economic and social developments, people have organized intimate relationships and made choices that define their views of themselves and their places in society, in reliance on the availability of abortion in the event that contraception should fail. The ability of women to participate equally in the economic and*

social life of the Nation has been facilitated by their ability to control their reproductive lives." The Center for Reproductive Rights, the abortion industry's legal arm, now states this idea explicitly in their self-definition. *"Reproductive rights, the foundation for women's self-determination over their bodies and sexual lives."* As the Center's website explains, *"are critical to women's equality and to ensuring global progress toward just and democratic societies."* In fact, the Center's connection between "reproductive rights" and democracy illustrates just how foundational abortion has become to the feminist philosophical edifice. This connective tissue is also now woven into feminist jurisprudence. For example, Justice Ruth Bader Ginsburg, dissenting from the Supreme Court's decision, by a vote of 5-4 with Justice Kennedy providing key "swing" vote and writing the majority opinion to uphold the ban on partial-birth abortions in *Gonzales v. Carhart,* 550 U.S. 124 (2007) wrote that women without the abortion right cannot *"enjoy equal citizenship stature." Id.,* at 172.

134 *See* C.D. Forsythe & S.B. Presser, *The Tragic Failure of Roe v. Wade: Why Abortion Should be Returned to the States,* 10 Tex. Rev. L. & Pol. 85 (2005), From *Planned Parenthood v. Casey to the "Day After Roe": Casey's Impact on Abortion Jurisprudence,* Americans United for Life, (May 31, 2012), http://www.aul.org/2012/06/video-auls-legal-symposium-from-planned-parenthood-v-casey-until-the-day-after-roe-caseys-impact-on-abortion-jurisprudence/

135 This is documented by James Davison Hunter's analysis of the 1990 Gallup Poll in his book, *Before the Shooting Begins* (Free Press, 1994). *See also* J.W. Dellapenna, *Dispelling the Myths of Abortion History* 970-972. (Carolina Academic Press, 2006).

136   *See* N. Difonzo, *Changing Minds, Saving Lives,* FIRST THINGS,
      (November, 2011), http://www.firstthings.com/article/2011/11/
      changing-minds-saving-lives

137   After abortion was legalized in 1973, the US abortion rate quickly
      rose from 16.3 procedures per 1,000 women aged 15–44
      to a high of 29.3 in 1981. Since, it has been on the decline.
      In the latest year for which data is available, the rate reached
      a low of 16.9 per 1,000 in 2011, according to the Guttmacher
      Institute. http://www.theguardian.com/world/2015/jun/08/
      us-abortion-down-new-survey. In the most recent survey done
      and reported by the Associated Press on June 15, 2015,
      several of the states that have been most aggressive in passing
      anti-abortion laws — including Indiana, Missouri, Ohio, and
      Oklahoma — have seen their abortion numbers drop by more
      than 15 percent since 2010. But more liberal states such as
      New York, Washington and Oregon also had declines of that
      magnitude, even as they maintained unrestricted access to
      abortion. Nationwide, the AP survey showed a decrease in
      abortions of about 12 percent (or about 120,000 lives saved)
      since 2010.

CPSIA information can be obtained
at www.ICGtesting.com
Printed in the USA
BVHW061517110319
542318BV00005B/137/P